D0399084

PURCHASED FROM
MULTNOMAH COUNTY LIBRARY
TITLE WAVE BOOKSTORE

Also by Howell Raines

Fly Fishing Through the Midlife Crisis

Whiskey Man

My Soul Is Rested:
Movement Days in the Deep South Remembered

THE
ONE *That*
GOT AWAY

~ *A Memoir* ~

HOWELL RAINES

A LISA DREW BOOK

SCRIBNER

New York   London   Toronto   Sydney

A LISA DREW BOOK / SCRIBNER
1230 Avenue of the Americas
New York, NY 10020

Copyright © 2006 by Howell Raines

All rights reserved, including the right of reproduction in whole or in part in any form.

SCRIBNER and design are trademarks of Macmillan Library Reference USA, Inc.,
used under license by Simon & Schuster, the publisher of this work.

A LISA DREW BOOK is a trademark of Simon & Schuster, Inc.

For information about special discounts for bulk purchases,
please contact Simon & Schuster Special Sales:
1-800-456-6798 or business@simonandschuster.com

Text set in Berthold Baskerville

Manufactured in the United States of America

1   3   5   7   9   10   8   6   4   2

Library of Congress Cataloging-in-Publication Data
Raines, Howell.
The one that got away : a memoir / Howell Raines.
p. cm.
"A Lisa Drew book."
1. Fly fishing–Anecdotes. 2. Raines, Howell.
I. Title.
SH456.R35 2006
799.12'4–dc22   2005057438

ISBN-13: 978-0-7432-7278-0
ISBN-10: 0-7432-7278-1

"The Grape Cure" by James Merrill, from *Collected Poems* by James Merrill
and J. D. McClatchy and Stephen Yenser, editors, copyright © 2001 by
the Literary Estate of James Merrill at Washington University. Used by permission
of Alfred A. Knopf, a division of Random House, Inc.

Lines from "The Tower" and "Why Should Not Old Men Be Mad?" by W. B. Yeats
reprinted with the permission of Scribner, an imprint of Simon & Schuster Adult
Publishing Group, from *The Collected Works of W. B. Yeats, Volume I: The Poems, Revised,*
edited by Richard J. Finneran. "The Tower" copyright © 1928 by the Macmillan
Company; copyright renewed © 1956 by Georgie Yeats. "Why Should Not Old Men
Be Mad?" copyright © 1940 by Georgie Yeats; copyright renewed © 1968 by Bertha
Georgie Yeats, Michael Butler Yeats, and Anne Yeats.

Lines from "A Battenkill Funeral" by William Herrick, from *The Gordon Garland,*
copyright © 1965 by the Theodore Gordon Flyfishers. Reprinted by permission.

For Krystyna

The One That Got Away

BOOK ONE

For two days feed on water. The third morning
Drink water and eat, some twenty minutes after,
The first of your grapes. In as many weeks as you need
You shall be cured. What happens, in plain words,
Is a purging, a starving not of yourself but of what
Feeds on you, hangs down like a crab from your heart.

JAMES MERRILL,
"The Grape Cure"

CHAPTER 1

On the Goneness
of Lost Fish

In a century of fly fishing, one thing has not changed. "It is our lost fish that I believe stay longest in memory, and seize upon our thoughts whenever we look back on fishing days." A paradigmatic Victorian gentleman, Lord Grey of Fallodon, published those words in a book called *Fly Fishing* in 1899. Over one hundred years later, there is still nothing as gone, as utterly lost to us, nothing as definitely absent and irretrievable as a lost fish.

"Seize our thoughts" is an apt phrase, for there are some lost fish that haunt us like old love. They live forever in what Izaak Walton called "the boxes of memory." Yet not all lost fish are equal. Sometimes there is a soothing completeness to the loss of a specific fish. The encounter has an accommodating narrative arc—a beginning, a middle and a conclusion, at which, for some reason, one does not feel robbed. These flashes of enlightenment are rare and a blessing when they come. But fishing in the main does not allow for such an absence of Avarice, such a deliverance from Desire and its handmaiden Regret. That is because, once a fish is on our line, we don't want the imperial feeling of possession ever to end.

The governing emotion of fishing therefore is not one of attainment but one of anxiety about incipient loss. Every moment that a fish is on the line, we dread the sensation of being disconnected against our will, of being evaded, escaped from, of grabbing and missing. Every fish that slips the hook instructs us in the surgical indifference of fate. For like fate, a fish only *seems* to be acting against us. It is, in fact, ignorant of us, profoundly indifferent, incapable of being moved by our desires, by our joy or sorrow. We regard the moment when the fish rises to a fly as a triumph of piscatorial artistry, and when the line breaks or the hook pulls out, we feel cheated, outfoxed, chagrined. We take it personally. But to the fish, such an encounter is simply an interruption, unremarkable and unremembered, in the instinctual, self-absorbed journey of fulfilling its fishhood. What we experience as an exercise of will and hope, the fish encounters as an accident, no more or less remarkable than meeting a shrimp.

So, perforce, each departed fish pushes us toward a dim, momentary and reluctant acceptance of that inescapable fact against which the mind constantly rebels. For against all reason and evidence, we try to believe that life is shaped by a process of acquisition. It is, in fact, a process in which our dear things slip away, slowly and elegantly if we are lucky, rapidly and brutally if we are not. We try to believe, in poor old Jim Dickey's mysterious line, that we can "die but not die out." Lost fish remind us that time, like an undertow or gravity itself, will pull us down, will confound every hope of lasting, every dream of possessing something—anything—wonderful for more than an instant. Lost fish chasten us to the knowledge that we are all, in each and every moment, dwindling. Imagine my surprise when I discovered well into my sixth decade that losing fish can prepare us for a blessing as well as for pain.

Accepting the latter, the hurtful, seemingly accidental losses that life imposes on all of us, did not come naturally to me. I remember the resistance I felt in college when my favorite professor, a wizened, erudite man named Richebourg Gaillard McWilliams, was making a point about one of Nathaniel Hawthorne's doom-clouded stories. "Everyone who lives has to accept something that may seem impossible to the young. At some point in your life, you will come to know great sadness. You will lose something precious. Remember this." He did not speak another word, but we understood that class was over.

The professor's son, Tennant McWilliams, was my closest friend, and I knew from him the piercing experience that lay behind the old man's words. When it came to sorrow, life had given him no grace period. Mr. McWilliams was three when his mother, pregnant with what would have been her second child, died in a fall down the hard, steep stairs of an antebellum house in the Alabama Black Belt. A dozen years later, Richebourg McWilliams's father died of a heart attack when the two of them were quail hunting not far from that fine, airy, oak-shaded house. Theirs was a plantation family tracing its roots back to fifteenth-century French Huguenots who had gone to the rack in Languedoc. But in the end these landed gentlefolk, who owned cotton fields, sawmills and steamboats, were as vulnerable as the blacks who served them or the white yeomen who scratched livings from patchwork farms in the Alabama hills. Richebourg McWilliams, indeed, was no luckier in respect to the wounds of mortality than my own father, who was haunted all his life by the early death of a parent on one of those hill country farms at about the same time.

I speak of these things in the context of lost fish, because in fly fishing as in life it is always possible to make things worse, through clumsiness perhaps or hubris. Say, for example, you tighten the drag on a fish that has just seen the net. Or perhaps the fish was well hooked and you say to yourself in the tiniest mental whisper, "Oh, yes, this wonderful creature is truly mine," when it has not yet been taken from the spacious, amniotic embrace of its watery home. If you conflate this kind of carelessness with unrepeatability—with knowing that you have blundered away a pleasing coincidence that will not come again—then, my friends, you have a departed fish that will never desert you. Certain of my lost fish—a largemouth bass in Alabama, a brown trout on the Missouri River, a permit in Belize—have been with me so long as to become icons of instruction about the importance of avoiding avoidable mistakes. I think of the respective mishaps by which they gained their freedom and I gained pedagogic memories—with the bass, an overtight drag; with the trout, a strike too hard by half; with the permit, a hook set slow as the thunder that follows lightning down a mountain.

Unlike Mr. McWilliams and my father, I knew little as a child about unavoidable losses, those to which one responds with courage or by being crushed. I had few occasions until comparatively late in life to consider the hierarchy of losses, to learn about assessing them in the way of Tennyson, who said that, while much may vanish from our lives at any given moment, much abides. Comrades, those words seem less facile to me now than when I first read them, for reasons I hope to illustrate. For the nonce, however, let us return to the subject of lost fish, if for no other reason than to prove how capacious a sentence was left to us by Lord Grey. For example, when I think of lost fish, I often turn in memory to the falsetto hotel keeper in Bellagio. The town is on Lake Como near the Swiss Alps. This is Mussolini country. Nearby, irritated Italians put an entire platoon's supply of bullets into Benito and his foolish mistress, Clara Petacci, and then hung them upside down, like marlin or tuna.

Unlike fish, they were dangled in a spirit of ridicule rather than admiration.

Anyway, that was the neighborhood, and the hotel keeper of whom I speak had a voice like a set of church bells. I knew, of course, that the age of the castrati was three hundred years past, but his voice had that kind of purity, a boy's voice pushed into an artificial tingling range beyond soprano.

The man with the wonderful voice and his mother owned a small hotel of austere, clean rooms. I spent a night or two there before moving into the nearby Villa Serbelloni, a writers' colony where I was to stay for the month of September 1991. The two of them, mother and son, radiated a kind of contentment you used to see among Southern families in which one or more unmarried sons or daughters remained at home and grew old with the parents. Down in small-town Alabama, these were often the most cultivated families. You would see them together—gardening, dining out, going to church or to musicales or to Birmingham for the symphony, cruising in their Buicks on Sunday afternoon—in a bond whose sweetness lay in a devotion that would be interrupted only by the rude fact of mortality and whose sadness lay in contemplating the terrible solitude that awaited the one unlucky enough to outlive all the others. Sometimes, of course, you wondered about the shadow side of such contrived domestic contentment, the parental selfishness or childish insecurity or lamentable romantic wound that demanded such a fortress existence.

The hotel, in any event, was a sociable place built around these two lovely innocents, the devout and scurrying and clearly doting mother and the trilling and unfailingly solicitous son. Perhaps because I was undergoing the predictable upsurgings of veneration and spirituality that casual Protestants often experience in deeply Catholic countries, I thought they seemed holy. Indeed, the severity of the hotel made you feel a little virtuous for staying there. It was built around a vine-shaded garden, and every morning I would awaken to the sonance of this gentle fellow fluting to the guests. He spoke in Italian or English, as if all he desired in life was their comfort. Was the room all right? Was there a need for more coffee or butter? Or for directions to the place for catching the tour boats? The man was an extremely polite musical alarm clock, rousing me gently, and when I went down for breakfast under the grape arbor, where I took my latte in an encompassing, almost aqueous green light in the incomparable Italian morning, and asked if there was a fishing tackle store in the town, he sang me to the right place.

I found it the first day, and many a mild afternoon after finishing my writing, I made my way down there to eye the owner's comely daughter and to try to wheedle local knowledge from her old man. The stock of fishing gear was limited, as was the proprietor's English. But in other respects, it was the ideal tackle store. The place was a combination working man's bar, coffee shop and news stand. It had beer, cappuccino and almost new British newspapers. There was supposed to be a game warden who would tell me about getting permission on the private trout streams in the region, but he never showed up. That was all right. By that time, my attention had shifted to Lake Como and my discovery that the water of the swimming beach at the Villa Serbelloni was home to a lot of fish.

It wasn't much of a beach, a rim of sand in a protected cove at the bottom of ancient stone steps. To the left as you faced the lake was a bluff that marched in ever higher ramparts toward a forested point of land that commanded one of the great views of Lake Como. In classical times, Pliny the Younger had a villa there, which he named Tragedia. To the right of the little beach was a piazza and towering boathouse—all of the same gray stone exposed on the flanks of Pliny's promontory. In back of the beach rose a sloping hill of tawny grass. It was spotted with fig trees and olive trees that looked dusty gray in the September sun. If you followed a winding gravel road to the crest of the hill, there, straddling the neck of Pliny's peninsula, was the Villa Serbelloni, a house that had over the centuries accreted outward from a fourteenth-century Saxon tower. What I am trying to say is that it was a damn fine place to be, and as a Southerner, I felt at home there, since the hospitality of the place, strangely enough, was financed by bourbon whiskey.

A little history is in order. Two noble families, the Sfrondatis and the Serbellonis, owned the place for four hundred years, each generation adding a wing to the house or improving the gardens with terraces, grottoes, chapels and elaborate plantings of boxwood, yew, cypress and bay. Over the years, the visitors included Leonardo da Vinci, various Holy Roman emperors, Queen Victoria and Kaiser Wilhelm. Flaubert, taken with the beauty of the place, pronounced it "a truly Shakespearean landscape." He added, "One could live and die here."

Ella Walker, an American heiress with a late-blooming, robber-baron hunger for European culture, did just that. Using the money her dad had piled up from the sale of Hiram Walker whiskey, she bought the place in 1930, and she died there in 1959. On her deathbed, she bequeathed the estate to the Rockefeller Foundation, stipulating that it be used as a retreat for writers, composers, artists and scholars. Since then, many famous names have passed through. But the only guest the staff still gossiped about was John F. Kennedy. On a state visit to Italy on June 30, 1963, he made a side trip to Bellagio, where he managed to arrive unencumbered by the First Lady. There ensued certain New Frontier recreational rites that scandalized the help.

I was first informed of JFK's misconduct by the stern Italian widow who supervised the household and kitchen staff during my visit. She stiffened, however, when I raised the subject again a few days later. In the interim, I had picked up some tantalizing details from other local gossips. Was it true that Marella Agnelli, wife of the Fiat chairman Gianni Agnelli, had journeyed from Turin to welcome the president to Villa Serbelloni in a deeply personal way?

"This could not be," she said. Not only was the beautiful Marella wed to the elegant Gianni Agnelli but she was, in fact, an aristocrat in her own right before they married. Someone from her fine Italian family would never sleep with an Irish-American, president or not.

Years later, Marella Agnelli was interviewed by Sally Bedell Smith for her sexual history of the Kennedys, *Grace and Power*. "Maybe yes, maybe no. It is impossible to say," Mrs. Agnelli said when asked about the rumored dalliance. "I am an old grandmother, and Gianni and I are still very much together."

I'm the last one to make excuses for the Massachusetts billy goat, but it's clear to me that President Kennedy, a man well versed in European traditions, can hardly be blamed for following the customs of the place in which he was a guest. Long before Jack and Marella arrived, Bellagio and the Villa Serbelloni had a rich history of what the guidebook calls "romantic sojourns." An eighteenth-century poet-priest, Giuseppe Parini, tutored the Sfrondati children at Villa Serbelloni and apparently cut a democratic swath through both the servant girls and the visiting noble ladies. He was eventually fired for taking sides in a mysterious slapping incident involving a chambermaid and a duchess.

A century later, the composer Franz Liszt took a house near the villa when he arrived at Bellagio after borrowing, rather permanently, the wife of a French count. The couple lived near my little beach, and their frolics eventually produced a daughter named Cosima, who was to marry Richard Wagner. I was not able to add to the amatory legends of the place, but so far as I can tell I was the first guest to arrive with a fly rod.

My thought was to practice my casting in the afternoons after I finished writing. The spacious grassy plateau behind the boathouse was an ideal place, and alongside it there were plum and fig trees with fruit ripe for the taking. So I practiced long, reaching casts, forward and back on the dry, sunburned grass, trying in a relaxed way to comb the familiar tics from my delivery. Then one day, taking a break, I ambled along the battlements of the tall stone boathouse, and there, twenty feet below, swimming lazily beneath the windless surface of Lake Como, were scads of fish. The best of them were large gray fellows of two to four pounds who loafed along in a way I came to think of as impudent.

So my practice gave way to an afternoon ritual of casting to these arrogantly cruising Italian fish with every fly and nymph in my box and then retiring to the tackle store/bar for consultation with the proprietor. He readily identified these fish by their Italian names, but he drew a blank when I tried him on the aquatic nomenclature I had learned in England. Were they loach or roach, barbel or tench or bream—all common warm-water or "coarse" species in England and elsewhere on the continent? I figured that if I could come up with the English name, I could call my fish-mad Cockney pal Derrick Seymour in London and find out what natural food these fish ate and then figure out a fly to match it. One thing I was certain of was that they were not trout, and in all my inquisitions about trout in the area, my friend at the bar had never mentioned trout in Lake Como.

So my drowsy, pleasant and almost fishless September progressed. Every morning, from my apartment on the slopes of the olive grove, I watched the mists rise from Lake Como and tapped away at my word processor. By afternoon, I waded out to a large gray boulder off the swimming beach or prowled the elevated terrace beside the boathouse. From these locations, I cast to the alluring gray fish that drifted along just under the surface. I knew they had to eat something because by now I had seen the Italian commercial fishermen in slim, high-bowed boats taking them on slowly trolled hand lines. One day I had a strike on a tiny Clouser minnow that my friend Dick Blalock, then in the last year of his life, had tied for our brook trout excursions on the Rapidan. My fish was a five-inch yellow perch, as unmistakable in its perchiness as if hoisted from a Vermont pond. I was cheered to think I had now caught a fish in Italy, but this little fellow was clearly not one of the Como cruisers.

I learned a bit about local fishing lore. In past times, the offshore commercial fishing rights on Lake Como had been controlled by wealthy townsmen called "masters of the lake." The locals developed several styles of nets and trotlines with lovely names like lina, sibiel, spaderna and mologna for taking perch, whitefish and herring. They also used long drift nets marked with small bells so they could be found in the dark. But the nastiest work was done with the frosna, or harpoon.

Even among adherents of the Redneck Way of Fishing, fish-gigging is way down the evolutionary scale. Who would have expected such a debased practice in such a classical setting? I attribute the popularity of the technique to the maddening effect of the gray cruisers, and I discovered that not even Liszt was immune. When he was not making babies with Marie de Flavigny, writing sonatas inspired by Dante or giving legendary concerts in Milan or Como, Franz liked to unleash his inner Good Old Boy. "Towards evening," he wrote, "we amuse ourselves fishing by torchlight. Armed with a long harpoon we glide across the waters looking out for drowsy fish dazzled by the lamplight hanging from the prow of the boat."

Across the 160 years that separated us, I saluted Liszt as a phrase maker. By day or night, "drowsy" was exactly the right word for these fish. I also vowed that, unlike the great composer, I would not be reduced to fish stabbing. I surrendered to the verdict of Lake Como. The lone perch would be all that I received. Each day after writing, I fished for a while, without expectation or angst, and the month moved along in a bending, autumnal rhythm. Cooler breezes jiggled the last fruit from the trees in the hillside orchard. With the changing light, the colors shifted subtly. The leaves on the olive trees somehow settled more deeply into that zone of gray-green color you see in the forested backgrounds of Renaissance paintings. Perhaps to punctuate His satisfaction with the heavy, sexy, wholly Italianate ripeness of the place and season, God decreed an intervention in the workings of Nature upon humankind or, more specifically, upon me. There came to pass an opportunity for me to interrupt my fishlessness. It was, by my lights, a miracle. I thought so then and I think so now. I was on my rock, not a speck of hope in my heart, when it happened.

Far out on the still surface of Lake Como, with nary another human being or boat in sight, fish began to rise. Not just to rise, mind you, but to strike savagely. I have never seen anything exactly like it in fresh water. Here was a compact school of fish striking in the roving marauder fashion of jack crevalle or bluefish. Then, it became clear that out of the fifty-six square miles of Lake Como's surface, a divine will was directing them to the patch of water in front of the rock I inhabited. They veered this way and that, feeding all the while, but always swung back toward me as if locked on a radar heading. I had on a dry fly, a number 16 caddis, and I cast, perfectly, if I do say so. The fly landed right in the path of the school. Soon my little fly was rocking on the wavelets of their frenzied feeding, and in a moment, I was taken, as the English like to say.

And oh, brothers and sisters of the angle, how I hate to tell what happened next. Since Franz Liszt did not cover this circumstance in his Lake Como diaries, I quote from another great composer, the late Mr. Roger Miller of Nashville, Tenn. To wit:

Dang me, dang me, they oughta take a rope and hang me.

For over forty years, since I learned to snatch crappies from the turbid waters of South Sauty Creek in North Alabama, a terrible, fish-levitating force had slept in my arm, like one of those alien pods you see implanted in the sci-fi movies. By steady effort, I tamed and controlled this monstrous reflex. Yet in that beautiful place, that site blessed by Pliny's poetry and Jack Kennedy's boinking and finally by a divine piscatorial intervention decreed for my sole benefit, this dormant muscular spasm chose, as if by its own malevolent will, to awaken. In this rare moment, this long-awaited taking by a mysterious fish ravenous for connection with me, I executed the South Sauty Heave. If I had been using marlin tackle, the fish would have sailed through the air and flopped on the sandy beach of the Villa Serbelloni. Alas, I was using trout tackle, specifically a leader so fragile it could barely lift the tail of your sleeping cat.

Back at the bar, my friend was sympathetic.

"This is very unusual," he said, leaning against the glass-topped counter that held cigars and tiny rubber shrimp.

"In what way?" I said.

"There are brown trout that live deep in Lake Como," he said with the weighty tone of a man revealing that there was a lost colony of Neanderthals in the rocky crags of the Simplon Pass. "They very seldom come up."

No, I thought. I do not want to listen. I won't listen. I fought back an urge to put my fingers in my ears. But he was into it now, swinging as relentlessly as a casket lid toward the inevitable closing of his story.

"But sometimes they do gather into schools on the surface and behave as you describe. No one knows why. They make a snapping sound when they feed."

"Like castanets," I said, snapping my fingers in a hopeless little motion.

"Yes, exactly." He beamed, as if proud of my observatory, if not my fishing skill.

I asked if it was likely to happen again. I thought perhaps my visit to the shores of Como had somehow coincided with the season of rising up and feeding with the sound of castanets. Hell, it's a romantic country, Italy. I do not know the Italian words for "You have the brains of a zucchini." But I know the look and body language that expresses the same thought. There's a kind of nonverbal Esperanto understood on fishing grounds the world over. That look told me I could stand on that gray boulder for as long as I liked, and I would see the ghost of Franz Liszt slinging a harpoon before I got another look at a brown trout.

Over the years, the trout that swam away with my caddis fly in its mouth has become one of the most prominent residents in that box of my memory reserved for fish lost despite a cosmic stroke of unrepeatable luck. I still wince at the memory of the exact moment in which I raised the rod too sharply, felt the tiny click of the line breaking and set that fish free beneath waters that once moved under the gaze of Pliny and Leonardo, which raises a question. How did I become a man who cared whether a bloody fish got away?

CHAPTER 2

My New Fishing License

If you read a book called *Fly Fishing Through the Midlife Crisis,* which came out in 1993, you know a fair amount about my life up to that point. I turned fifty that year, and I started this book as a sequel, exploring what it feels like to move into the later, supposedly calmer stages of life after a sometimes stormy, but stimulating Middle Passage. *Fly Fishing Through the Midlife Crisis* traced my rediscovery, as a restless thirty-eight-year-old White House reporter, of a boyhood passion for the sport of fly fishing. The book records the fishing adventures that my young sons, Ben and Jeff, and I had under the tutelage of our Falstaffian fly fishing guru, the aforementioned Dick Blalock, a retired diplomat-gourmand-raconteur. The quest for wisdom in fly fishing—to move from the greedy Redneck Way of Fishing practiced in my native Alabama to the higher ground of catch-and-release angling for pure sport—parallels in time other more arduous personal trials and passages common to life in our time and country: feelings of entrapment in the midst of a promising career, a restlessness too elusive to diagnose or treat, painful marital journeys like the one that led my wife and me to divorce in 1990. That's *Fly Fishing Through the Midlife Crisis* in a nutshell.

In starting this sequel, I planned to explore the passage that comes after midlife. Once again, fly fishing would provide the context for talking about dreams of freedom in the natural world, about my work as a journalist and about the task that confronts everyone who survives long enough—how to conduct honorable, pleasurable, productive and graceful lives as we finish out our working careers and move toward old age. The final topography of *The One That Got Away* turned out, like most things in life, to be far different from anything I could have imagined.

I started at *The New York Times* as a national correspondent in 1978. It was the sixth newspaper for which I worked and, while not the most vigorous, certainly the best in overall quality and in the rewards it offered for people who liked to work hard. I was determined it would be my last newspaper. I never expected to stay so long, since I spent a lot of energy during my first ten years at the *Times* plotting an escape from its sometimes stifling embrace. But stay I did. Under company rules, I faced mandatory retirement no later than February 4, 2009, one day before my sixty-sixth birthday. I was appointed to the top job in the *Times* newsroom, executive editor, on September 5, 2001. Those were eventful times, full of death, suffering and pain for the *Times*'s home city and for our country as we moved from the calamity of 9/11 to the grinding wars in Afghanistan and Iraq.

The *Times* staff of 1,100 reporters, editors, photographers, artists, designers, researchers and clerks produced magnificent newspapers during these events. For its work in 2001, the *Times* set the all-time record for Pulitzer Prizes won in a single year, seven in all, five for coverage of 9/11 and the war in Afghanistan. The seven included the Pulitzer board's highest honor, the Prize for Public Service, which the paper had earned only five times in the eighty-nine-year history of the Pulitzer competition. The *Times* won the Prize for Public Service again in 2004, for work published during my twenty-one months as executive editor.

But something else happened on my watch. If you were following the news in mid-2003, you may remember that I was fired as executive editor after a reporter named Jayson Blair published dozens of lies in the form of made-up or plagiarized facts in our paper. I had not hired Blair or promoted him from clerk to reporter. None of the voluminous memos produced by the *Times* bureaucracy about Blair's lax professional and personal habits ever reached my desk, probably because we were all working so hard to handle the rush of breaking news that followed the attack on the twin towers. I did approve an editor's suggestion to use Blair on the large team of reporters covering the Washington sniper story, in which position he established himself in the liars' hall of fame. Newspapers are hierarchical. When the ship hits a rock, the captain may have to walk the plank. Such was my fate. Some people thought I got a raw deal. Others were glad to see me go. That is not what this book is about.

Mainly, this book is about what happens when you get what you wanted most in the strangest possible way. It's about the unpredictability of luck, love, lies and, of course, life in all its glorious, heartbreaking, quicksilver mutability. Years before I got fired, back when I was writing *Fly Fishing Through the Midlife Crisis,* I recounted with approval the tale of Carl Jung congratulating one of his patients on losing his job. Now, Jung said, you can get on with making your life interesting. Actually, I thought about that on Wednesday, June 3, 2003, when the *Times*'s publisher, Arthur O. Sulzberger, Jr., called me into his office and let me go. "This is not going to be an easy conversation," he said. It was a considerate thought, but he was wrong. The meeting was short and cordial, a time of dashed hopes we shared, understood and did not need to discuss. I had run enough people off the paper to know that going on about whys and what-ifs is tedious and undignified.

Besides, after forty years of going to the office day after grinding day, I was curious to know if Jung was right about the joys of abrupt liberation or simply blowing that old psychoanalytic smoke. I had loved the sustaining "truths and ideals," to use Jung's language, of the life that was ending for me that day. "But," Jung added, "we cannot live the afternoon of life according to the programme of life's morning: for what was great in the morning will be little at evening, and what in the morning was true will at evening have become a lie."

Now when it comes to talking about my new programme, there's only one place to start, where the Gulf of Mexico's green-crystal waters wash upon soft silver sands.

CHAPTER 3

Snapshot I:
Beyond the Second Sandbar,
the World's Most Beautiful
Bathing Beach, 1947

I almost drowned once. That could be the source of my enchantment with creatures of the watery world. The event alarmed everyone in our family who witnessed it, yet it is one of my happiest memories. Actually, if my companions and I had enough sense to worry about anything, we should have been more worried about sharks than about drowning that brilliant long-ago summer day. But in those days at Panama City Beach, Florida, the people who owned the cottages and tourist courts, for this was before the age of motels, said that the only sharks along the World's Most Beautiful Bathing Beach were sand sharks, and sand sharks do not bite.

On the part of the local authorities, promoters and possibly even average citizens with a decent memory, this was a lie of considerable magnitude. The northern Gulf of Mexico is one of the world's great shark hatcheries. In the years leading up to World War II, there was a commercial shark-liver-oil factory in Panama City. It closed only because the market for shark-liver oil collapsed, not because Panama City was running out of said livers or the hammerhead, bull, blacktip, blue, spinner, mako and tiger sharks that produced them.

But believing as we all did that there were only pacifist sand sharks in our waters, my brother and sister and cousins, all teenagers, made long trains of automobile inner tubes, using a few feet of rope between each tube. With the big boys up front to do the kicking, this string of young Raineses ventured far from shore, a half mile or more, way out beyond the second sandbar. My parents and aunts and uncles, being from the Alabama hills and trusting uncritically in the fictional affability of local sharks, thought this was a healthful recreation for the young people and gave it their blessing. Sometimes they would sit proudly on the patios of their new waterfront cottages and watch their little darlings bob toward the horizon. Sometimes they didn't watch but went about whatever business it was that occupied adults at the beach in those easeful years after World War II. This happened on a day when my parents were not watching.

I was four. Someone, my parents, I suppose, had bought for me a child-size circular float tube at the beach store. I remember it well. It had a printed design on one side and was clear plastic on the other. There was a tiny navel on one side of the tube, from which unfurled a plastic straw by which the device was inflated. My siblings and cousins inserted me in the tube, which fit up under my arms, and trailed me along as the caboose in our jolly floating train.

Far offshore, they looked back to check on me, and I was gone.

I can remember being under the sea. The water was clear and colorless near the surface, then fading to an emerald transparency nearer the bright sand bottom. I don't remember seeing any fish, but I knew that the surf held darting, shining fish that would nibble your toes when you waded in, and I had a sense of entering their world. It was peaceful. I don't remember breathing water, but surely I must have. I do not remember being afraid, but surely I must have been. I remember, as I said, clarity and white light that seemed to expand in all directions. I do not recall flailing back to the surface. I did bob up after a while, however, and of that moment, bursting into the sunlight to the unabashed jubilation of my minders, I have a sharp and distinct memory. They report that I was splashing around but not terribly dismayed. They put me back in my tube, and I remember the words "Don't tell Mama and Daddy" being spoken over and over, and I never did.

For all my childhood summers after that, there was no keeping me out of the sea along the World's Most Beautiful Bathing Beach. I prowled its shallows relentlessly with buckets and a long-handled net. I was a collector of blue crabs, sand dollars, bullhead minnows, coquinas, sand fleas, anything that could be dipped from the water. Then my attention turned to the problem of trying to pull things from the waters of Florida, things that pulled much harder than the twenty crappies I caught at South Sauty, back home in Alabama.

I hooked a shark while fishing for spotted sea trout with my father and brother in a rented boat. They were using the casting rods they used for bass in fresh water. I had a big cane pole. My brother reports that he heard me grunt and looked around to see me hanging on grimly while a fish longer than I was cut tight circles with the green line in the green water over the green eelgrass of West Bay. This I remember extremely well.

"It's a shark! Give me the pole!" my brother shouted.

He rose from the transom seat of the boat and reached toward me. I did not want to be helped. I had not asked to be helped. I was transfixed by the sight of the shark's cutting didoes in front of me as if the whole bay was my personal aquarium. As far as I could tell, my shark and I were doing all right. I remember the feel of the pole's thick, gnarly butt in my hands, and I remember pulling the pole as hard as I could toward the vertical and the sharp bend that put into the tip. Before I had time to figure out how to avoid the unsolicited brotherly assistance now headed toward me, the knot on my line failed. Either my father or brother had tied it. Before too long, I learned to tie my own knots.

Still, I was indisputably at their mercy when it came to getting out to sea. Usually when my dad and his brothers chartered Bert Raffield for their king mackerel trips, I was barred on the spurious grounds that I would get seasick and ruin everyone's trip. I wasn't buying that, of course, because I had been on pleasure boat cruises with no problem. Jerry, by contrast, had been known to spew like Vesuvius when his shoes touched a boat deck. Such was his passion for ocean fishing that he learned to cure himself at sea by force of will. For many years, he was the only person I knew who could accomplish that. My passion was just as strong as his. Finally, when I was seven or eight, my father and my uncle Erskine chartered Captain Emil Frudaker and his boat, the *Miss Muriel,* since Bert Raffield's boat was already booked. I was allowed to go. I do not overstate when I tell you that it was one of my happiest days on this planet, a perfect— nay, supernal—undertaking for a journey-proud, land-bound boy who longed to plumb the bleak ocean sea.

Even before we left the dock, Captain Frudaker proved him- self a masterful utterer of profanity. Nor was Erskine a slouch in this regard. While we were still crossing the smooth waters of the bay, Uncle Erskine hooked a big black grouper, and as he cranked he said, "It pulls like a goddamned bale of cotton." I filed this sentence away in my memory as soon as I heard it, and still trot it out from time to time in homage to a particularly hard- pulling fish.

At the time, I expected my father to shush his cursing brother and our fulminating captain in respect of my innocent presence. He didn't say a word, however, and all day the captain and my uncle competed like trapeze artists, turning the air blue with triple somersaults of profanation. The entire experience was educational, and not just in respect to my ability to express frus- tration or offer colorful tributes to worthy fish. Because Emil Fru- daker proved as skillful at fishing as at malediction, I also learned the addictive power of two sensations that hold me in their thrall to this day.

One is the motion of a big boat going out to the fishing grounds. The grouper had come aboard just after daylight. Now, as the sun lifted from the ocean beyond the jetties, Captain Fru- daker pointed *Miss Muriel*'s bow dead south and throttled up her twin Chevy engines. I felt *Miss Muriel* climb and slide, climb and slide as she forged through the flattened, inbound rollers in the pass between St. Andrews Bay and the open Gulf. The second stroke of my enlightenment came once we were a mile or so offshore, and the boat had slowed to trolling speed.

The mate put out four lines and handed the second portside rod to me. The two people holding the stern lines had fishing chairs. But those holding the side rods were put on long benches that ran almost the length of the cockpit. I was sitting on a small cushion on one of those benches when a strong fish took my lure, a Japanese feather dressed with a cigar minnow. The boat was running one way, and the fish was going another. Since I weighed all of fifty pounds and since I was sitting atop a loose cushion on lacquered wood, I began sliding rapidly toward the stern. I was, in fact, being pulled overboard. It never occurred to me to let go of the rod. Quicker than it takes to tell, I had been dragged off the bench and toward the transom of the boat. I would have gone slam over it if my shoulder had not hit a roof post near the rear corner of the deck. That gave the adults time to grab me before I made the second accidental entry of my young life into the sea off Panama City.

Eventually I cranked in a toothy, silvery king mackerel over three feet long. I caught four of the monsters that day, but it was not the sight of my four dead fish on the dock that I remember most sharply or that made a sea fisherman of me. It was the jolting strike itself, the synaptic speed of that righteous moment when you feel the abrupt weight of the fish on the line, the sudden, unmediated ascent from vacancy to sanctified connection with creature, ocean, sky, the juice of life, with a miracle so sublime, so brand new in this world that it feels utterly unpredicted and unrepeatable. Oh, joy without mitigation! Oh, thunder of expectation in the blood! Oh, this shimmering mystery, this glimmering surprise! Oh, moment of cathexis eternal!

That is to say, it felt pretty good to me—so good, in fact, that I quickly discovered I could remember how good the last strike was only in the fleeting instant when the new one was going on.

Of course, there are people who say feeling a fish take your lure is like coming. We've all heard that. Such comparisons were beyond the ken of the rescued and thoroughly transformed little boy aboard the *Miss Muriel* as she climbed and slipped over long, mackerel-rich swells while his incomparable uncle and the Ahab of the World's Most Beautiful Bathing Beach shouted goddamns to the heavens. Besides, it felt better than that.

CHAPTER 4

Among the Manhattoes

I was born in the winter of 1943, and fifty years later, in the same bleak season, I moved to New York. Mayflower brought my furniture. The fly rods traveled with me in an Isuzu Trooper that would eventually be eaten by Manhattan. The city, I was to learn, whittles you down. It wants you to travel light. If you come by automobile, it also wants you to cross some grim territory to get there. Pat Moynihan liked to speak of the days when even a poor man "entered New York like a king." Train-riding yokels from small-town America never forgot the vaulted spaces of Grand Central or the old Penn Station, where black engines lay panting like big dogs beside the teeming arrival platforms. When ships bound for Ellis Island slipped in on the swirling tides of the Narrows, the gazers from steerage felt blessed by their first sight of the islanded statue and the islanded invincible city beyond.

It's a whole lot different when you come thumping along the New Jersey Turnpike in an SUV. Instead of Lady Liberty, you get the Joyce Kilmer Service Area, last chance to buy gasoline and Whoppers before the tunnel. The Kilmer, with its teeming throngs of galosh-footed hoi polloi and its lot of rusted and busted cars parked between rows of gray snow, made me grumpy. Then, upon reflection, I decided that you need to allow downtrodden areas a little room for boosterism. The South, after all, raised plenty of monuments to generals who specialized in losing battles. Why shouldn't murky old Jersey build memorials to its bad poets? Brooklyn, after all, had a stronger claim on Whitman.

To get to the Kilmer, you pass through the Meadowlands, historic dumping ground for PCBs and surplus members of La Cosa Nostra. Corpses are certainly the least toxic substances hidden in these tidal creeks, yet you can still glimpse mallards in the potholes. Nature persists. It presses at the urban fringe, stubbornly convinced it can outlast the city.

Neither you nor the ducks should bet on New York going easily. Not even the crazed Saudis of Al Qaeda could erase the insistent, even magisterial fact that at some point in every transit of New Jersey, out there on the northern horizon, the works of man, with a mountainous steel authority, rise up as abruptly as the east front of the Rockies where they leap from the grassland plain around Choteau, Montana. These are the cliffs of Manhattan, mournfully snaggletoothed from the loss of the twin towers. But even in their falling and rising, even when they stand outlined against the sky of memory, the buildings of Manhattan remind us that in a world where the loftiest peak is on its way to becoming a pile of sand, our New York is the renewable mountain. For pilgrims from the outback, of any age and from any place in that vast Podunk that is the rest of America, the fact of the gleaming city is forever new for us, nascent and jolting for each generation in its turn, a permanent surprise. And at some point it hits even the most jaded and well traveled of newcomers that there is an arresting name for what lies at the end of the Holland Tunnel.

Home.

For my part, I never thought it would come to this—actually having to live in Manhattan, I mean. My cushy time as an expense-account visitor was over. Now I'd have to pay for shelter from the scrum. Years ago back in Alabama, when I accidentally became a newspaper reporter, no one could have told me that, at the age of fifty, I would approach New York with a sense of Fitzgeraldian awe that I never felt on arrival in the other imperial cities—Rome, London, Beijing, Paris, Tokyo, Delhi, Moscow. And certainly, no one could have convinced me that I would arrive as one of those who come down out of the hills to bayonet the wounded. That is to say, I was there as an editorial writer, a breed that I, like most career newspaper reporters, viewed with suspicion. Alabama's rogue-giant governor, Big Jim Folsom, used to say that reporters were the "workin' press" and editorial writers were the "settin' press"—a bunch of old hens forever clucking and puffing their feathers and counting the eggs in their nests.

I had, as it were, talked my way into the henhouse. By the 1992 presidential campaign, I had been the *Times*'s Washington bureau chief for four years, and I was getting restless. On January 16, 1992, Arthur Sulzberger, Jr., succeeded his father Arthur "Punch" Sulzberger, Sr., as publisher. I told Arthur that the *Times* needed a liberal columnist strong enough to serve as a counterweight on the op-ed page to William Safire, the masterly conservative pundit who was a franchise byline at the *Times* and, despite our differing views on politics, my good friend. It would be fun to see if I could hold my own against Safire, with his network of sources, tireless reporting, witty prose and his killing instinct for ripe targets. Arthur said since I was interested in opinion writing, he had a better idea. I should become editor of the editorial page. Surprised, I backpedaled. I seldom read the *Times* editorial page and had no ambition to write in that stolid way, even as the boss of the whole operation.

Arthur swore he wanted to change the page. He wanted editorials with greater muzzle velocity and a sharper, more distinctive style. He wanted the page to "have a voice," and he said he was willing to take the heat if we took a tough, independent line with Democrats as well as Republicans. About one thing I was not worried. I felt he had an instinctive feel for my politics. I have always voted as a liberal, but I have never been a party man. In assessing politicians journalistically, integrity and truthfulness always counted more than party for me. Coming of age when George Wallace and Barry Goldwater were trying to out-seg each other, I regarded both parties as flawed vessels unworthy of holding the precious bodily fluids of democracy. I hated the way *The Wall Street Journal* editorial page whored for the Republicans, and I wasn't about to do the same thing for the Democrats.

I told Arthur he should think of me as a mean-spirited liberal, opposed to the abuse of welfare by individuals and by corporate America as well. You could total up the pennies stolen by every welfare cheat since 1776 and you wouldn't have a patch on the public subsidies for steel, railroad, oil companies and defense contractors in any given decade since 1900. The *Times* didn't need a knee-jerk Democratic page, he said, citing its endorsements of Dwight Eisenhower and, more recently, of New York's splenetic Republican senator, Al D'Amato.

"Just give it some thought," Arthur said. "I'm in no rush to make a decision."

The South in my day had produced a few heroic editorialists, and I had worked for and admired one of them at *The Tuscaloosa News.* In the fifties, Buford Boone had supported the admission of a black woman to the University of Alabama. Because of the death threats, Buford slept for much of the rest of his life with a shotgun under his bed. And even though a few friends knew he feared for his life, his editorials continued to sound like they had been written by an armed man who wasn't scared to shoot. When he wrote that Bobby Shelton, the imperial wizard of the Ku Klux Klan, was a "jackal," the jackal sued and won a $500 libel judgment at the Tuscaloosa County Courthouse. Shelton said that wasn't much of a penalty for ruining a citizen's good name. Buford said that if he had known the price was going to be so reasonable, he would have gone ahead and called him a worthless son of a bitch.

Still, admiring a courageous small-town editor and wanting to write editorials are two very different things. On the other hand, it would be a hell of a thing to give the *Times* editorial page a literary voice and make it a force for campaign finance reform, health care, the environment, civil liberties and social justice. Not that the *Times* was wrong on any of these issues. It was simply too polite in its support. The environment was my favorite example. The *Times* wanted clean air and clean water and wilderness protection, but it was also for wise use and cost-benefit analysis, an approach that offered huge loopholes for polluters and developers. I wanted a page that would respond to Jack Welch's laments about the $500 million GE was supposed to spend to dredge its PCBs from the Hudson by pointing out what every legislator in Albany knew. Considering what GE's slovenly waterfront factories did to that river over the course of thirty very profitable years, his stinginess was an insult to the taxpayers.

As a young reporter in Southern capitals, I was part of the first generation to write insistently about "sunshine laws" and campaign finance. The pork-chop legislators and the lobbyists who fed them in Tallahassee and Atlanta had laughed at us, right up until public pressure forced them to support reform. In our day, someone needed to bang the war drum for those issues on the national stage and try to shame the members of Congress into acts of virtue.

By and by, I convinced myself that this might be fun. Firing up the editorial page also fit into my theory that the *Times*'s traditional stodginess was no longer a charming eccentricity. It was a threat to the paper's long-term prosperity and influence. The *Times* could boost its stagnant circulation—and thereby increase its newsroom budget for quality journalism—only by attracting the nation's best-educated, most affluent, most sophisticated readers and the advertisers who needed them as customers. To do that, a newspaper that liked to wear its dullness like a merit badge had to become livelier, smarter, more modern, more authoritative on a broader range of subjects and, of course, less painful to read. I could also see how the editor of that kind of editorial page might have trouble holding on to his job. The prevailing creed in the newsroom was that any effort to improve the paper in any way other than cosmetically was "un-*Times*ian." It was heresy to suggest that the paper could become livelier without sacrificing its traditional seriousness of purpose. The *Times* did much of its journalism by the numbers. A new emphasis on creativity was a direct threat to the journalism of tireless repetition that represented professional rectitude and personal economic security for many of its editorial employees.

Journalism that is essentially mimetic and has only to be as good as what was done the day before is dog easy to make. By instinct, mimetic journalists are widget makers. Many had barely recovered from the makeover that Punch Sulzberger and Abe Rosenthal carried out in the 1970s. This segment of the staff—and it was large and influential—was an automatic constituency for editors who wanted to preside, not innovate. I couldn't imagine a more boring life than that of a journalistic gym teacher leading the same calisthenics every day.

But I was titillated by Arthur's claim that he wanted to pep up the paper. He had adopted the cajoling, tongue-in-cheek motto "Change sucks" as a way of preparing the staff to think the unthinkable. At its simplest, the message was that the paper could be better if we thought more about the news and less about the *Times*'s endemic struggles over turf, titles and perks. It wouldn't hurt to work harder, either. The institutional response was, predictably, We think the paper is good enough the way it is, which is the way it was, which is the way it ever shall be if we can help it. Still, Arthur had the look of a persistent fellow. I figured what the hell, this guy says he wants to step on the gas. Let's see how fast he wants to go. What sealed the deal for me was that I had nothing to lose. I was certainly the first and probably the last graduate of Birmingham-Southern College to be offered the editorship of the nation's most influential editorial page.

Once, in an interview for a feature story filed from London, I had asked a retired safari hunter named Hilary Hook why he decided to spend his life in Kenya. He was the last of the breed and something of a cult figure in England as the subject of a BBC documentary called *Home from the Hill.* Hook and I were in a pub in Wiltshire, about fifty miles from London. His eyes got dreamy. He had been sent as a young army officer to train native troops, first in India, then in Africa. He said once he got to Africa and saw how good the hunting was going to be on the Serengeti and in the Masai Mara during his lifetime, he had said to himself: "Why not have it?"

So why not write editorials for six months? If I hated the job, I could go back to the newsroom or quit. If Arthur didn't like the way I ran the page, he could fire me. My taste for smash-mouth journalism had almost gotten me fired a couple of times at other papers. Any journalist who wrote as if he had a shotgun under the bed had to know that there was always a sword over his head. That's the way the newspapers work.

In those days, Punch Sulzberger's East Side buddies liked to denigrate Arthur as "Pinch." The nickname was meant to wound. Mainly because Arthur looked younger than his years and had a flippant attitude toward high society, it was fashionable among the old guard to depict him as too light for the job he had inherited. Once I got to New York, I seldom missed a chance to tell those dinner-party mandarins that they were underestimating Arthur. He and I had met in the Washington bureau of the *Times* in 1981, when I was thirty-eight and he was twenty-nine, and we hit it off immediately, not as buddies but as colleagues. We were both true believers in the inherent superiority of the *Times,* but we were close enough in age to take a satirical, sixties view of its foibles and pretensions. Arthur was a competent writer who would have had a decent chance of getting a job on the *Times* even if his name was not Sulzberger. I thought he wore the mantle of future leadership in a graceful way. After two years on the paper, I was just beginning to recover from the shock that hits most newcomers from high-energy newspapers. We admired its rigorous standards and ability to attract smart people, but our admiration could not offset the frustration and puzzlement caused by the *Times's* dilatory response to the news and by its collective, institutional willingness to stand around and get scooped, as it had been by *The Washington Post* on Watergate. I felt intuitively that Arthur might be the man to change the paper's entrenched culture of indolence. In any event, we laughed at the same kinds of ridiculous people, whether they worked in the Reagan White House or in the Washington bureau of the *Times,* a collection of savants and nerds that felt like a cross between the Faculty Club and the Junior Electrons Science Club.

I always felt that his sonship was a mixed blessing to Arthur. He had been around long enough to learn that if you want to run a newspaper, the best thing to do is inherit one. But the question of whether he would have been there without the benefits of nepotism nagged at him. Once, years later when we were both in executive suites in New York, I congratulated Arthur on creating something entirely new in *Times* history, a management team in which every member was there on the basis of merit. I wanted to bite my tongue as soon as I saw the frozen look on his face. "Yes," he said, "everyone but me."

Whatever his insecurities, Arthur had brass balls when it came to editorials. I took over the editorial page three weeks before Bill Clinton was inaugurated, and we started blasting him almost immediately for his first round of wiggles, stretchers, flip-flops and sellouts. When the new president called Arthur to the White House for a private lunch and a bitching session, Arthur told him to think of our editorials as "tough love."

"I can see the tough," Clinton complained. "But where's the love?"

Arthur came right back and told me the story, but he didn't tell me to tone down our criticism. I was impressed. Standing up to presidents is not easy. People in journalism and politics, including our critics and surprised competitors, began to comment about the signs of life on the editorial page. The Sunday talk shows began quoting the *Times* editorial page where in the recent past they would have quoted *The Washington Post* or *The Wall Street Journal.* When network news shows regularly track your paper like that, it's a sure sign that you are a step ahead of your print competitors.

Not everyone was happy when we began to let it rip. Bullies manqué like the columnist George Will and Bob Bartley, the late editor of *The Wall Street Journal* editorial page, had gotten used to the silence of the liberals. Suddenly there was plenty of bleating from them and other conservative cheerleaders. When I wrote an editorial depicting Rupert Murdoch as a threat to American journalism, he ordered the *New York Post* to begin a weekly column attacking the *Times* in general and, often, me personally. Both *The New Yorker* and the *National Journal* ran stories about how unhappy the White House and the Democratic leadership of Congress were with our editorial page. They expected passing grades by virtue of not being Republicans. A *Times* reporter was quoted as saying that the whiners on Capitol Hill could expect no relief. "Howell eats gunpowder for breakfast," he said.

There was a lesson in the politicians' feedback and in the complaints from journalistic traditionalists inside and outside the *Times.* Both groups are happy with a *New York Times* that is dull but worthy. The last thing that other news organizations want to see is a *Times* ready to leverage its advantages in resources and prestige. Executives from the newspaper chains joked among themselves about our stuffiness, but deep in their hearts they wanted the *Times* to remain slow, tedious and self-important. If the *Times* gave its readers journalism that was quick, witty and creative as well as intellectually sound and serious of purpose, its example would put too much pressure on the entire newspaper industry and on media companies like Knight Ridder, Gannett and Newhouse that prided themselves on their frugal newsroom budgets.

Beyond raising Cain and attracting attention, there is little an editorial page editor can do to improve the overall quality of a big paper. The real power rests with the executive editor. By my reckoning, it would be almost ten years before I got a shot at the job. I would be approaching sixty and would have only five years or so to raise the paper's energy level and its circulation.

I developed what the political reporters call a two-pronged strategy. If I got the top job, I would stay until I reached mandatory retirement age as I approached my sixty-sixth birthday. I would put every fiber of energy and creativity I could muster into showing that it was possible to "turn the battleship," to use the metaphor constantly invoked, in the negative, by the paper's most talented journalists. If I didn't get the top job, I would try to figure out some way to afford early retirement and put that same amount of effort into the book-writing career I had put on hold so many times.

Although I wanted to win the top job at the *Times,* I knew I could live without it for the simple reason that I had already fulfilled my burning boyhood ambition, which was to publish a novel before I died. The novelist Scott Spencer spoke for me when he said that "nothing has ever really quite matched the complete sense of vindication of having my first book published." *Whiskey Man* came out from Viking to good reviews in 1977. It was a Depression yarn based loosely on my great-grandfather on my mother's side. "Doc" Fell got his nickname from his sideline occupation as an herbalist. But his real calling was as a stalwart in the production and consumption ends of the moonshine business.

The financial pressures of raising a family and the success I was having at the *Times* caused me to abandon my dream of leaving newspapers altogether to devote myself fully to novels and serious nonfiction. As for my immediate prospects, editorial writing is not a bad life. It is far less tiring than most kinds of real work, including news reporting. The hard part was being honest with myself about the fact that I might be saying a final farewell to the creative life I had once imagined. Who knew if I would have enough juice left at the end of my newspaper days to write this book, for which I signed a contract in 1994, and the big Civil War novel, the big civil rights novel and the ambitious nonfiction books that stood queued like neglected children in my guilty imagination?

It was a pragmatic decision—the money was good—and a timid one. The odds on writing a good novel are daunting. The odds on writing a novel that would make more money than the *Times* would be paying me were pretty damn long, too.

There was an idealistic component. Even if journalism was my second love, I had felt from the start an unfeigned passion for newspapering and an almost religious sense of mission about the *Times* as an institution. Whatever its flaws, the *Times* best embodied the kind of journalism that is essential to the future of the American nation. Helping the paper make the changes necessary to assuring its own future was a worthy life's work, and I was curious to see just how good the *Times* could be if energy and creativity could be wedded to its ideals and superior resources.

Plus, making a newspaper is terrific fun, at least for me. A newspaper is a daily miracle of birth through the agency of scores of midwives and great barns of tireless robots and thundering machines. As for the people, every newsroom is a ship of fools. Some are mad, some are funny, some brilliant, some priapic, a few tragic and, of course, a good many drunk or stoned. The best of them are haunted by the knowledge that newspapers don't create anything that lasts. In the next rank down, you find those capable of true enjoyment, riding the daily adrenaline rush and not caring a whit that the next day's work will vanish into the maw of time before they have their next scrambled egg. For the likes of me, newspapers became our Hotel California. Wanting to leave was a chronic whisper in the back of your head, but the gang in the bar was fun and checking out seemed just about impossible.

At least four times over the years—1969, 1974, 1977, 1984—I had made serious escape attempts. I freelanced for eighteen months in 1974, finishing two books that failed to make me rich enough to quit. I had always gone back to the newsroom for the steady money I needed as a family man and for the daily deadline rush that was methadone for my unfulfilled literary cravings. As I turned fifty and settled in as editorial page editor, I had no illusions of escape, but I liked contemplating some newly available consolations. The final payment of my divorce settlement was in sight, and my sons, Ben and Jeff, were both out of college. A really good raise with hefty bonuses and stock options came with the promotion. For the first time in my adult life, I had the means to fish anywhere I wanted for any fish that caught my fancy and to pursue the diversions available to an unattached heterosexual male in the world capital of smart, beautiful, stylish and/or rich women. So no one was more surprised than I when I was hit, not long after I'd settled into my new New York kind of life, by a failure of desire in regard to angling. It happened in the office of the Sinus Doctor to the Stars. Who knew what might fail next?

I became very fond of the Sinus Doctor to the Stars. He had a select clientele, some living, some dead. He had signed photos and letters of thanks from JFK and LBJ (dead) and Sinatra (then living) and Pavarotti. He was the guy who the White House or the Metropolitan Opera or the Broadway producers called in when the stars were having voice trouble at showtime. My Washington, D.C., sinus doctor told me that the guy was an incorrigible social climber, but that he was also the absolute best in the business and that he'd take me as a patient because I was a top editor at the *Times*. Sure enough, I strolled right in and became a pampered patient. The day of my first appointment, Mick Jagger was in the waiting room. I figured if this guy could fix those sinuses he had the real uptown mojo, and it turned out I was right.

The other thing about Sinus Doctor to the Stars was that he was a truly nice and caring man. The autograph collecting that bothered the other doctor was pretty standard behavior for carriage-trade physicians in Manhattan. After looking into congested orifices all day, why shouldn't the guy get a signed picture from the Chairman of the Board or a cushiony hug from a diva? I liked him a lot, and I listened when he told me in May 1993 that I could not go on a wilderness canoe trip with a sinus infection. You have to delay the trip, he said, and to my surprise I let him prevail even though a week's delay would mean we would be there after the smallmouth bass had spawned. Catching five-and six-pound bass was the reason for the trip. The way fishing works in northern Minnesota and southern Ontario is that if you get there too late, the big female fish have gone back to deep water and mostly you catch the pound-and-a-half males that are guarding the nests. The fact that I would follow the doctor's orders given this set of circumstances was the first sign I might be becoming tabescent as to fishing.

Here's the sad part. Not long after he ordered me to sleep in my own bed rather than a tent in the North Woods, the Sinus Doctor to the Stars got the flu. Although he didn't look it, he was in his mid-seventies. He insisted on coming to the office every day, waving off the nurses' increasingly urgent warnings that he go home for uninterrupted bedrest. After several days of this contrary behavior, he died in his sleep in his nice East Side apartment.

Flu is very dangerous for older people. In Doc's case, there's a lesson about Manhattan that goes beyond the great universal truth that no one gets out alive, even on the upper East Side. Perhaps it's because having 1.5 million people crammed onto one little island shakes up the odds, but in any case, I was to find evidence time and again that there is definitely some kind of galactic statistical glitch in the areas of luck and mortality in Manhattan. I soon learned that the deadliest diseases in my new hometown turned out to be irony and paradox. Look closely at the Doctor to the Stars, who was certainly the best upper respiratory disease physician in New York, maybe in the world. In my view, he stopped breathing altogether because the Manhattan Luck Warp, what we might call the irony odds, means that sometime, somewhere a doctor has to die of not following his nurses' orders. Some rainy day, sooner or later, a Con Ed vice president is going to get electrocuted by a hot manhole cover. Similarly— perhaps tomorrow, perhaps after we're all gone—some veterinarian or dog walker is going to die on the sidewalk on York Avenue and East Eighty-fourth Street after being struck by a twenty-pound Persian cat falling from the forty-third-floor window of a $5 million co-op apartment. It could happen. There's even a name for the plummeting-cat "epidemic," to use the term chosen by the American Society for the Prevention of Cruelty to Animals. It's called "high-rise syndrome." Three to five cats a week bail out of New York buildings. In one sample, more than 130 cats fell from heights of two to thirty-two stories in five months. Forty percent of them fell at night, which means that you might never know what hit you.

There is another way, I suppose, of looking at the paradoxical death of the Sinus Doctor to the Stars. Leaving the nurses out of it, you could say he died of not staying home when he should have. I mention this because it reminded me that just the opposite is what usually happens in the South, especially in my family.

CHAPTER 5

Hereditary Reasons for Leaving Alabama

If there was such a thing as Debrett's Guide to Redneck Royalty, you can be assured that my kinfolks and I would merit a line or two. On this point I refer you to John Martin Dombhart's *History of Walker County, Alabama, Its Towns and Its People,* published by the well-remembered Cayce Publishing Company of Thornton, Arkansas. Dombhart, born and educated in Washington, D.C., arrived in Alabama in 1929 and made a life's work of recording the history of "those hardy pioneers, who came into the 'hill country' with little or no possessions, and through the work of their own hands, alone, created the county." And quite a county it became, too, producing in due course a Speaker of the United States House of Representatives, the legendary actress and cocaine snorter Tallulah Bankhead, the man who played Goober on *The Andy Griffith Show* and several important football players at the University of Alabama.

According to Dombhart, my great-great-great-great-grandparents were Thomas and Susan Keys Barton, the first white settlers to locate in Alabama Territory north of the Tallapoosa River. It had been inadvisable to farm on the north side of the Tallapoosa until Andrew Jackson subdued the Creek Indian nation. In every root and branch of the family tree that I've been able to trace, the pattern is the same; the Fells, the Walkers, the Keyses, the Abbotts, the Bests, the Flannagans and Gordons and Raineses rushed into Alabama at the earliest possible moment and stayed.

Among them they represented the main bloodlines of what was to become Hillbilly America—the English, Scottish, Welsh, Irish and, of course, the Scotch-Irish, whose penchant for dressing their women in short skirts shocked Ben Franklin and all of Quaker Philadelphia.

Thomas and Susan Barton's eldest son, Moses Barton, got to Walker County by 1822. His daughter Milia married James Raines, builder of the second gristmill on Blackwater Creek. They named their son Hiram. Reaching draft age at an inopportune time, he took to the woods around 1861 to "lay out" until the Civil War was over. Praise be, this young man of sound political judgment and intact body parts emerged from the woods to father in 1872 Hiram Howell Raines, the long dead grandfather whose name I carry.

Howell Raines, for that was the name he went by, continued the family tradition of staying in Walker County. It was through a study of his life that I assumed what I regard as a hereditary obligation to contemplate the relative importance, in both our personal and our familial lives, of staying and leaving. I took this obligation freely and gladly, in tribute to the hard, truncated, striving life of the first Howell Raines.

By all accounts, he was a smart man and an unusually curious one for his time and place, a progressive farmer. He had saved his money until he could buy 160 acres of prime land between Curry and Sunlight. He ordered brood stock, seeds and plants for his orchard from the best catalog houses in the Midwest. Such agricultural ambition was a rare thing in the hills in those days. He had a fun-loving side. He liked feasts of whole roasted goat. He made his boys a goat-drawn cart and hand-cut the goat's bridle and reins out of a cowhide. When rain raised the creeks, he'd take his family camping on Blackwater, setting trotlines and frying the fish on the spot in a big iron pot, fried them so crisp and mealy you could eat fins and all. On one such outing, he cut a hook out of my five-year-old father's thumb with a pocketknife. He was a blacksmith and, according to my father, such a keen shot that he could stand way back from a tree and drive a nail into it with rifle bullets.

Whether or not this feat of marksmanship is true or the

product of a boy's adoration, it is certainly a fact that, in the one surviving photograph of Howell Raines, it is the eyes that grab you. He was a man with an intense, almost burning gaze, hawk-like in the old homesteaders' way. Which is to say, he looked like a willfully calm man who could be provoked by unreliable promises or rude behavior. He was a Methodist. He made the communal wine for his church in a big pottery crock that I've inherited. In my house, I have a chair that he carved and caned. In my closet is his rabbit-eared shotgun made by the Baker Arms Company of New York. Like my father, I've tried to hold on to every available bit of evidence about this man I never knew.

The first Howell Raines liked newspapers. He read the Jasper *Mountain Eagle* and subscribed to the Memphis *Commercial Appeal,* too. He wanted to know more, it appears. For all his striving, he spent much of his life following a mule up and down cotton rows. At night, from the porch of his house, he could see on the southern horizon a vast annulus of light thrown into the sky by the blast furnaces in Birmingham, forty miles to the south. He led, in sum, a nineteenth-century agricultural life within sight of the fires of the industrial age.

He lived in a place where in cases of extreme illness doctors made house calls, arriving from Jasper, the county seat, by horse and buggy to announce, in his case, that there was not much they could do. There was, to be sure, already an up-to-date hospital in Birmingham in 1913, when he contracted this undiagnosed illness. From time to time, as he weakened, his favorite bird dog was allowed into the sickroom, and Howell Raines would rest his hand upon the animal's head. After weeks of decline, after scenes of even greater poignancy, he died, without complaint and without any visible breaking of will, in his own bed of an illness that was never identified.

His four boys had worshiped him. Not one of them ever forgot his grief. To honor his memory, several of his grandsons were given the middle name Howell. The Hiram was not doled out until the birth of the last of the six male children born in that generation. It was regarded as a stiff, countrified name.

My father and his brothers were city folk by the start of World War II, businessmen who, having worked their way up from carpentry, were beginning to be able to afford good cars and nice suits. In their world, during the boom years that made Birmingham the "Magic City," anything redolent of the farm life was not a business asset. Nonetheless, my father made an announcement to my two older siblings while my mother and I were still at the West End Baptist Hospital, where I was born on February 5, 1943.

"Y'all aren't going to like this," my father quoted himself as saying, "but we're going to name him after my daddy." It was, as it turned out, the last chance in my generation to perpetuate *both* of the ancestral given names that had been written into family Bibles since pioneer times. That is how I, the last of the old man's grandsons, came to be the only one who would be called Howell, as he was.

To soften the old-fashioned look of it a bit, they reversed the order of the given names, putting Howell first, assuming that a city boy with the country name of Hiram out front might come in for some teasing. So Howell Hiram Raines was written on the birth certificate, and as a small boy I got my share of teasing for Howell. After all, the more urbane of my two given names has a formal sound to it, and I was born in an era of Bobs, Jims, Bills, Billy Rays, Larrys, Juniors and the occasional Randy. I became a student of names. I regarded most Randys as unsound and never met a kid named Jay who was worth a damn. The teasing made me fierce. I'd let people shorten it to Hal, but never to Howie. I learned to keep altogether quiet about the Hiram. Actually, it didn't make a bit of difference, but it's the sort of thing kids worry about.

From an early age, I wanted to hear stories about Hiram Howell Raines. My father was six at the time of his father's death, and he told me that he had dreamed about the funeral in cinematic detail throughout his adult life. I asked what seemed the obvious question. Why did they let the man lie there and die? Why had they not simply carried him by wagon to the railroad station in Jasper, only eight miles away, and put him on the train to Birmingham for a second opinion? That was the first thing I noticed when my father took me to see the old home place. They were not way, way out back in the sticks as I had always imagined them to be when they spoke of being "up in the country." Yet Curry, the village where they buried Howell Raines, was so close to Jasper, and the train ran between Jasper and Birmingham every day. For all we know, a simple surgery at Hillman Hospital in Birmingham, which was fully capable of such procedures by 1913, might have saved his life. In any case, a more precise diagnosis by a city doctor in a teaching hospital couldn't have hurt. Why not try it?

"I've always kind of wondered about that myself," my father said. Just that.

I could tell the question pierced him. Fifty years later, the loss was still fresh, as was the memory of being a powerless country boy with no recourse against the remorseless negligence imposed by ignorance and a few miles of dirt road. I dropped the subject, never to return to it with him.

As far as most folks were concerned, my hard old grandmother was not a lot of fun, but Jane Best Raines doted on me because I had her husband's name. We would sit for hours on her swing in the shade of a big elm tree and she would tell me stories about this quiet, rectitudinous, industrious man. She saw him one evening after he came in from plowing. He unhitched the mules and then, instead of washing up for supper, he stood for a long time by the barnyard fence, looking across his fields and into the distance. She went to him, and he said, "Jane, I've worked my last day." The point is, she said, he *knew*. He knew he had worn himself out getting that farm into shape. He was a demon for work. In hot summertime, she would put on her sunbonnet, and I'd follow her into the garden for tomatoes or the henhouse for eggs. I made her tell the same stories over and over. The church doors never opened without her being there. She read a magazine called *The Gospel Trumpet*. So I was stunned when she became the first person I ever heard say "shit" and "damn." I couldn't have been more than six. She wanted to tell me what Hiram Howell Raines said one day when a man approached him during a political campaign. He said, "Shit, here comes one of those damn Democrats."

In those days, Democrats used to talk about the Solid South, but in regard to our family history, we weren't part of it. The Raineses were hereditary Republicans. My grandfather was, after all, the son of a man, Hiram Raines, who hid out in the woods until the war was over rather than fight for the Confederacy. I'm sure it was largely because he didn't want to get shot, but the fact is that Hiram and his father-in-law, old man Hial Abbott, were Lincoln-loving Unionists by conviction. So were many of their neighbors in the hill country. By night throughout the war, Hial (later spelled Howell) Abbott carried food to the draft-dodging country boys who were laying out in gullies and branch heads all over Walker and Winston counties. Some of them, he ferried in his canoe across the Sipsey River, so they could make their way to the Federal lines and enlist in the Union Army. After the war, the Southern Claims Commission of the United States government certified Hial Abbot as a cast-iron Unionist who risked death by hanging by neighbors who regarded him as a "damned old Lincolnite." The commission ruled in 1871 that Hial Abbott should be paid for "his one good mare" and the four hundred bundles of fodder, thirty-five bushels of corn and fifty pounds of bacon he provided the Union cavalrymen in Wilson's Raiders when they passed his farm in 1865 on their way to Tuscaloosa to burn the University of Alabama. Hial Abbott billed the government for $220.50, arguing that the horse alone was worth $150 and "corn was very scarce and hard to get at any price" in those days, but he settled for $178. At this remove, I can only surmise that my grandmother was willing to burn my tender ears with profanity to make sure I understood the true political faith of my forebears.

She was, without dispute, the final authority on all matters relating to her husband, especially his death. Until she herself died in 1967, she said the man had killed himself with labor. His work paid for the farm they had bought in the 1890s. Selling the farm after his death enabled the family to move to town, where my father and his brothers found prosperity. Grandpa Raines's sacrifice came to be the foundation fact in the family myth–"He worked himself to death." Period.

Early in life, weighing all I could glean from my father and grandmother, I came to a different diagnosis, so to speak. I figured the man died of not leaving home when he should have. Hiram Howell Raines died of not going to town, just as surely as the Sinus Doctor to the Stars died of not staying home. Knowing the power of paradox, I wasn't going to make the same mistake my grandfather did. That was another reason, I guess, that, when Arthur presented the opportunity, I moved to the biggest town I could find.

CHAPTER 6

The First Editorial:
On Fun*

It took a woman, of course, to give us one of our best fictional portrayals of the suppressed rage American men feel about being worked to death. It comes in Caroline Gordon's 1934 novel, *Aleck Maury, Sportsman*. The title character is idling around a country store near a boat landing, waiting for a friend to arrive with the new bateau that will carry them downstream on a leisurely fishing and camping trip. Nearby, a Tennessee farmer is digging fence holes, an arduous task in his state's rocky soil. The farmer sees Aleck Maury lounging about enjoying the river view and the fine day.

> Between intervals of post-setting the old man looked at me with deep-set crafty eyes.
> "How you goin' to get down the river?" he asked finally.
> I replied that [my friend] had had a boat made.
> "You goin' to fish all the way."
> I nodded. Just then somebody called out to me that the boat was ready and I turned to go. The old farmer suddenly left his posthole digging and leapt up on the [porch of the store]. He was shaking his fist and his chin beard waggled with suppressed fury.

*This editorial and those that follow represent the beliefs, views and opinions of the sole proprietor of this book.

49

"I'm sixty years old," he yelled, "and I ain't never went a fishing in my life."

What does this kind of anger tell us? The emotion is more complex than the working-class resentment captured in the country song "Take This Job and Shove It." It has to do with the familiar trade-off that confronts most of us in kindergarten and never lets up: mandatory attendance versus doing what we like in the pursuit of fun. The bargain that the United States presents most middle-class workers is nothing if not stark: Around the age of twenty-one, you will be enrolled in the American economy; after forty or fifty years of diligent post-hole digging, you will be freed to play, to dance, to fish or to die, as it suits you.

The Inner Baby is strong in American men. Even those who like their work feel life contains too few play periods—too little gambling, too little honky-tonking, too little sex, too little pure, unclassifiable, heart-lifting joy and way, way, way too little recreation that is *specific to our whims and desires*. That can include too little golf or, God help us, too little bowling or NASCAR racing. But in these matters of fun preferences, it is dangerous for one man to judge another, as perhaps can be seen looking into the two main compartments of my own vision of Manhattan life, a vision springing from desires "in the heart long-pent, now loose, now at last tumultuously bursting," to borrow a phrase from Whitman.

For me, there would be in one compartment more glossy, glamorous fishing of the kind that had shaped my fantasies since I first picked up *Field & Stream* and *True* and *Esquire* long years ago. The other compartment would contain an ample, continual, unrestricted serving of the pleasures available to an affluent, unattached male in the supreme city of recreational love.

Just as my professional trade-off was clear to me—a last abandoning of literary dreams in return for an extremely fine newspaper job—so was the personal trade-off. That had to do with the other kind of love one hears about—the deep, abiding, permanent love of the heart that a man and woman are supposed to want, the kind arriving with a thunderclap that never stops reverberating.

I thought no amount of searching would bring that to me, probably because of some flaw in my nature in regard to uncynical, long-term adoration. It was a matter of accepting this shortcoming and seeing that it was not without its compensations. I knew that I had not been a particularly gifted husband. I lacked the requisite placidity. Like Huck Finn, I was forever itching to light out for the territory. Reaching the age of fifty did not tamp down that restlessness. As Yeats said at an even greater age,

> *Never had I more*
> *Excited, passionate, fantastical*
> *Imagination, nor an ear and eye*
> *That more expected the impossible—*
> *No, not in boyhood when with rod and fly,*
> *Or the humbler worm, I climbed Ben Bulben's back*
> *And had the livelong summer day to spend.*

So I accepted that for reasons of temperament, inclination and firm choice a captivating, everlasting, heart-filling, ship-launching, sonnet-flinging love was not in store for me. I was moving to the Island of Beautiful Women, and I would have to get by as best I could on the Manhattan kind of love.

Such was my planning process: no doomed pursuit of the Great American Novel, no Love Eternal, just a damn fine time. I won't be offended if you call it a male fantasy. That was the whole point. It was just sitting there, waiting for me. Why not have it?

CHAPTER 7

Ennui in the Promised Land

At that point in my life, the most numinous place in the world for me was Darky Lake in the Quetico Provincial Park in Ontario. There I learned to handle heavy fish on fly tackle, an event that confirmed my conversion from fish murderer to a fly fisherman who put fish back into the water rather than into an Igloo cooler. The magic of Darky Lake captured me on my first voyage through the waters of Quetico, remote Darky with its yellow-streaked cliffs and hieroglyphs, home waters of the Ojibway and their invisible brothers, the Maymaygwayshi, Paleo-Indian elves who lived in cracks and crevices along the stone-bound shore and survived by theft, trickery and the bartering of a powerful healing substance called rock medicine with the shaman who knew how to summon them. As soon as the Sinus Doctor to the Stars declared Ben and me fit to travel, we lit out for Darky.

We arrived a week too late for the best fishing, and day after day the lake was wrapped in brattices of gray drizzle. Soaked to the bone after an afternoon of fruitless casting, I was toiling up a muddy bank at our canoe landing when I fell in a tangle of fly rods, paddles and tackle boxes. My right shoulder ached from the ungainly fall. I mixed a Jack Daniel's and lake water and retired to my tent. I was not having a good time, and I tried to talk myself into believing it was because, having just turned fifty, I was getting too old for slamming around the wilderness.

But I could not conjure a plausible snit about my age. As I pondered the roots of my discontent here in this place that had brought me such joy, a subtle and sinister realization marched

53

across my mind. I was bored. Here in the place of my deepest imbibing of the joy of fly fishing, I was apathetic about doing more of it. I prayed that I was not bored with all fishing, but I was definitely bored with this fishing. What had looked so appealing from Manhattan struck me as somehow extraneous. I had loved this place because you could go for days without hearing a manufactured sound. Now the call of the loon and the clatter of the C train were of equal interest. Any smart person knows what he or she seeks with the little games we choose—that effortless marriage of passion and curiosity by which the mind, ceasing to think, is fleetingly at one with the flow of the soul. Without that, the lot of us—fishers, runners, shooters, trekkers, climbers, jumpers, surfers, knitters, ropers, riders, seekers of birds, strikers and rollers of balls—are ridiculous figures watched through an iron fence by a Mississippi idiot.

My spirits lifted somewhat on the flight home. Ben said that he had enjoyed the trip and thanked me for it. But, he added, the sameness of the Canadian fishing was beginning to get to him. Maybe it was simply a matter of our having done the world's best smallmouth bass fishing to a fare-thee-well. Suddenly I felt a twinge of hope. Perhaps I was not burned out. Maybe all I needed was a change of venue.

I tried to think of a big one.

Back in New York I called my friend Tennant McWilliams with a proposal I was sure he would reject. Every long friendship has a contract. The contract in our friendship, which began when we were fifteen, was that I was the radical and Tennant the conservative. I make up my mind quickly. He ponders. In college, he would say he had to study when I argued for cutting class in May because the bream were bedding and it was possible to catch a hundred or so in the course of a ravishing spring afternoon out in the blossoming countryside. Later, when I would suggest we take a break from our wives and kids for a fishing jaunt to Florida or Louisiana, it was Tennant who said that a birthday party or a soccer game made it impossible. So I was just going through the ritual of an old friendship when I called to report on our Canadian trip and to lob another feckless proposal his way.

"Let's go fishing at Christmas Island," I said.

"Where is that?" he said.

"In the Pacific Ocean, eleven hundred miles south of Honolulu, just above the equator."

"What do they catch there?"

"Bonefish and a local fish they call the giant trevally. It looks like a big jack crevalle and pulls like hell."

"How much will it cost?"

"Two or three thousand plus airfare."

"I'm in," he said. "Let me know when you get the departure date."

Well, I said to myself, Tennant's getting adventurous in his old age. Now the thought occurs that perhaps I simply failed to factor in the impact of his second divorce.

CHAPTER 8

An Evening Stroll Through
the Intersection of Forty-third Street
and Memory Lane

For the first few months of 1993, as I settled into my new job as editorial page editor, I took temporary quarters in a residential hotel at Broadway and Fifty-first. Every night, I walked through the heart of Times Square from Forty-third Street to Fifty-first. This was in its *Road Warrior* period, before the Giuliani clean-up turned midtown into an urban theme park. Having not yet mastered the beeline walk of a veteran New Yorker, I was like live bait to every pimp, dope peddler, card shark and would-be pickpocket. Fat, sweaty Irish guys called at me through the open doors of the porn houses. Pakistani camera sellers tried to drag me into their shops for a stolen Canon at double the list price. One cold night a young man fell into step about fifteen feet behind me as I left the *Times* and followed me into the winter darkness of a seedy stretch of Forty-third Street near Eighth Avenue. He walked in my blind spot, so I couldn't catch a glimpse over my shoulder. I jammed one hand deeply into the pocket of my topcoat and kept it there, as if I might be carrying. Then, without breaking stride, I spun around and walked backwards for two steps, the way the British soldiers in Belfast do when they're on sidewalk patrol. I got a good clean look at the guy, and as I turned again toward the front, he began talking to me.

"That's good," he said. "See who's back there. I like that. What you got in that coat? You got a gun? You a cop?"

Then he veered across Forty-third to work the other side of the street.

Graduation day! A Times Square coyote was letting me know I no longer walked like a tourist. Editorial writing had settled into a routine, too. As I said earlier, it's absolutely the most relaxing kind of newspaper writing as long as you don't mind being denounced by important citizens. Usually the lights of Times Square were ablaze by the time we locked up the editorial page and sent it to the printers. One day I finished early and encountered real daylight. The sidewalk vendors at Seventh Avenue and Forty-third Street had yet to fold their card tables. There, in the gritty huckstering heart of Times Square, I encountered a touchstone of my boyhood, the irreducible totem of my youthful ambitions, an exact replica of an object not encountered for forty years and yet upon the stroke of that moment remembered utterly in its every tattered detail down to who said what and how the weather was.

This object, as venerable and potent for me as Rosebud had been for Charles Foster Kane, was a copy of *Life* magazine. It lay amid a spread of incense sticks, elderly issues of *Look* and *Colliers* and piles of *Dungeons and Dragons* comic books with covers showing the armored brassieres and the impossible Valkyrie cleavage of the warrior maidens of yore.

The guy was asking twenty-five dollars for the magazine I wanted, and he settled for twenty-three. He could have asked a hundred and made the sale. I had the exact change. I even got a receipt for the tax man. I had just purchased what was, I realized, the trigger for my becoming both a writer and a man who would travel halfway around the world to torment fish and be tormented by them.

It was a copy of *Life* dated September 1, 1952. Across the upper right corner of the cover was a diagonal yellow banner. It said:

The One That Got Away

An Extra Dividend in this issue
'THE OLD MAN AND THE SEA'
By HEMINGWAY
A Complete New Book
First Publication

When that edition of *Life* arrived at 1409 Fifth Avenue West in Birmingham, I was confined to bed with mumps, the least painful of the Big Three childhood diseases, the others being chicken pox, with its intolerable itching, and "German" measles, which carried high fevers and, with World War II only seven years past, a faint resonance of Nazi malice. I was nine years old. It was dry and hot at that time of year in Birmingham, and our house was not yet air-conditioned. I remember the oscillating fan, with friction tape around its frayed cord, and the open windows. The pecan trees in the backyard had not yet dropped their leaves. Summer does not give up easily in Alabama, and for a small boy confined to his room, the afternoons are interminable.

Late in the day, when Grady Hutchinson's housework was done, she would sit by my bed and read to me from "The Old Man and the Sea." Grady was eighteen and more full of sass than was prudent for a black person in Alabama in those days. She was the first card-carrying member of the NAACP I ever met. She had been working in our home for the past two years to save money for nursing school in New Orleans. I have written elsewhere of the impact she had on my racial views and my subsequent journalistic career by teaching me about the human reality of segregation. But I was rounding fifty before I realized that Grady had also shaped my idea of the kinds of work and life that were possible in the world beyond Birmingham by reading aloud those chiseled sentences about the old man, Santiago, and his tattered sail that "looked like the flag of permanent defeat."

It took her several afternoons to get through the book. It was laid out across nineteen open pages that began with a photograph of Hemingway, unbearded and relatively sober looking, standing in front of the harbor at Cojimar, Cuba. I remember being aware that Ernest Hemingway was famous, but our response to the work was anything but "literary." Certainly the Jesus symbolism eluded us, or at least me. We were simply absorbed with the story and would stop to discuss parts of it. I remember dwelling, for example, on Santiago's commentary on "the great Dimaggio who does all things perfectly even with the pain of the bone spur in his heel." I remembered specifically how Hemingway went on and on about bone spurs: "Can it be as painful as the spur of a fighting cock in one's heel?" And what of the cocks themselves? How could they fight with one or both eyes pierced by steel? When I got the old magazine home that night and scanned the Dimaggio paragraph again after so many years, another sentence leapt out at me. I had forgotten the conclusion of Santiago's meditation on pain and endurance: "Man is not much beside the great birds and beasts."

Other bits came back to me, Grady reading about the old man's curious habit of talking to his paralyzed hands and to the fish, the slight tension in Grady's voice as she read about Santiago and the black man who arm wrestled until blood ran from under their fingernails, Grady giggling when she read that Santiago "stood up and urinated over the side of the skiff."

We liked the parts about baseball. Grady and I were both baseball fans. She was devoted to the Dodgers because of Jackie Robinson and also to the Giants, since Willie Mays was from Fairfield, a steel-mill village just outside Birmingham. Grady and her friends used to make fun of the hapless Fairfield girl who jilted Willie Mays because he had no future. We were shocked when Santiago dismissed John J. McGraw, the legendary manager of the Giants, as a mean drunk.

I was fascinated by the description of Santiago's baits. I had never seen a marlin, of course, but I had been to sea with Bert Raffield and Emil Frudaker. The sardines that Santiago used seemed a lot like the cigar minnows that we trolled for king mackerel off Panama City. I was astounded by the matter-of-fact way in which Santiago caught a bonito, another fish I knew from Panama City, and ate it raw. It would be decades before Birmingham heard of sashimi, and I was convinced that Hemingway was lying. No one could eat raw fish and live, even if they could choke it down.

Southerners learn to write by listening to spoken language, and I have come to believe that hearing so much Hemingway read aloud at such an earlier age was a kind of lucky inoculation, for I grew up among Faulkner cultists. Faulkner was an omnipresent and dangerous model for young Southerners since he writes so much like we think we talk when we get drunk. The temptation is to think you can just rear back and write like that, too. And no one can, because drunk or sober, Mr. Bill was a genius. Hundreds of Southern writers have drowned in the swamps of Yoknapatawpha. Of course, imitating Hemingway can be ruinous, too. Platoons of storytellers have died on the slopes of Mount Ernest, mumbling that in the fall the war was always there, but we did not go to it anymore. But if you are born in Faulkner country, a few gulps of early Hemingway can be a useful influence in the same way that imbibing one singularly cold, stingingly astringent martini is better for your head than a whole bottle of bourbon.

The old *Life* magazine fetched from the wells of memory another thing that happened in our old house in Birmingham. It had to do with fishing and writing, too, and with the most precious thing my mother ever did for me. On another summer afternoon, a year or two after Grady read "The Old Man and the Sea" to me, a subscription copy of *Field & Stream* arrived with the day's mail. My mother and I were alone in the dining room, where the mail was always piled for sorting on the big table. As she divided the bills and letters, I picked up the magazine and made a declaration that had suddenly popped into my head: "I would like to write for this magazine when I grow up."

I know I have remembered the moment accurately for it set the compass of my life. Yet as I read the words I spoke, they still surprise me. I was not a little boy who spent a lot of time confiding in adults, including my parents. For my part, I was a private dreamer. For their part, they were not given to offering a lot of advice about what the future might hold. What astonishes me now is not simply that I had formed an aspiration so fully removed from my family's history and employments, but that it was an aspiration that also embodied a precocious, inchoate desire to escape the buffet of choices then on offer in Birmingham.

For at about that time, my brother and his pals were going off either to the University of Alabama to major in something called business administration or to our state cow college, Auburn, to major in an even more unappetizing pursuit called engineering. I cannot recall a time when I did not think a life devoted solely to making money sounded tedious and trivial. Not even the entrepreneurial grail of so many in our corporation-dominated town—to own your own business, as my father and his brothers did—enticed me. My father went to his cabinetry plant every day, directed men in how to turn lumber into showcases and sawdust. By some mystery known to him and my uncles, they figured how to finish the day with more money than you started with, and over the years you were supposed to pile it up as high as you could. Then you'd die and what did it matter? What had you left to the world that counted? I describe these feelings now in the language of an adult, but at the time they were simply attitudes, unformed surely, but indisputably present in my thinking from the very beginning. I simply thought a life lived for business would not matter, just as from my earliest hearing of the Bible stories—the parting of the waters, the walking on same, Jonah and the whale, the Flood, the whole bit—I thought this: I doubt it.

Clearly, even before I had a philosophy I was ripe for the seductions of literature and, perhaps more specifically, those of journalism. I was a born cynic, and a restless one at that. In the fifth grade, our neighborhood's legendary teacher, the austere and demanding Miss Johnnie Stott, had written me a note saying I was such a bright lad I could aspire to a lofty position in life, "perhaps even mayor of our city."

Miss Johnnie was a stern piece of work. She favored polka-dot dresses for her blocky frame and wore sturdy shoes that made a clumpetty-clump sound when she raced toward the desk of some hapless daydreamer. With her scroll of white hair and stern, powdery face, she was a dead ringer for Gilbert Stuart's unfinished portrait of Washington. I remember her note about being mayor because she issued few compliments, and I was proud to have this. Yet being mayor of Birmingham was just about the most trifling ambition I could imagine.

This lack of interest in politics may have reflected the fact that Miss Johnnie had earlier in the year stolen an election from me. My sin was using too large an "X" to mark the ballot beside the name of my main competitor, Mike Sherman. I thought it was a generous gesture to vote for my opponent, who was getting trounced. But Miss Johnnie saw something that needed squelching in the way I swaggered to the blackboard and made my mark. She disqualified me on the spot. I think she thought she was giving me a lesson in the dangers of hubris.

In any event, I had a different career in mind, an ambition suddenly given shape by a magazine that seemed the magical, living conflation of the two things that moved me most, words and fish, an ambition that vaulted from dream to possibility when I told my mother I wanted to write for *Field & Stream* and she said she didn't see why I couldn't. Then, as I recall, she went back to sorting the mail. I don't think we ever talked about writing again, except for when she caught me reading *Tobacco Road* and sniffed that Erskine Caldwell was no friend of the South.

No matter. With that first comment, a few words she could not remember, in a moment buried in the thousands of unemphatic transactions that pass between parent and child, she put the ropes and poles of possibility inside the loose tent of my fantasy. And she taught me something that I tried to keep in mind when I became a parent.

You must be careful what you say to your children. They think you know what you're talking about.

CHAPTER 9

Because It's There

When the plane lifted off from Honolulu, I got the Panama City Feeling, and that is when I first began to suspect that Christmas Island was going to be very, very good to yours truly.

I speak here of a specifically joyous emotion I experienced as a child when our family headed for Florida. The Panama City Feeling would come over me like salvation when we cleared the interminable outskirts of grim and grimy Birmingham, and my father would put his foot to the accelerator in a serious, prolonged way and let that baby blue 1949 Oldsmobile begin to eat. It sucked in the infinite, two-lane distance like a string of spaghetti. It consumed black asphalt and convergent white lines and piney, red-clay hills and Speed Kills signs and every sun-blasted hick-a-Bama hamlet that separated us from the heavenly sands.

In my memory, the Panama City Feeling is connected to a visual image of what I imagined to be happening behind us as that big V8 engine pushed me back against the blue-and-white basket-weave seat cover. I pictured bits and pieces of our mundane daily life being dislodged by the rushing force of our departure and sent swirling behind us like so many leaves in the slipstream of our mighty Rocket 88. It is sort of the opposite of Wordsworth's idea that we enter the world "trailing clouds of glory." We were speeding toward paradise, leaving as our contrail the hundred blasted pieces of the imprisoning, ragtag reality of Birmingham.

On this day many years later, I toasted the thought of putting another gritty city, New York, far behind us. Here's to casual old

Air Nauru on its weekly jaunt from Honolulu to Christmas Island, jetting us into the placid Pacific sky. Here's to our fellow passengers aboard this silver bird representing the entire fleet of the national airline of the Republic of Kiribati. Here's a blessing in particular for the sprinkling of earnest and unobtrusive Japanese honeymooners. These great-grandchildren of the men who raided this self-same Honolulu have returned to Hawaii in peace, as sweetly tentative scuba-diving Yuppies bearing yen not bombs from the Land of the Rising Sun. As for my own nation, it had provided a remarkably homogeneous group of citizens on this flight to Christmas Island. That is to say, we were middle-aged to semielderly white people carrying fly rod cases and deeply receptive credit cards.

From observations and interviews, I have gleaned several sociological, financial and psychological facts about the Americans encountered in exotic fly-fishing locations. There are enough of us in the United States to support a constellation of fishing camps around the world and good travel agencies like the Fly Shop in Redding, California, and Frontiers in Wexford, Pennsylvania, to get us there. Nobody knows exactly how many of us there are. Nowadays an estimated 25 percent of this free-spending, far-traveling band of fanatics are women. Some are wives or girlfriends who followed men into the sport, but a growing number are there independently, living proof that women don't need to depend on men for expensive mindless fun. The unattended men—whether they be escaped husbands, self-indulgent bachelors or confused widowers—run toward the fanatical and obsessive. They are bound by a common thought. Perhaps this is true of the women you see in fly-fishing camps, too. But I'm sure about the men. That thought is:

Before I die, I want my slice of adventure pie.

Once you pass fifty, you realize with a jolt that the sand has run through the glass much more rapidly than you ever suspected it could, and the years which would have been spent in some dashing way had you been born in another age have gone into the endless, impersonal, forward grinding of our Great Enterprise.

In our fifties, we cannot escape an understanding of what Mr. Jagger, my mate from the waiting room of the Sinus Doctor to the Stars, was talking about.

You better get it while you can.

This line of reasoning led me to a contribution to the economic growth of America. I call it the Manhattan Deathbed Principle, and I developed it during my deskbound years in Midtown. It works like this. Let's say I take a lunchtime stroll from Times Square over to the old Orvis store off Madison Avenue or taxi downtown to the Urban Angler on lower Fifth Avenue or simply thumb through one of the fishing catalogs. Let's say I spy a new piece of equipment, whether it is a $4.95 gadget for tying a knot that I already know how to tie, or a slightly better version of a $695 rod that I already own. I ask myself a question: On my deathbed, will I be happy that I did not buy this radiant object?

Hearken to this, my brothers on waters faraway and near! In the privacy of my own greed, I ask, Will I be truly satisfied when I cross the last river that I denied myself and instead hoarded the money it is going to cost me, a piddling amount in comparison with the obligatory expenses of even a modestly financed life in the third millennium? If I find that I am still undecided, I compare the price of the desired object with what it cost to straighten the teeth of my sons or send them to college for a year or the indisputably fair but nonetheless weighty amount that I paid by way of exiting my marriage.

When you put it that way, such a modest object of desire is incontestably no more than you deserve. You may say that this is a selfish and self-indulgent attitude and that a grown man ought to be embarrassed to write down such a sentiment. I say to you that America would be a happier, healthier, saner nation if more men felt they were breaking even in the pleasure department. That's the reason the men's movement petered out in the '90s. They kept saying men need more masculine love, more mentoring, more grieving for their lost fathers, more drumming and more dancing in the green glade. They got it wrong.

Men need what they always have needed—more toys and

more time to play with them. I don't mean to be taken as excusing any man who indulges any hobby, including fly fishing, by being stingy with his family. But there is a bigger problem in America than the thousands of young deadbeat dads. It is the millions of old ones who are simply dead beat once they get through raising their families and serving their time at work. Florida is full of them. They are the gouty coots sitting beside their Airstreams saying they wish they had bought a Harley or gone to Pago Pago.

The Manhattan Deathbed Principle could have helped these men. It's too late now for them, of course. But it's not too late for you and me, my work-lashed brethren from coast to coast. The principle has both its philosophical and its practical applications, and it is the latter that makes it indispensable to the fisherman intent on curing his pleasure deficit. Here at last we have a proven system for avoiding the most maddening of all angling emergencies, being in the right place with the wrong gear.

I arrived at Christmas Island bearing, in addition to my flyfishing tackle, an eight-foot spinning rod for the giant trevally that I had read could be caught in the surf during cocktail hour at the Captain Cook Hotel. I also had a trolling rod and a reel spooled with thirty-pound line for the small tuna that I had read could be caught outside the reef line if you hired one of the local boats. These rods were contained in a traveling case, also newly purchased, that looked like the barrel of a small cannon. Tennant, who shares my philosophy, had a similar case that looked like the barrel of a larger cannon, as he had come equipped with a twelve-foot spinning rod.

Alas, no system, not even one founded on so solid and simple a rock as the Manhattan Deathbed Principle, is perfect. There are, unfortunately, always variables, especially when it comes to the United States Post Office as it functions in New York City. As in the movie *Men in Black II,* it is staffed entirely by aliens.

So I arrived with the nagging knowledge that for all my care there was a critical gap in my gear arsenal. For Christmas Island's ubiquitous bonefish, I had sturdy workhorse tackle, an 8-weight Orvis rod and matching Orvis DXR fly reel I had purchased several years earlier on the daydream theory that I would someday need it. But you also need a heavy fly-fishing outfit for the giant trevally that sometimes cruise onto the bonefish flats from the reefs and deep channels. Here is a fish of folkloric pugnacity. Japanese fishermen travel all over the Pacific to catch them on spinning gear. Under the name ulua, they are also the favorite heavy-tackle fish of Hawaiian surf casters. In the brief history of fly fishing on Christmas Island, trevally have established a Vandalic reputation for wrecking the tackle and nerves of visiting Americans.

So I sought the recommendation of Bob Clouser as to what outfit I would need for this fearsome creature. Bob is the inventor of the most important wet fly of the twentieth century, the Clouser Deep Minnow, and also the owner of a mail-order fly shop in Middletown, Pennsylvania, where my Visa number is well known.

"I have just the outfit," Bob said by telephone. "A Sage ten-weight rod and a Fin-Nor Number Four reel."

Fin-Nor makes trolling reels as big as ice-cream freezers for the offshore fishing boats that go after tuna and marlin. Their fly reels are famous for smooth, powerful drags, but I always thought they looked a bit heavy and clunky for prolonged casting. I said as much to Bob.

"That's the reel that Lefty and I use in Central America for tarpon," Bob said. I was trumped. Clouser himself is a demigod in the fly-fishing world, but Lefty is the kahuna. Also known as Bernard Kreh, former outdoor editor of the *Baltimore Sun,* he is one of the best fly casters in history. As it happened, Mr. Kreh has been angry at me since he read the galleys of *Fly Fishing Through the Midlife Crisis,* because of my condemnation of the payola arrangements between certain famous fishing writers and the people who own tackle companies, fishing resorts and fishing magazines. Lefty took it personally. So did the editor of a leading fly-fishing magazine. He banned any review of or reference to my book from his pages. He told a mutual friend that because my book questioned the veracity of fishing writers, it would be bad for the fly-fishing business. It's an amusing idea—that you could cure people of fishing by exposing them to facts. The truth can only make you free. It can't stop anyone from doing what he wants to do. This guy's theory on true facts, if correct, would mean the end of a lot of things more dangerous than the fly-fishing business. The Bush political dynasty and weddings photographed from helicopters come immediately to mind.

At any rate, I operate on the theory that any gear that's good enough for Lefty Kreh is good enough for me. He and my late friend Ernest Schwiebert, author of *Matching the Hatch* and *Trout,* are the two greatest fly fishermen of our day by my reckoning, and I'm proud to have known both of them. So I bought the Fin-Nor. Admittedly, I suspected that Bob recommended the reel with such fervor simply because he had one in stock, but there is no question that its drag would be up to the test of any fish I would encounter on Christmas Island.

Unfortunately, on the day before my departure for Christmas Island, my precious four-hundred-dollar Fin-Nor was in the possession of the aforementioned postal workers somewhere between Middletown, Pennsylvania, and New York City. I will cite in passing one of my few beefs about life in Manhattan. The mail delivery is not up to third-world standards. No doubt the post office has statistics to show that its performance in Manhattan is just dandy. So let's just say that, when it comes to getting mail delivered in New York, I have the same kind of luck as the several thousand air travelers who die every year using the safest form of mass transportation in the history of mankind. In any event, I was ready to leave for the trip of a lifetime, as they say in the travel biz, and I did not have my reel.

So I telephoned Paul Dixon at the Orvis store, who suggested I buy Orvis's budget saltwater reel, the Battenkill. As reflected by its $120 price, the reel was less precisely engineered than the Fin-Nor, and its drag was not nearly as strong. But Paul pointed out that the Battenkill was probably tough enough to hold up to anything I would encounter on a one-week trip. The difference we're talking about here is like that between a hundred-dollar Kodak and a thousand-dollar Nikon. Both take fine pictures under most conditions, but at the extremes you will see why the Nikon costs more.

"When you get back, if the Fin-Nor has shown up, you can use the Battenkill as your backup reel or give it to one of your sons," Paul said. "I can have it ready for you in an hour."

"How much backing does it hold?" I asked.

Here it is worth pausing for a technical note for readers unfamiliar with fishing tackle. The line on a saltwater fly reel consists of three sections joined together in this order: the leader at the end nearest the fish, then the fly line and finally the backing. The leader, seven to twelve feet long, is usually made of thick, clear monofilament. It is the weak link in the chain that connects the angler to the fish. The next section is a fly line of 90 to 120 feet that is extended during the act of casting. The fly line is connected to the backing, a much longer section of thin but strong Dacron line that is tied, in turn, to the hub of the reel. Without the backing, a large fish would simply run to the end of the fly line and break off, since the leader in flats and ocean fishing typically has a parting strength of ten to twenty-five pounds and cannot hold a large, muscular fish swimming away at high speed. Landing such a fish, then, becomes a matter of letting it go "into the backing." That simply means that, as the fish swims away, this reserved line "in back" of the fly line winds off the reel. It does so against the force of the drag, and the effort gradually tires out the fish so that the line can be cranked back onto the reel and the fish brought close enough for landing.

"They say those big trevally make long runs," I told Paul. "I want to be sure to have plenty of backing."

"The Battenkill ten-eleven holds two hundred yards of thirty-pound backing," Paul said.

"Is that enough?" I asked, remembering that the Fin-Nor would hold more line.

"Look," Paul said, "that's two football fields of line. If you can't catch a fish in two football fields, you probably don't deserve it."

When I was sitting in the mahogany-paneled comfort of a corner office on the tenth floor in the Italianate corner tower of the Times building on West Forty-third Street, Paul's argument sounded hard but fair—and a hell of a lot more reasonable than it would slightly later in my life.

CHAPTER 10

A Short History of Christmas Island, or Testing the Likely Effects of Global Thermonuclear War on Birds

At Cassidy International Airport, the modern traveler encounters a paradox. The terminal, if such we may call it, is an open-sided, tin-roofed shed that would have served very well as a set for *Donovan's Reef* or, for that matter, *Fantasy Island.* Yet the landing strip is long enough to accommodate the world's largest airplanes.

The concrete strip, like the rusting bulldozers and abandoned radar dishes that clutter the jungle, is a relic of the time when the best minds in the strongest nations in history were planning, for what then seemed to be compelling reasons, to obliterate one another. They needed a place to practice, to perfect the tools of the exercise.

This island, named for the official birthday of the Prince of Peace, was it.

From 1956 until 1963, British and later American thinkers were exploding nuclear weapons in the sky only thirty miles offshore. Luckily, the warrior empires that have kept us free did their bang-bang downwind, leaving the island itself unradiated. Millions of seabirds, going about the daily business of prawn and minnow collection and crab pecking, were blinded. The human residents, then subjects of Her Majesty Queen Elizabeth II, were thoughtfully reminded to cover their heads, so their sight was spared. In 1979, the inhabitants of Christmas Island joined those of thirty-two other islands scattered over 2 million square miles of the central Pacific to form the independent socialist nation of Kiribati (pronounced kiri-bass). The capital, Tarawa, is over two thousand miles away and does not enter the daily thinking of Christmas Islanders to any detectable degree.

Their thinking seems to me reflected in the sign over the customs shed. It says:

Welcome to CHRISTMAS ISLAND
Paradise of fish and birds
110 miles north of the equator
5 feet elevation

To the side of this text is a silhouette of a fly fisherman and the national seal of Kiribati, which consists of a yellow sun rising from the sea into a red sky. I personally would have gone for a blue sky, but otherwise the sign artist pretty well nails what they've got plenty of on Christmas—fish and an equatorial sun that at midday expands one's understanding of light. The brightness wallops all the way back to the base of the optic nerve. For some reason, both Tennant and I emerged from the Air Nauru 727 without our sunglasses, and there is a nice shot of us in front of the sign, looking devil-may-care, in a squinty way, in our tropical shirts. Tennant is carrying a duffel from which protrude the aluminum cases containing four fly rods that were, when it came to bonefish, pristine.

The next revelatory sight to greet us was a pair of bare feet sticking through the window of a pickup truck parked outside the customs shed. The feet were attached to the body of a man who was sleeping on the seat of the vehicle. In due course, he roused himself to participate in his employment, which was the hauling of our luggage to the Captain Cook Hotel. He turned out to be a harbinger of the spirit of service on the island, which is to say there when you really need it but barely noticeable otherwise. At first, I suspected that this wholesome indifference to stress stemmed from the local fondness for ganja, joints of which were publicly and matter-of-factly hand-rolled in good old hippie-dippie cowboy fashion. Soon enough, I decided that the work habits of the Christmas Islanders were based less on cannabis than on sound economic analysis.

When you live on an island located two hundred miles from its nearest neighbor, there is not much use in dashing around in a frenzy of industrious activity. You must wait for a large macroeconomic wave to wash over you. Three such waves have hit Christmas Island in this century. In chronological order, they were (1) copra farming; (2) World War II and the aforementioned preparations for nuclear war; and (3) fly fishing.

It seems ridiculous to think of American fly fishers as a force in globalism, but we do play our tiny role as best we can and, for my part, without complaint about the cost. The mathematics, at its simplest, is this. The number of fly fishers has increased so rapidly that the traditional elite destinations in Alaska, and the Rockies, the Bahamas, Argentina and New Zealand, could not accommodate all the people who had the dollars, the appetite and the minimal skill needed to catch a glamorous fish in a strange land. The result has been speedy change in a lot of lazy places. The first fly-fishing explorations of Christmas Island took place in 1982. Ten years later, by the time Randall Kaufmann included the island in his comprehensive international guidebook, *Bonefishing with a Fly,* American fishermen were second only to the government-owned copra plantations in the economy of Christmas Island.

Wherever you encounter them—rather, us—in the airports of the world these days, American fly-fishing tourists are recognizable by an affected swagger of world-weary expertise and the faux casual dropping of exotic place names. We are all lugging the same expensive equipment and the same books, in this case Mr. Kaufmann's.

I knew from the book that Randall Kaufmann had been

coming to the island since 1985. What I didn't know was that, unlike a lot of celebrity fly fishers, he is quiet and unassuming, so quiet that it took me a day or two to figure out that the lanky fellow who resembled the jacket photo on my book was, in fact, Randall Kaufmann. So I was able to quiz him directly.

Is this, all things considered, the best bonefishing in the world?

"Yeah, I think so," Randall said. "That lagoon is so big and so fertile there just isn't any habitat that compares to it in the South Seas. For the first-timer who just wants to get out there and experience some wading-the-flats bonefish action, it's the best spot going. It's easy. It's pleasant. If a person can cast thirty feet, you're going to catch bonefish. You just can't help it."

"Easy" is the operative word here and one not frequently associated with bonefish. *Albula vulpes,* "the gray ghost of the sand flats," is one of the most lied about and lusted after fish in the world. Catching one is not as hard as devotees like to pretend, but in the clear, shallow waters of Florida, the Caribbean and Central and South America, it is plenty hard enough. As Rick Ruoff, a famous guide in the Florida Keys, puts it, "If I took you out in Islamorada, and we caught three fish in a day, I'd say we had a great day." On Christmas Island, he added, "you catch three before the first sandwich."

The ease of the fishing is purely a matter of abundance, and the abundance springs from geology. Between ten thousand and 1.8 million years of postvolcanic activity has created a sheltered place—the lagoon to which Randall Kaufmann referred—that is an ideal bonefish hatchery. Christmas Island is the world's largest coral atoll. The lagoon is actually the flooded caldera of an extinct volcano. The 140 square miles of low, sandy land surrounding the lagoon are the remains of the rim of the volcano. This bracelet of volcanic land has protected the lagoon from the pounding Pacific surf for aeons, allowing the lagoon to develop its bottom of silky sand and coral and its vast herds of crustaceans and fish.

In the Florida Keys or the Bahamas, it is possible to fish hard all day and get only one or two chances at a bonefish. Then, by casting badly and moving abruptly, it is possible to motivate the fish into the bye-now state called "spooked." At Christmas Island, the bonefish can be spooky, too. But because of the vastness of the flats, these fish see fewer people—and flies—so they are not as tightly wound as their hypersensitive cousins in the Gulf islands and Central America. Besides, if you spook one fish there will be another one or a pod of fifty or even a school of several hundred along in a few minutes.

I do not want to belabor the point, but the place has got the bonefish.

Even so, our first afternoon proved to be a frustrating one. After dumping our luggage at the hotel and donning our wading shoes, Tennant and I were driven to an inlet and instructed to wade across a small neck of water and fish around an island that lay about a hundred yards from the beach. We spent a couple of hours carefully stalking and casting to a slow-moving school of fish to no avail. Back on the beach, I could see our guides enjoying a smoke in their pickup truck. Finally, in a mellow mood, one of them joined us with an announcement.

"No, man, those are milkfish. Look just like bonefish except they've got a black tip on their tail. They won't take a fly. You've been wasting your time."

I was new to international saltwater fly fishing and had not yet learned how to express myself with suitable clarity to lazy guides. Otherwise I might have pointed out that *he* had been wasting my time. But perhaps my diplomacy paid off. The guide led me over to the little island, and we walked slowly along its crusty shore of volcanic rock. The dark bottom made for poor sight fishing, but in short order he told me to make a cast into the shallows, and presto, I caught my first fly rod bonefish of the trip and, as it happens, of my life.

It was a small fish. The earth did not move, but at least the deed was done. Over the next four days, we mastered the difference between bonefish and milkfish and caught our share. The latter, by the way, have since been proven quite amenable to biting flies of the right design. Few things change more quickly than the absolute certainties of sport fishing. Tennant and I also discovered that, depending on whether you are on the lagoon side or the ocean side, Christmas Island has two distinct fishing metabolisms.

The miles of flats inside the vast protected lagoon are placid to the point of indolence. Think of a white-sand desert covered with knee-deep water. Under this water the bonefish are prospecting the bottom with their piggy little snouts, hoping to get lucky on shrimp, crabs, slugs or whatever. Sometimes the bonefish blow water out of their mouths to uncover creatures hiding in the sand.

If you wear amber polarized glasses, a bonefish looks like a neon blue cigar. It is pretty and also exciting to see a half dozen or so of these swimming cigars coming at you in a random, shifty formation. You start working out false casts—bang, bang, bang. Then, if you remember the diagram in Randall Kaufmann's book that shows you exactly how far in front of the cigar to drop the fly, you do that. Or perhaps you are so excited you put too much line into the back cast and you drive the rod too hard on the forward cast and the fly and an ugly ball of line land on top of the fish and they scoot away across their watery desert.

That is when a guide like the gentle and highly expert Tabaki Kobae says, "Oh, man, why did you throw there?" Most places in the world, guides say this sort of thing testily. At Christmas Island, they speak with a kind of heartbroken resignation. My theory is they picked up the intonation from the Dolly Parton album that plays every morning in the Frigate Bar of the Captain Cook Hotel, where the guides gather to wait for the fishermen to finish breakfast.

In any event, the guides had turned out to be much better than our first afternoon led us to expect. There is one guide for every four fishermen on the flats, and for an additional eighty dollars Tennant and I hired an extra guide each day to cater to us. That turned out to be Tabaki, a squat fellow, now deceased, whose locally tied flies were much more effective than those we had brought from the States.

I was moved by Tabaki's sighs to ask him to critique my casting, which after a winter's layoff was not up to its usual mediocrity. He took my 8-weight Orvis rod and began shooting out majestic casts, punctuating his backstroke with a distinctive upward stab of his arm.

"Where did you learn to cast like that?" I said suspiciously.

"Lefty Kreh taught me," Tabaki said proudly. "Every day after we fished, he gave me a two-hour casting lesson."

Tabaki's remark oppressed me more than I can say. Even though I had praised the great man's angling skills to the heavens, there would be no lessons from Lefty in my future. I did not resent Lefty's expertise, which would be as pointless as resenting Tiger's swing or Serena's serve. Nor did I feel oppressed because Tabaki, who had never seen a fly rod until a few years ago, was casting better than I could after forty years of intermittent effort and a decade of intensive, or at least expensive, concentration. No, I was oppressed by the sheer weight of something more personal—my own amateurishness in the face of this new kind of fly fishing. I had gotten cocky about my ability to catch trout and bass, including some large ones. But in saltwater environments, the heavy rods and lines, the persistent winds, the greater distances needed in even routine casts—all these factors converged to form a nexus of neuromuscular chaos. Whenever it was mentioned that I had written a book about fishing, I made a point of telling people that my skills were modest. Then I would pick up a rod and prove it.

But hell's hammers, I didn't want to think of myself as clumsy either. Somehow the abundance of Christmas Island, where it is possible to catch plenty of easy fish, sharpened the contrast between those fish and the hard ones that Lefty or the other experts might catch. I'm talking about the ghostly torpedoes you sometimes glimpsed on the turbulent rim of the islands, where the easeful shallows brushed up against the fertile, brute surge of the blue Pacific. I particularly liked these ocean flats, which were bands of shallow, protected water between the coral reef and the shore. It is an environment of great violence, beauty and motion: gulls, terns, pipers zipping by within inches of your head, angelfish and blacktip reef sharks at your feet, and always the big combers marching in to die in shuddering explosions against the coral ramparts of the barrier reef. Fishing those flats, with the cannonade of the waves always in your ears and the spirals of white spume leaping incessantly toward the sky, was a little like standing behind a fortified line during a battle, protected improbably from a world of violence that stretched to the horizon. In those spots, if you trained your eyes on the area where the clear water stranded off into the deeper green underbelly of the incoming waves, you'd see the most intimidating bonefish, the sovereign loners, a full yard long, which didn't need to slide into the knee-deep flats to nibble little stuff. In their passing, these fish put me in mind of what Isak Dinesen said about elephants. They moved along as if they had an appointment at the end of the world.

In the precincts of such fish, one day Tabaki spoke.

"Big bone. He's coming along the edge of the deep water."

Sure enough, moving steadily through the green murk was a gray shape five or six times the size of the fish we had been catching in droves in a long march across an amiable flat.

"You can't reach him from here. Let's move out. Don't splash."

We took an intersecting line to try to get ahead of the fish. It was coming steadily on an unveering course, out there in about four feet of water.

"Cast now, as far as you can," Tabaki said, in that voice guides use when they suddenly care whether a particular fish is caught. It is a voice very different from the one they use when they are saying, in effect, you paid your money, here's your shot, I do this every day.

He was watching the relationship between my false casts and the fish. On the fourth or fifth stroke, he said, "Let it go."

I did. To my surprise, the fly landed in the edge of the deep water. Maybe my best cast ever. Not dead-on, but plausible.

"Let it sink," Tabaki said. "He might see it."

I let it sink without hope, satisfied simply that the cast had not been a humiliation.

"Now strip, strip, strip," he said.

Dear hearts, I wish to tell you that this lordly fish swung toward the fly as inexorably as doom's pendulum, not hastening in the least until the last instant, when it closed on the fly in a rush and took it and was the biggest fish of our trip and one of the biggest ever taken at Christmas Island, where a seven- or eight-pound fish is a large one.

I wish to tell you that and I suppose I could, but it did not happen. The cast was not quite good enough, or my luck was not the supremely obliterating luck you need to make up for a cast that is not quite good enough. A few times in a fishing life that kind of luck will come along, but it did not come to me on this day in the Republic of Kiribati.

Nor was my casting good enough for the other edge-cruising gorillas we spotted on the ocean flats where the big ones would from time to time come looming along under the combers. Just as well, Tabaki explained, since a bonefish that strong and that close to the reef will simply bore over the edge and cut you off on the coral and that would break your heart more cleanly than a bad cast. I would have been willing to take my chances on that kind of heartbreak.

In any event, my casting perked up a bit, and with Tabaki's coaching, both Tennant and I took very nice fish on the ocean beaches. Tabaki and I walked the beach and found the bonefish prospecting in singles or small pods along the edge, where a mild surf surged against the shore. I made a cast to the best fish we encountered, then crouched to lower my outline against the sky. I pulled the fly in short spurts, and the bonefish made a lazy approach, tipped down and picked the fly off the bottom.

I pulled the line tight against its weight and then lifted the rod. The fish, realizing it was hooked, streaked off toward the reef. Coming to the breaker line, it swung right and ran a hundred yards or so along the deep trough in front of the breakers. The fish stopped and bulled around for a bit, then took off in an even more extravagant run. I thought it was simply a very strong fish.

"Uh-oh," Tabaki said, pointing by way of explanation toward what had really inspired the second spurt.

A gray shark of about five feet had come out of the boiling water of the reef and was quartering the shallow ocean pasture in front of us, swinging its head like a pointer bird dog that has winded quail. It was swimming very fast. My fish was honking along. Suddenly, there did not seem to be enough room in the ocean for both of them. I had read somewhere that when a shark gets on the trail of a hooked bonefish, you should release your drag and allow the fish to run freely. I think that's what I did, but I'm not entirely sure, for I found the sight of the shark quartering back and forth on its long sweeping searches to be absolutely transfixing.

Anyway, the shark veered back toward the ocean. It had lost the scent. I could gain line. The shark disappeared under the foam at the base of the incoming waves. The fish measured twenty-five inches, which meant it weighed about six pounds. Tabaki left me to join Tennant on another section of the beach, and they got a fish of twenty-seven inches, or almost eight pounds.

Those were our best Christmas Island bonefish, and while nothing to retire upon, they prodded us into thinking about other, bigger fish that lived beyond the breakers. Tabaki said he would take us outside the reef in one of the hotel's outboard boats. He said he knew a good spot for tuna, and we stopped at one of the island stores to buy some wildly expensive steel leaders and swivels, since Tabaki didn't think the stuff we had brought was heavy enough for the fish we would encounter. Our little plan unfolded neatly and quickly until, back at the hotel, we encountered Big Eddy Currie, the chief guide and well-known local character.

Big Eddy arrived at work each morning on a swaybacked motorcycle that was barely up to its task. The "Big" in Big Eddy referred to NFL-size bulk. He was the great-grandson of a Scottish gun trader who figured long ago in arming the winning side in the Gilbert Islands' bloodiest aboriginal war, and I don't think

Big Eddy much liked me. I didn't much like him when he told me that Tabaki couldn't take us offshore because Big Eddy wanted him to guide a Frenchman with whom it was clear Big Eddy had been doing some heavy tip business.

"Tabaki must take another client tomorrow," Big Eddy said. "Guides must learn they can't make their own arrangements."

If Big Eddy had been only 50 percent smaller, I would have given him a good talking to. I would have pointed out that his interest in guide pedagogy and employee discipline seemed entirely foreign to everything else I had observed on Christmas Island. Instead I retired to the Frigate Bar to whack away at the island's limited supply of Jack Daniel's.

Clive Gammon of *Sports Illustrated,* one of my favorite fishing writers, says they ought to call the Frigate the Somerset Maugham in tribute to its lazily swinging fan and gamy collection of expatriates, sailors, fishermen and islanders. The pastimes in this bar, in addition to drinking, are tying flies for bonefish, telling true stories about bonefish, telling lies about bonefish, and asking Big Eddy where you are going to fish for bonefish the next day. Since I had already exhausted the last possibility, I started watching one of the tiers, a handsome islander who looked like a younger, much less dissipated version of Don Ho, the singer once billed as "Hawaii's Dean Martin."

Upon introduction, the fellow turned out to be Tuna Smith, a well-known guide I had read about and tried to book in advance. But I had been informed by our travel agent that Tuna was on the outs with the Captain Cook, and could not be located or relied upon. The reasons for this situation proved to be unknown or unknowable. Yet here was Tuna, looking chipper and being tolerated by the Captain Cook, and to tell the truth, looking more reliable than your average American Senate candidate.

"Are you booked tomorrow?" I said.

"No, I'm free. You want to go bonefishing? I got great flies."

Tuna held up a Crazy Charlie tied with the oversize eyes and a bit of the bright hair favored by the Christmas Island guides.

"No, my buddy and I want to go outside to try for tuna or big trevally. We're a little tired of the flats. Can you get one of the hotel's boats?"

"I don't need to," Tuna said. "I got my own boat, better than theirs. A hundred and fifty dollars for the day."

"You're on," I said, and with that fortuitous meeting, I was at long last on my way to the definitional adventure I had sought on so many streams, lakes and oceans.

CHAPTER 11

Not an Albatross

The next morning, Tuna picked us up at the hotel, which is in Banana, and we set out in his truck for the boat dock in London, the island's biggest settlement. The two-lane road between Banana and London is lined with a number of churches entirely out of proportion to the island's population of three thousand. In a way, it is soothing to see so much chaste ecclesiastical architecture, so many clean, palm-shaded lawns, so many walkways lined with whitewashed rocks.

But do not be deceived.

These establishments attest to a fact omitted from the travel brochures. Christmas Island is a churning urn of religious competition. The islanders have a perfectly serviceable animistic religion. It involves determining what creature is your "devil" and then avoiding it for the rest of your life. The religious bureaucrats of the world saw an irresistible opportunity in the simplicity of the indigenous faith and its lack of formal organization. They have divided the island's amiable inhabitants into competing sects. There are Roman Catholics, various kinds of mainstream and holy-rolling Protestants, Seventh-Day Adventists, Jehovah's Witnesses and Latter Day Saints. As a result, you never know when you're going to run into an evangelist.

For example, one was driving our truck. We were rolling along pleasantly toward our day's fishing when Tuna emerged in that role, although his agenda was not immediately clear. He first observed that my job at *The New York Times* was an influential one. I responded modestly, as is my wont, and tried to change the subject, as I always do when the subject of work intrudes upon my fishing time. I asked if Tuna thought we should try for tuna or trevally first. But Tuna's thoughts were not on the world of fish but on the condition of the world. He observed that a newspaper could play a powerful role in spreading healthy ideas.

"Hmmmnnn," I said. I meant to sound deeply noncommittal. Tuna apparently took this moaning sound as an expression of interest as to what ideas might be spread.

"My religion teaches that the world doesn't have to be in such a mess all the time with fighting and people not having enough to eat," he said pleasantly.

Just then, we were passing a small round tabernacle, and Tuna allowed it was, in fact, his place of worship. Tennant, who is a historian and implacably curious, asked what kind of church it was.

"Baha'i," said Tuna. "Have you heard of it?"

"I have," I interjected. I observed that its practitioners were being tortured in Iran. Tuna did not take my meaning.

"Yes, exactly," he said. "We have a plan for world peace. The problem is there are too many bad people and too many governments in the world. We need one big government."

"Sort of like the UN," said Tennant.

So, just that quickly, I found myself in Editorial Writers' Hell. After only a short time in the opinion business, I had discovered that E.W.H. is a place that travels with me. It works sort of like *Tales from the Crypt* or *The Twilight Zone*. I think that I am on vacation and that I am going to be doing something intensely pleasurable which will take my mind off work. I encounter people who appear at first interesting and cooperative, but just when I get my hopes up about having fun, these people turn out to be members of a vast international network, the Rampant Opinion People. They operate like reverse vampires. They can live only by injecting their opinions into someone else. Their entire life is a restless search for host bodies. Finding themselves within range of an editorialist is the equivalent of Lestat spying an unattended thirteen-year-old virgin.

The first few times I was R.O.P.-ed while fishing, I thought about pleading that I was on holiday, which by definition means taking a break from *Times*ian opinions and, perforce, the opinions of others as well. In my testier fantasies, I saw myself assume the painfully polite manner, if not the vocabulary, of a spokesman for the British Foreign Office. "I'm terribly sorry," I said in this fantasy, "but I'm afraid there's been a mistake. You seem to have me confused with someone who gives a shit what you think."

Of course, I never said that. I share with most Southerners the trait of being pathologically polite. I had observed that politeness was not a regional habit in my new hometown, but I was never able to kick it. More relevant in regard to free-associating opinionists, I am anchored to what Helen Jacobus Apte, a memoirist from Atlanta, called "the clear stone of duty." All newspapering is based on a sacred civic contract in which the reader is invited—and, on the editorial page, exhorted—to be engaged with the fate of his or her city, state, nation and world. This calls for a certain tolerance on the part of a journalist who is confronted with a sincere and mannerly expression of that engagement. It's another case of knowing the rules when you sign up.

Although I am a sort of hymn-singing heathen who hopes Cotton Mather et al. were wrong, I often found myself wondering in such situations whether God might be a somewhat judgmental and peremptory editorialist. What would He say upon hearing my complaints about Editorial Writers' Hell?

"Listen," God would say, "through a happenstance that even I do not fully understand, you have wound up as Editorial Page Editor of *The New York Times*. Next time I'll be more careful. It's hard to keep all of creation running perfectly, and I've got more important personnel crises in your general area. For example, what the hell am I going to do about fire ants and the Christian Broadcasting Network? So here's the deal, as ordained by me, the Lord God Almighty, the Great I Am or, speaking editorially, the Great We Are, whose dominion extends to the birds that tread the air, the fish that swim in the waters and the creatures who type into word processors. Every day you get to parade your opinions before 1.1 million subscribers. On Sundays, you have

1.7 million. So the least you can do is recognize your obligations and not go around insulting people who want to mention *their* opinions. As for those opinions that are tedious, redundant, predictable, ill-informed or intrusive into moments that you have set aside for pleasurable experiences, be they piscine or carnal—I give you this commandment: Complain not about the paying if you have chosen to join the playing."

I took His point. There's always a wild card in the deck we call free will. Even so, I was surprised to stumble into this storm of unsolicited opinion on the road from Banana to London. The last time I looked, Christmas Island was well outside the *Times*'s circulation area, and I figured this was the one place in the world I could go fishing without running into someone who wanted to talk politics. By this time, Tennant, damn him, was flagrantly and sincerely inviting a minute explanation of the Baha'ist worldview. Tuna, for his part, clearly saw that a man in my profession could be, if converted, an extremely useful promulgator of the Baha'i solution to the timeless problem of global coexistence.

So Tuna lectured as he drove. No, he said, the United Nations was not really the model he had in mind. They just talked and had no power. The way he saw it, the world needed an international police force under the theological supervision of Baha'i elders. They would also run the world's one government and, if necessary, use the police to make sure everybody got along.

"So," he said, "if a bad man started causing trouble somewhere in the world, the police would go to that place and tell him to stop. Why wouldn't that work?"

I suppressed the thought that World War II had followed a not dissimilar script and that the part about telling the bad man to stop had proved a considerable task. Upon reflection, I was impressed with the sweet, untutored heartiness of Tuna's concern. His desire for theocratic police seemed out of keeping with the placidity of his daily life on Christmas, but then I thought about what Tuna saw when he looked around his island. He did not need a subscription to the *Times* to understand the global reach of bad men or good ones who leave behind rusting war machines and memories of bird-blinding nuclear flashes.

Tuna was proud of the low promontory of coral rock where he stopped his truck. There, under construction, was a two-story palm-thatched house where his family would live close enough to the sea to feel the salt spray through the windows. It would be a trig little domicile, anchored at the corners by authoritative, heavily bolted posts, since its location would give it plenty of chances to taste high water in typhoon season. There was an open shed where scuba gear was strewn around aerated fish tanks. Tuna explained that these and the twenty-foot outboard boat anchored nearby in the lagoon were the main tools of his tropical-fish business. The entire plantation was perhaps thirty feet by fifty feet. In the middle of the yard, between the house and the shed containing the fish tanks, were a couple of gazebolike structures formed by heavy worktables whose legs had been extended upward to support roofs of palm fronds. Two workers, obviously taking their first look at the day, had emerged from curtained sleeping perches under the tables to carry our gear and respond to Tuna's instructions about readying the boat. This was Tuna's world, a place where people did not take for granted a dry place to sleep. Once the house was completed, he, his family, his workers would all be gathered in one tidy compound.

He approached one of the worktables and swept aside a piece of canvas with a triumphant gesture. "Would you like to fax someone?" he said. "I just got this. Anywhere in the world, I can send or receive a fax."

Sure enough, there was a nice machine all hooked up and ready to go, although it seemed to me an open question as to how long its casual cover could protect it from the salt mist that, according to Tuna, rose like a white curtain on any windy night when the waves battered the pocked white coral along the edge of his property.

"Actually, I'm trying to avoid faxes," I said. "What do you use it for?"

"Fish orders," Tuna said. "From Honolulu. They tell me how many triggerfish or clown fish they need on the next flight."

"Do your fish go to the States from Honolulu?"

"Mostly to Japan," he said. "The Japanese are crazy for tropical fish."

Tuna clearly was a cyclone of entrepreneurial zeal and one-world philosophy. I was touched by his determination to wring every fair penny out of the island's grim little economy, and I suspect that was what got him crossways with the Captain Cook Hotel and, perhaps, with Big Eddy himself.

"If you were here in a couple of months, I would have a twenty-eight-foot Boston Whaler. I think I'm going to get a business partner in Honolulu. He'll send it in by freighter. Right now we go in my diving boat."

The craft in question was an open fiberglass skiff much like the pangas used in Mexico and Central America. It had high sides, wooden bench seats and a tiller-steered Yamaha outboard of forty horsepower. Tuna's helpers had brought it next to the shore from its mooring spot, and we got aboard. Soon we were climbing the long blue rollers in the island's only pass between the lagoon and the open ocean. The first white men to come through that pass did so in a long boat on December 25, 1777. They were from Captain James Cook's ship *Resolution,* but they coasted into the lagoon under the immediate command of the ship's twenty-two-year-old navigation officer. He was William Bligh, a seaman of undisputed mettle, although like other assertive leaders, he has been depicted as lacking in people skills. I have no idea whether this was a fair depiction. It probably depends, at least in part, on the reliability of mutineers as witnesses. Bligh's group found the island devoid of people, because it had no source of fresh water, but they scooped two hundred pounds of fish out of the lagoon and returned later for a big load of sea turtles.

Following Captain Bligh's paddle tracks was not the healthiest of omens, but it was a cheery one compared with what happened next. We ran outside the reef to an area Tuna thought would be good for trevally. Tuna worked the boat as close as he dared to the booming surf and had us loft big plugs onto the smooth, humped backs of waves that were just about to turn to foam. Then we cranked as rapidly as we could. Trevally like a fast bait, they say, but I can report with undisputed certainty that seabirds love those lures, or maybe they just feel companionable in that part of the world. At any rate, there were so many birds it was spooky in the Hitchcockian sense. We're talking big black birds with wicked beaks and six-foot wingspans and V-tails. They wanted to get close to us and then chase the lures as they arced through the air. Sometimes they would swoop down and lift the plugs from the water with their feet. Luckily we did not snag any of the beasts. I have a nonviolent, indeed, even reverential feeling toward giant birds of prey, so you know what happened next was not intended, at least by me.

I unleashed a ferocious cast, unaware that a bird was swooping toward me with such timing as to intersect my heavy plug at its moment of maximum velocity, about ten or fifteen feet from the end of my rod. Bird and plug fell to the sea, entangled, and I cranked them over so Tuna could reach them.

As our craft rose and fell on the long-breathing humps of the ocean, Tuna lifted the bird by the fishing line. Its head was held by the embrace of the treble hooks.

"Don't worry," Tuna said. "I will revive it."

"I don't think so," I said.

For when Tuna lifted the creature, its head lolled around with the unmistakable, terminally relaxed motion of a neck-wrung chicken. Once you have seen it, you know what it means.

I felt a sinking sadness at the black sack of feathers to which I had reduced this creature of soaring majesty. The bird floated in a posture of profound finality which repudiated Tuna's speculations that it was just stunned. It looked much smaller now that it was splayed instead of soaring, smaller and forever beyond the reach of avian CPR.

"Let's try another place," Tuna said with the authoritative gaiety of a guide who knows his clients need a fresh start. That suited me. I wanted to get as far as I could from the dead-bird karma of the waters off Poland, a coastal hamlet a few miles from London. The area struck me as a theological collision zone. If we were playing under Christmas Island rules, I needed to pray that this bird was not my devil. But being an English major, I was also thinking about Samuel Taylor Coleridge. Tuna identified my victim as a frigate bird. Frigates, I knew from reading British sea novels, were also known as man-o'-war birds. Did this species have others aliases? Albatross, for example?

I pressed Tuna closely about this question. No, no, he assured me, the albatross is much bigger, an entirely different bird. I felt mollified, but I couldn't shake the thought that a bird which had two names might somewhere, in the vast spaces of human literary effort and the South Pacific Ocean, have a third.

"I know a place where we sometimes see schools of small tuna in the morning," Tuna said. He yanked the string that awakened his Yamaha. As our course lay parallel to the shore, we ran according to the undulation of the sea, sometimes sneaking along in the troughs of the waves and sometimes lifted up to play ridge runner along the crests. Up top we had sweeping views of unsullied beach and the big combers marching through Captain Bligh's pass. Perhaps it was those big waves surging toward the pass that stirred a question in Tennant's mind.

I heard him shout at Tuna over the buzz of the engine. It was something about life preservers.

"Don't worry about life preservers. We won't need them," shouted Tuna, our trusty guide, entrepreneur, Baha'ist prophet and, I hoped, infallible ornithologist.

CHAPTER 12

Not a Bonito Either

Out on the lawless frontier of the vast Pacific, under the revolutionary spell of Tuna's world-federalist preachments, perhaps touched by the same equatorial up-yours spirit that made Fletcher Christian turn on Captain Bligh, I broke the Manhattan Rules of Fly Fishing. I'm willing to admit right up front that I knew the rules were important. One of the first things I learned upon moving to New York is that people you run into at the Anglers Club and the Theodore Gordon Flyfishers may look easygoing, but when it comes to the rules of fly fishing, they are about as relaxed as Charlton Heston on gun control. The general view in such quarters is that humankind has received four great charters of cosmic guidance, those being the Ten Commandments, the Constitution, the Dow Jones Industrial Average and the Manhattan Rules of Fly Fishing, not necessarily in that order.

So let the record show that I am not pleading ignorance of the rules. I cannot even claim the defense outlined in Merle Haggard's song "Mama Tried," that was I was born the "one and only rebel child / From a family meek and mild." Up until that moment, I had a pretty good record on rules in general. I was dead solid perfect on observance of the U.S. Constitution. I was also clean on the Ten Commandments in the areas of killing, stealing and bearing false witness.

How then, given a generally tractable nature, did I come to violate the most sacrosanct standard of my sport? I will resume my narrative with this observation. Like so many of the deeply pleasurable occasions of sin in my life, this one began with a simple question that had not occurred to me before that moment. It came from a respectable source, the observant Baha'ist in the rear of the boat.

"Have you got any big streamer flies?" he said.

We had been trolling with conventional tackle off the northwest corner of the island, where ocean currents boiled against the steep flanks of the old volcano. The water was hundreds of feet deep here, and its upper stories were trafficked by schools of bait fish that, in turn, pulled in schools of small tuna. From time to time, we could see the splashes of feeding fish, but we had no takers on our big plastic lures. So Tuna thought a fly, being more streamlined, might attract a strike.

As it happened, I had a brand-new, tandem-hooked billfish fly purchased by mail order from the Fly Shop of Redding, California, for what I took, then and now, to be a bargain price of $4.95. A nice fly it was, and I had bought it, as I buy so many pieces of tackle, prophylactically. I felt that someday, somewhere I might need it, never mind the fact that I had never caught a billfish and had, in fact, seen damn few in my life.

"How's this?" I said to Tuna, holding up a concoction of green and white plastic filaments tied like a ponytail.

"Perfect," he said. "Put it on your ten-weight fly rod, and let's troll for a few more minutes before we go inside the reef for bonefish."

Perhaps if I had been born under the ennobling influence of the Manhattan Rules rather than into the Redneck Way of Fishing, things might have taken a different turn at that point. Perhaps then I would have given Tuna a stern but loving look and reminded him that he, of all people, should know that what the world needed was not rank and random adventuring but good rules and a vast, benign mechanism for their enforcement. I should have told him that trolling is not fly fishing, unless perhaps you are president of the United States and get reduced to arguing that you don't know "what the meaning of 'is' is." For my part, I understand all forms of the "to be" verbs, and I know that fly rods are made for casting. I understand, too, that you must be casting when you hook a fish for it to count as a fly-rod fish. For years, people in New England have trolled flies from rowboats for yellow perch, trout and landlocked salmon, and it is a serviceable way to get something for the frying pan. But it is *not* fly fishing, of which the cast from a still position is the sine qua non.

Right then I had my chance to explain the Manhattan Rules to Tuna, to evangelize, as it were, to a man with a proven taste for things spiritual, evangelistic and orderly. Instead, I tied my Fly Shop billfish fly to my twenty-pound Orvis leader with the eighty-pound shock tippet. I paid line from my Orvis Battenkill 10/11 saltwater reel, and within minutes I was trolling with my nine-foot, 10-weight Sage fly rod. I confess again that I was not casting my line as intended by the designers of all the products named above and as mandated by the Manhattan Rules of Fly Fishing and the International Game Fish Association of Fort Lauderdale, Florida. I think of myself as a fly fisherman and so present myself to the world, but I was trolling as openly as any wire-lining, beer-gutted, bowling-shirted New Jersey plumber on his annual outing to murder a Cape May bluefish.

I think Tuna was explaining again the fine points of how the international police force would operate when the strike came. He talked about that a good deal to fill the odd moments of the day. As ocean strikes go, it was gentle. The fish made a short run, pulling line from my fly reel, and then turned docilely and began swimming toward the boat and then past it. I had to wind rapidly to take the slack out of the line.

"What kind of fish is it?" Tennant asked.

"Probably a bonito," said Tuna.

At that precise moment, an astonishing blue-and-silver creation came out of the top of a Pacific wave that loomed above our puny boat like a hillock of cerulean jelly. There is something impressive about looking uphill at a fish that seems half as long as your boat. In *The Outermost House*, Henry Beston wrote about big rogue waves "coming like a king" out of the sea. That is how I think of that moment. The wave rose above us like a king, and an impossible fish climbed into the sky like the Son of God. What

I'm trying to express, I suppose, is that on the stroke of that moment something rolled over within me, something at the center of my chest. It was, I think, the tumblers of my heart.

"It's not a bonito," I said.

Tuna, whose attention had been elsewhere, saw the second of three greyhounding leaps.

"No, it's not a bonito," he agreed in a tone of calm acceptance that I assume is taught in the temples of his faith.

I, having been raised in the shrieking heebie-jeebie land of Jimmy Swaggart, have not achieved astral consciousness. I fear that my voice betrayed a lifetime of belief that if God has a plan, it will be revealed through trials, complications and afflictions, rather than through the ministrations of a traveling band of Good Cops who show up when things get sticky.

All of which is to say that at this crowningly intense moment of my fishing career, I babbled.

"It's a sailfish," my mouth announced foolishly even though my brain knew with perfect clarity that it was not. I remember this dysfunction with precision, because it did not feel like a slip of the tongue. Instead, I felt that the abrupt appearance of this fish to which I was so intimately and horrifyingly connected had jarred my mind and my tongue into separate modes of operation. They seemed to respect each other, but not to care any longer that they were lodged in the same body.

"It's a marlin," I finally managed to say, feeling a foolish sense of triumph at being able to state the obvious.

It was, indeed, a Pacific blue marlin, and by every available sign, this particular marlin was in fine fettle. It was a young marlin at the brimming height of its powers. Scientists of human aging would have to report that I, a stocky, graying man just past fifty, could not be regarded as being at the height of my physical powers. On the other hand, I had reached through calculation and steady effort the ability to fish in some of the waters about which I had dreamed. So it came to pass that the marlin and I met in the roomy precincts of the far Pacific. Now we were both doing what we had to do. I was holding on. And the marlin, having gotten its introductory leaps out of the way, was hauling ass.

Its course lay toward the equator, the imaginary midline that girds our common home, the lovely, unpredictable and inadequately policed planet we call the earth.

CHAPTER 13

Blueness and Bolts Therefrom

According to *The World of the Southern Indians* by my fellow Alabamians Virginia Pounds Brown and Laurella Owens, the Cherokees believed that there are seven directions: north, south, east, west, up, down and where we are now. Between us, the marlin and I were covering all the points of the Cherokee compass. The fish had taken control of the first six—especially up, down and south. I figured that left me in charge of where we were, which was feeling intensely alive on the heaving bosom of our dispassionately fecund mother, the sea; and if you interpret the Cherokee idea of location to include all aspects of consciousness—everything that is thought, felt or seen—I can tell you exactly what I learned as my fish showed itself in those three arcing leaps that exist on the screen of my memory as a definitive celebration of blueness—viscous blue sea, vague blue sky, the final dead-end, blood-clot blacky blue of the fish's snout, back and tail, everything blue before me not opposed but affirmed by the valuable under-slice of the fish's silver belly.

I learned that this was in no sense "my fish," even though I could not then and cannot now drive that "my" from my interior vocabulary. I learned something about the face of true longing. Being hooked to a wonderful fish that you are sure you cannot hold inspires the same feeling of lust and dread you get from falling in love with someone you are fairly sure is not going to feel the same way about you. Indeed, I cannot adequately express to

you the blistering speed and rank power with which the marlin—
"my fish," as I longingly thought—was rejecting the idea of near-
ness to me.

Yet hear this, brothers and sisters of the angle.

In this supreme moment, with the fatal fist of doom and
desire clutched tight around my throat, I did not fuck up.

Indeed, a series of formidable thoughts announced themselves
in my consciousness. True, the scene in our little boat was one of
disorder, a mélange of feckless shouts, self-abrogating instruction,
of engine gunning and headlong pelting up and down the indifferent cleavage of the sea. Yet my rod, as inadequate as a daisy
stem in comparison with the muscular capability of this fish,
had not broken of its own accord, nor had I broken it through the
brand of clumsiness endemic among fishermen in such moments.
That is to say, I did not heave back against the fish with all my
might. Nor did I yield to the temptation to try to snub the fish off,
like a rodeo roper with a bolting calf. The reel handle went
round and round in a blur. My reel seemed as hardy as it was
cheap. The marlin had not thrown the hook in the first moments
after being hooked or on the first jumps, as they often do. The fish
was still on. I had survived the first and most burning run without
getting spooled or tangling the line. But mainly, I had not pan-
icked. I had babbled, to be sure, but I had not done anything terminally stupid.

Forgive me, but I must dilate on the lattermost point, the
total absence of disastrous actions on my part. The anglers among
you will understand. For my entire life, I carried an image of failure in my head, a script of what would happen if I got struck by
a truly significant fish. I think most fishermen carry such an
expectation of failure within them, because luck in fishing does
not give you any warning, and your ingrained response, which
can only be overcome with years of effort, is to jerk away from
good luck as if you had touched a hot stove or a raw electric wire.
Many, perhaps most fishermen remain jerkers and snatchers at
heart, lifelong prisoners of the South Sauty Heave. Sometimes I
think it is because we want to get the losing done with one cleanly

fatal stroke rather than through a humiliating storm of unforced errors. In World War II, psychologists called this the "riddance syndrome." Pilots would actually fly into deadly danger to rid themselves of the awful anxiety over where and when they would finally be shot down.

But I hereby give witness to the fact that another kind of thing entirely occurred. Hubris be damned. I must say again what was then and is now and will be until the day I die the anchoring fact of my fishing career.

Out on the far Pacific, luck struck me like lightning and I did not fuck up.

And not only that.

I became as calm as the hit man played by Richard Bright in *The Godfather.* His was the character who checked into a Midtown Manhattan hotel, changed into a policeman's uniform, then strolled around writing parking tickets until Don Barzini appeared on the steps of St. Patrick's Cathedral. Thereupon he dropped to one knee, grasped his pistol with both hands, aimed slowly and steadily and brought Barzini down with a long, clean shot. I was just such a picture of cold-blooded competence.

I had always wondered what it was like to fight a big fish for a long time, and the moment of my education was at hand. I had the tangible sensation of learning new things, moment to moment, and it became apparent that the things came in two categories, those that are surprising and those that are boring. I also had the feeling that time had slowed down, and that while the pressure of the fish is always there, the mind wanders. When someone speaks to you, you hear what he said, but you also hear its echoes inside your head. For example, Tennant said something, and I immediately thought of his father.

On pleasant mornings in the school year, Mr. McWilliams liked to stand beside an open window while he lectured. From time to time, he would turn away from the class and into the mild air of an Alabama autumn or spring. Beyond him, you could see the blackjack oaks on Enon Ridge turning orange or green, depending on the season. He spoke in formal, elegant sentences that reflected the way he engaged the world. His was the unquenchable, embracing curiosity of a Victorian scientist. Everything made by man or Nature fascinated him, and he was as apt to comment on a mortised joint in the window frame as on the tight carpentry of a Robert Frost poem. That was Mr. McWilliams's greatest gift as a teacher—the ability to impart to his students a ravenous curiosity about all that could be observed and about the forces, seen and unseen, that shape surface reality. I consciously emulated him. I wanted to meet the world with a searing intensity for the most basic of reasons. Mr. McWilliams said no one could become a writer without it.

He was also a great believer in adventure, in exploring the world. As a young man, he had studied in Germany and remembered sitting in a theater in Munich when Hitler and his party clumped down the aisle to take seats in front of him. He did not believe in being contained, either physically or mentally, by Alabama. Well into his fifties, he carried the green book bag he had acquired at Harvard. He spoke often of the tropical seas off Cuba and Miami, both places he had lived. When I was still in high school, I heard Mr. McWilliams refer one day to a person as "beautifully educated," and the comment awakened in me the thought that there was perhaps more to be mastered in life than what was readily apparent in my first glance around Birmingham. The adjective "beautifully" was used a lot in the McWilliams home, which I visited first as a teenage friend of Tennant and later as a favored literature student of his father. There were beautifully prepared meals where one was coached to refer to the green beans as *"les haricots verts"* and comment on the freshly caught *"poisson rouge"* from the Gulf. There were beautifully written books to discuss, and eventually the ambition that one might become educated in the spirit of that adverb. So there was a long historic echo when Tennant spoke a sentence after the fish had been on the line for several minutes, and the affair began to settle down into an orderly struggle.

"You are handling this beautifully," he said.

I thought not of the fish or of my friend's generosity but of how much he sounded like his father and how pleased the old man, who was born in 1901, would be that, over ninety years later, these two boys he had shaped so forcefully, his son and his student, were still friends as we passed into our fifties. I thought also that, in the becalmed waters of middle age, American men yearn for a certain amount of chaos. We will travel far and pay dearly to get it. And I thought that I, by God, was getting my money's worth.

CHAPTER 14

The Ocean Comes
to Look Us Over

In the first chapter of *The Garden of Eden* by Ernest Hemingway, the protagonist hooks a large sea bass on the French coast on a cane pole. He prevents the fish from breaking off by chasing it along a jetty, following the fish out toward the sea. A waiter from a nearby café, observing the battle, hurries down to offer advice.

> "Softly does it," the waiter said. "Oh softly now. Softly for us all."
>
> Twice more the fish forced his way out to the open sea and twice the young man led him back and now he was leading him gently along the jetty toward the café.
>
> "How is he?" asked the waiter.
>
> "He's fine but we've beaten him."
>
> "Don't say it," the waiter said. "Don't say it. We must tire him. Tire him. Tire him."
>
> "He's got my arm tired," the young man said.
>
> "Do you want me to take him?" the waiter asked hopefully.
>
> "My God no."
>
> "Just easy, easy, easy. Softly, softly, softly," the waiter said.

The way you whip a big fish is to chase it for as long as it takes. The trick is not new. Izaak Walton, writing in the seventeenth century, recommended throwing the pole into the water and letting the fish drag it around until it was exhausted, a trick that I sometimes saw replicated by Alabama cane polers during my childhood. Tuna planned an open-sea version of this strategy, with our boat as the cane pole. We learned in short order that he was a marvelous boat handler. We raced through the ocean's hills and valleys behind the marlin, and it was thrilling to be up in the high bow of the boat, tasting the warm, salty spray and feeling the relentless pulse of the fish, leading us south. Tuna was a believer in softly, softly, too. He coached me constantly not to put too much pressure on the line. We would tire the fellow out in due course. All we had to do was be patient.

There was something else about Tuna that I apprehended in those first pelting minutes. He really wanted to catch this fish. Beyond that, he believed we were going to catch it. A guide cannot fake conviction, and there is nothing worse than being in a boat with someone you are paying but who does not much care, one way or the other. Right off, I sensed something elemental in Tuna's response to our situation. I can only describe it as the primal optimism of someone who has grown up conquering sea creatures of all sizes and for whom there is no business other than living the life that the sea and the world have put in front of him. More than anything I did not want to disappoint him.

The fish had slowed in its swimming a bit. It was still going steadily away, running about six feet under the surface, out to the side of the boat so there was a long bow in the line. I asked Tuna to move in more directly behind the fish to reduce the drag on the line. I was afraid the weight of the curved line would pull the hook or break the tippet. Even though the seas were running ten feet or better, the waves came in long swells, without a lot of surface chop. So Tuna was able to gun the boat ahead, closing on the fish and enabling me to regain a hundred yards or so of backing.

After we had been engaged with the fish for some time, perhaps a half hour of bouncing along the waves, up and down, I heard a strangled noise from the rear of the boat and glanced back over my shoulder. Tennant's head was hanging over the gunwale, and from time to time, he shouted passionately at the sea. He is not a large man, but he seemed to hold quite a lot.

Seeing my friend in the embrace of mal de mer reminded me of a comment I had read that compared being seasick to a lover's jealousy. You think you're going to die and everyone else thinks it's funny. One glance at Tennant, who had ceased shouting at the ocean and had fallen back into his deck chair, convinced me that this would not be a good time to share this witticism. My main attention was on the marlin, but I still found time to make mental note of a scientific observation. In my life, I have seen only two people who were green with nausea, in the sense that there was actually a faint but unmistakable green tint to their skin. One was Tennant, whose head was now rocking around on his shoulders with something of the glazy-eyed, lolling look of that murdered frigate bird. The other was my cousin Joe Raines, who acquired motion sickness on the roller coaster at Kiddieland Park in Birmingham in 1953. Joe wanted to go home the moment he turned green. I hoped Tennant didn't have any illusions about going home. So far he was keeping his mouth shut. Even so, I felt a surge of irritation toward Tennant. Not that I don't love him like a brother. I do and don't mind saying it. But what if we needed him to do something other than moan and loll?

"Drink a Coke," I told him.

"I don't think I can keep it down right now," he said.

Even so, I was encouraged. He had spoken a sentence free of complaint and containing no mention of the shore. Good thing, since there was no way in hell he was going to touch the shore before this fish was caught or escaped.

More time passed. We had kept gaining on the fish until now it was only about a hundred feet off the starboard bow, swimming steadily just under the surface, the point of its tail slicing out of the waves like a scimitar. Sometimes the boat would slow against an incoming wave, and without its mediating speed working on my behalf, I could feel the chained energy and weight of the fish and ponder the profoundly unbalanced relationship between it and my fly rod. I was peacefully contemplating such matters and silently congratulating Tennant for suffering in silence when Tuna spoke.

"Do not worry about the boat," he said.

I had not been worrying about the boat, but Tuna's introduction of the concept prompted me to turn toward him. I saw that he was standing shin deep in clear Pacific ocean water that had somehow managed to get on the wrong side of our hull.

"Just pay attention to your fish," Tuna said. "The drain plug came out. I think I can find it."

Ah, the drain plug.

If you are not a boater, you may not understand the centrality of the drain plug. Most outboard boats have a hole in the transom for the purpose of draining the bilge when the boat is lifted clear of the water or, more commonly, when it is moving ahead smartly enough to cause the water to be sucked out into the wake. But we had been moving slowly for a while, inviting water to enter the boat in the absence of the plug. There was already enough water in the back of the boat for a grown man to lie down and take a bath. I'm no naval architect, but it was clearly necessary to find the plug and return it to its home, a one-inch hole in the transom, in order to interrupt the nautical activity known as sinking.

In fact I did not much worry about the boat or the unalterably absent life preservers. I paid attention to the fish. I continued to handle it carefully, but with a certain airy absence of anxiety that I had never known before in the presence of a fish for which I harbored such lava-hot desire. I felt calm about our situation. We were far from land, having followed the fish steadily away from Christmas Island for over an hour. There were no other boats in sight. We had no radio and no flares. So it did not require Baha'ist clairvoyance to know what might happen if we went into the water. Tennant would recover from his seasickness. I would drop my rod. Tuna would tell us not to worry. We would do the survivor float. We might be rescued. Or we might meet some of those big untutored open-ocean Pacific sharks that, unlike their relatives in the Atlantic and the Gulf of Mexico, have not learned to associate people with danger and instead seem to associate them with "easy to chew."

CHAPTER 15

Snapshot II:
The St. Johns River, June 1956,
a Captive Boy, Alone on a Dock,
Dreams of Escape

On the long ago June day that I will lay before you, I was part of a secret event on the gasoline dock at Kinard's Fish Camp near Palatka, Florida. By shaping the quality of desire I would feel as man and boy, it changed the fishing part of me. The scene on the St. Johns, with its sharp edges of nostalgia and frustration, surfaced in my memory when I found myself, many years later, at another fuel dock. Tennant and our college classmates Ed Hardin and Mike Atchison and I took Ed's Bertram sport fisherman, the *Abracadabra*, into the cup-shaped harbor at Man-O-War Cay in the Bahamas. It's a place where you encounter a number of people, including some young families, who live aboard their boats and drift around from one anchorage to another in the islands. It is a fine life if you like to read and know how to fix a marine diesel. Some of these live-aboard folks are unapologetically wealthy. Some are seagoing hippies with an attitude—I'm too smart to work—that makes you suspect them of having an insurance policy from the great international firm Daddy's Money. At Man-O-War that day, a sun-browned couple of the first category tied up their expensive motor sailer near the *Abracadabra* and strode purposefully along the dock that led to the island's well-known boat repair yard. I was feeding the sea turtles and groupers that inhabit a live pen beside the dock, and as the couple passed me, the man shouted a sharp come-along-now over his shoulder.

Looking back toward their boat, I saw a spidery, tanned boy of six or seven. He was barefoot and in swim trunks. He was dawdling along the very outermost edges of the dock's warm planks, watching the water intently, as if he was afraid of missing something fleeting and unrepeatable. It took persistent urgings from the father to lure the boy past the grouper cage. He went on down the edge of the dock, arms spread for balance, his body tilted out to the left like that of a tightrope walker, never taking his eyes from the clear Bahamian waters and the darting wrasses and baby snappers that live in the shadows of every dock down there.

That boy's fascination with the alternative world that is wrapped by water reminded me that before I was a fisherman I was simply a boy who could not stay away from the sea, lakes, ponds, puddles, rivers, creeks, brooks, branches and springs, and up until I was eight or nine years old I could happily be around water without fishing in it. The gift for being the companion of water rather than a flailer of it deserted me, but I remember those days as possessing a peacefulness that lies beyond the reach of incurable fishermen. For them—for us, I should say—every stretch of unfished water is a missed opportunity. In that happy, earlier time, all marine pleasures—swimming, dam building, collecting and liberating newts and minnows and crabs—were equal.

I had several favorite venues, none of which lay near my home. Indeed, one of my chief grievances against the part of Birmingham where I grew up was its lack of ponds and creeks. Between them, the municipal sewage system and the United States Steel Company had polluted every stream within bicycle range. But once I could get down to the Gulf coast at Panama City or back into the hills of Winston County, Alabama, I was in the kingdom of joy.

My mother was from Winston County, and my grandparents still had a good-size farm there when I was a boy. The county was called the Free State of Winston, and long before I learned to admire the antislavery tradition that had earned it that title in the Civil War, I loved the Free State for the deep ferny hollows and freestone streams where it was possible to forget the smoke-stacks and flue dust of Birmingham. Had there been any brook trout native to Alabama waters, they would have lived in Winston County. It is the footstool of the Appalachians, where the south-ernmost reach of those mountains plays out in a terrain of ridges and upland plateaus, some of them partitioned by formidable lit-tle canyons ringed by gray sandstone bluffs. It looks cool and trouty in the canyons, not only because of the clear fast streams but also because of the vegetation. The deeper ravines support spruces and firs, remnants of the boreal forests that thrived there in the last Ice Age.

The creeks had names like Brushy, Dismal and Clifty. There was a place called Wolf Pit, and under some of the bluffs you could see holes worn in the boulders where the Indians had ground corn with rock pestles. On the low backside of my grand-father's pasture, a spring leapt from under a mossy bank and ran into the forest through a series of pools and small waterfalls. This was salamander water. You had to follow it down to a bigger creek in the next deep hollow to see the fatheaded chub minnows that were shaped like little baseball bats.

The chub minnows looked a lot like the bullhead minnows I used to catch at the Slough in Panama City. The Slough does not appear on any map. It was simply an outlet canal between J. Manning Vickers's lake and the Gulf of Mexico. It ran straight across the beach, and like most outlet streams of that sort, some-times it ran freely into the sea and sometimes it was blocked by the shifting beach sands. It changed daily, depending on wind, tide, wave action and rainfall. Every morning I visited the Slough to check on its latest wanderings and to net a daily harvest of blue crabs that migrated in from the sea. I played in those waters with an absorption about which I had forgotten until I observed my own sons and, after that, the lad on the dock at Man-O-War.

But try as I might, I cannot remember when I changed from

a prowler of waters to a fisherman. I want to recall the exact moment, but I simply cannot. I think it had to do with a piece of equipment, a tiny rod and reel with an ingenious antibacklash device, that my father bought me at Fisher-Stinson Hardware on Harrison Avenue in Panama City. My brother, Jerry, tells me that, when little more than a toddler, I was coached by him and others in the catching of pinfish and catfish from the surf at Panama City, first on a cane pole and then on my rod and reel.

Those were such happy times. I could not know that I stood on the threshold of my long captivity among the bait fishermen. I have only myself to blame, of course. We all choose the life we want. That is my philosophical position. In reality, I blame my father and my brother. Here we must pause to contemplate the powerlessness of the baby brother—in all families perhaps, in Southern families for sure, in sporting families most especially. In my earlier book, I mentioned the rage I felt when my brother and father went fishing at Tate's Hell Swamp, the Florida Panhandle's greatest redoubt of snakes, gators and fish, and barred me from going on the grounds that, at six years old, I was too young. Once you have imbibed the bitter broth of abandonment, the taste never leaves your mouth, even after you are deemed old enough to tag along. That is the lot of baby brothers. We tag along and we go along with the program, no matter how silly, for we never forget that we can be dropped from the manifest of any trip at the whim of someone with a driver's license.

It can be an instructive experience. I learned, for example, to listen passively when nonsense was being spoken by my elders. For I was thrown early and often into the company of men who had firm convictions, great rhetorical skill and little knowledge. I learned that among certain of my relatives and their hunting or fishing buddies a particular introductory clause—"I'll tell you one damn thing"—was almost certain to be followed by a profoundly misinformed statement about the habits of fish and game, strategies relating to women and football, the contents and interpretations of the U.S. Constitution, circumstances under which it was possible to shoot a trespasser and not be convicted of murder, rock and roll or the political preferences of the American people. It was, in many ways, ideal training for a future journalist, especially one who was to come of age in Alabama during a time when the ignorant statement delivered with passionate conviction comprised the entire coinage of public debate. An innate skepticism in regard to the old, powerful or charismatic, a skepticism first honed in the hunting lodges and fishing camps of my native South, also proved to be a durable tool for dealing with the managing editors of Southern newspapers, for analyzing the Vietnam War policies of Presidents Johnson and Nixon, and for covering the "impossible" presidential campaigns of Jimmy Carter, Ronald Reagan and Bill Clinton.

When it came to fishing, there was a price to be paid for this constant early exposure to feckless teaching. As with smoking, that price was addiction and stunted growth. What I realize from the distance of forty years is that, long before I suspected it, I had developed a subversive attitude toward the Redneck Way of Fishing. I recognize now, at the remove of a half century, that the first stirrings of rebellion came near Palatka, Florida, in 1956. It was the spring that my brother completed his army tour in Germany. His return filled me with joy because I idolized him and, more practically, because in Jerry's absence, my father's energy for organizing fishing trips had tailed off. But with Jerry back in the States, we piled all our gear and a ten-horsepower Johnson motor into the back of the Chevy wagon as soon as school was out and embarked on a slow ramble through the heart of Florida. The mission was fishing, but it seemed to take my father and brother a long time to figure out where we were going and what we would fish for.

Even so, I was happy for the simplest of reasons. I had not been left behind. Finally we fetched up at Marathon Key, drifting the pellucid reef waters aboard a party boat owned by a husband-and-wife team of dropout New Yorkers named Ed and Clare. We did not believe Yankees knew what they were doing by land or by sea, but we signed on anyway for a half day with Clare and Ed on the edge of the Gulf Stream. Clare was a loud blonde with skin that looked like saddle leather. She said we could bottom-fish for snapper or we could fish a ballyhoo near the surface on the chance of catching something more glamorous.

Dad and Jerry opted for the sure thing of snatching snapper and grouper off the bottom, and in the seminal mistake of my fishing career, I emulated my elders. To tell it now, I feel regret swell in my chest like the ache of a lost love. So many subsequent pleasures disappeared into the whirlpool of that innocent moment. For Clare herself had put out a line with a big float, under which was suspended, at the depth of about three feet, a silvery minnow. For a couple of hours, we caught yellowtail snapper and grouper and ridiculed the exertions of a fellow passenger, a Tennessee hillbilly who thought bottom fishing meant that your bait had to lie flat on the bottom. As a result he was constantly hung up, and finally managed by main force to winch up a chunk of living coral the size of a washtub.

Then, suddenly, there was an explosion. The sheetlike surface of the tropic sea was split by a formidable iridescent creature. It was a dolphin of about thirty pounds, and it had Clare's bait, and hook, in its mouth, and Clare proceeded to put every hillbilly bottom digger on that boat to shame. She moved as economically as a cobra. She took the rod from its holder, cranked down tight to the fish and set the hook with a smooth, clean stroke. Round and round the boat she went, dodging customers and passing the rod from one hand to the other when she came to the stanchions that supported the boat's sunroof. I had never seen a fish jump so much or pull so hard. It outshined even the mighty king mackerel I had caught with Bert Raffield and Emil Frudaker off Panama City.

The sad part is that I understood instantly the meaning of Clare's catch. In fishing, you must wait for something wonderful. Moreover, in waiting, you must pass up the easy temptation of the common catch. Alas, I had been born into a family that believed in instant gratification, another useful characteristic, as it turned out, for journalism. "Easy to catch" and "good to eat" were the standards by which we rated fish, and in Palatka, Florida, where we fetched up for some freshwater fishing after leaving the Keys, the fish were sinfully easy to catch.

The St. Johns River swings to the east at Palatka, and in the cove of that turn was a huge shallow area the shipping companies had turned into a dumping ground for old barges. It was called the Boneyard. The skeletal timbers of the sunken vessels poked through the surface like the limbs of a drowned forest, and the muddy, cluttered bottom was ideal spawning habitat for all kinds of sunfish—particularly the spectacularly colored "red-bellies" and a huge local variety of bluegill called "copperheads" after a band of brassy color across their steep foreheads. The St. Johns River was famous for its bass fishing, but during the first full moon of May, the fishing for sunfish over the vast spawning beds in the Boneyard was so easy as to be irresistible, at least for my family. We were not alone. Kinard's Fish Camp was jammed with out-of-state fishermen, including a fellow Alabamian named Walt, who each year froze hundreds of fish for sale in his restaurant back home. It was illegal to sell game fish in restaurants in Alabama, but Walt lived in a small town where the authorities had—dare I say it?—other fish to fry.

I thought Kinard's a little paradise of sandy roads and cabins scattered in a grove of moss-dripping oaks. Quail whistled in the orange groves. I had a line of credit at the snack bar. Every day at fish-cleaning time, I ran up there from the dock and ordered thusly: "A Coke for me and a Falstaff for Curly." Curly was the dipsomaniac dockhand who cleaned our fish and sometimes ran our boat. He was not exactly a guide, but he knew his way around the Boneyard and had also put us on to a deepwater spot called the Pilings, where it was possible to catch crappies on tiny freshwater shrimp locally known as "humpbacks."

Even among the efficient fish killers at Kinard's, our family had a certain status. My father proudly reported an overheard conversation in which a newcomer who inquired about where to fish was told to "follow that old man and his two boys." It was the first time I had ever heard my father refer to himself as old, even though he was younger at the time than I am now. For reasons that I assume had to do with his pain over his own father's death at forty, my dad was always in a hurry to think of himself as elderly. It was as if by living to a great age, he could protect himself and all of us from the pain he knew at losing his own father so early.

In any event, it felt good to be regarded around the camp as experts, as outriders, as scouts who could lead others to where the fish were. Yet when I think back to that long ago summer now, the snapshots are rearranged. I can hardly recall the sight of those teeming hordes of captured copperheads finning slowly in our live well. Instead I remember a solitary moment that I never revealed to Jerry or my dad.

One morning I was at the dock by myself, waiting for them to come down from breakfast. Our boat was in the stall at the end of the dock nearest the gasoline pump. The water between the boat and the palmetto-fringed shore was calm and black with tannin. I took one of our cane poles and stripped the hook, sinker and float from its wispy monofilament line. In place of the hook, I tied on a small popping bug that I found in one of the tackle boxes. I had made a crude but serviceable fly rod. Had I known anything about angling history, I would have recognized my bamboo wand with an unweighted line as being very similar to the English rods described by Walton in *The Compleat Angler*.

With a short, flipping cast, I settled my little fly on the still water along the bank. Almost instantly, there was a slashing strike, and I had caught a dark, chunky bass of about three-quarters of a pound. I remember that fish's glistening ebony back, its white belly and that distinctive smell of musty fertility acquired by bass in the leaf-dyed waters of inland Florida. I knew that smell from the much larger bass that my father and brother had caught a few years earlier in Mr. Vickers's lake on Panama City Beach. In those days, they had fished with top-water plugs on their casting rods or popping bugs on bamboo fly rods for big, glamorous bass and had decreed that I was too small for such fishing.

Then, maddeningly, just as I got old enough to be admitted

to the company of men, they switched techniques. They abandoned artificial baits for worms, gave up on bass and became ardent worm fishers in pursuit of bluegills and shellcrackers. I was too timid to protest. Indeed, when my father and brother arrived at the dock that morning, I did not tell them I had already caught a fish on a fly. I did not say what I believed, that we should go fly fishing for bass in the cool of the morning rather than waste those precious hours dunking worms in the Boneyard. For I did not dare to strain the thin webs of tolerance by which younger sons lash themselves to adventures planned by their elders.

In other words, I knew my place and kept my peace. But something had happened that morning on the dock at Palatka. Like Clare, I wanted to catch a more exciting fish, and I had sneaked out and done it. Moreover, I wanted to catch it on something more elegant than a worm, and I had done that, too. In other words, there was a fly fisherman inside me, trying to get out.

CHAPTER 16

Some Case Studies
in Marine Maintenance

Through the third hour and into the fourth, I was feeling pretty good. True, the marlin still felt very strong, but we were cruising along at its pace, which eased the pressure on my arms and shoulders and created in me two illusions. One was that the constant, pestering weight of the taut line over what you might call the fish's left shoulder was bound to wear it down. The other was that our tribulations had ceased.

"Do not worry," Tuna exclaimed in what I initially took to be the spirit of troubles laid by.

"The water is out of the boat," he added.

I craned my head around and looked over my own left shoulder. Sure enough, he was not standing in water. He was proud of himself.

"How are you doing up there?" Tuna said.

"I feel good," I said. "We've passed four hours and I'm not tired at all."

Tuna had no way of knowing I was not just another soft vacation fisherman. I wanted to assure him that I had been waiting a lifetime for this moment and that conquest resided in my soul. I desired to communicate, in the subtle, modest yet firm way of the Appalachian people, that for all the gray hair on my head, he had a gritty Dixie boy on his hands, a dead-game sport, as my dad would say.

"We'll wear him down," I said. "I think he's tiring a little. He doesn't have as much zip as he had when we first hooked him."

Yet this report did not cheer Tuna as I had hoped. He stood at the tiller, steering us up and down the blue Pacific hillocks. I took him to be curiously unresponsive to my report on the fish, whose pulsing weight was vibrating in my hands at every moment. It turned out Tuna had something else on his mind.

"Do you have a screwdriver?" he said.

I said, not testily but firmly, that I wondered why he needed a screwdriver.

"I have to pull up the floorboards," Tuna said. "I think the drain plug floated under the floorboards while the boat was full of water. Now all I have to do is find the plug."

Oh, yes, yes, indisputably, we still needed the drain plug. As long as we kept running along at half throttle or better, no water could enter the boat. But once we stopped to land the fish or when we, inevitably, ran out of gas, we would start sinking without delay. It was news to me that the plug had not only come dislodged from its hole but gone missing entirely. If it was not under the floorboards, that would be additional news of a very bad kind. It was also news, of a surprising sort, that our drain plug was suspected of floating, since these items are customarily constructed of sinkable materials such as brass and hard rubber. If one comes out, it falls to the bottom of the boat and you pick it up.

"Float?" I said. "Why did it float?"

"It's wood," Tuna shouted back. With a touch of pride, he added that he had carved it himself.

"It has to be under the floorboards," he concluded.

It was time to rouse Tennant from his postpartum apathy. His color had shifted from green to pasty gray, and he moved when roused like someone swimming through an atmosphere that was thicker than that experienced by other humans. Nonetheless, he made a good catch when I swung my Orvis fishing bag toward him.

"See if I brought my Swiss Army knife or Leatherman tool," I said.

He rummaged unhappily through the bag's several pockets. The zippers seemed deeply mysterious to him. As I suspected, the desired items were not in my fishing bag but rather on my dresser back at the Captain Cook.

"Don't worry," Tuna suddenly exclaimed. "I found my screwdriver."

He held the welcome object aloft. It was cheap-looking, like the tools you see in the ninety-nine-cent bucket beside the cash register at True Value. It was rusty. But it was, by God, a screwdriver. Tuna instructed Tennant to take the tiller and fell to work in the bottom of the boat, removing the half dozen screws that pinned the plywood floorboard to the raised ribs of the hull. I want to be fair to Tennant. When you have been seasick, you do not feel like running a boat. Besides, steering a small boat up and down Pacific swells all the while keeping a precise, tight-line distance between the boat and a departing marlin is not a good situation for a novice helmsman, even if said novice has not been throwing up.

Complications ensued. When we slid down the face of a long wave, Tennant failed to back off on the throttle. The boat gained suddenly on the fish.

"Slow down, slow down!" I shouted, too late. There was a big belly in the line. I cranked rapidly to try to take up the slack before the fish could slip the hook. But my cranking was rowdy and undisciplined. It caused the rod tip to jiggle, and this, my first crude move, threw a loop of slack line around the tip-top guide on my fly rod. I knew instantly that this meant trouble, and sure enough, when the boat slowed on the uphill side of the next wave, the fish took off, yanking the top section of the three-piece rod from the ferrule where it joined the middle section. The jerk of the separating rod apparently inspired the marlin to try out its overdrive. Line peeled from the reel and I watched the end section of my rod, firmly looped into my line, disappear into the waves, taking along with it my claim not to have done anything clumsy in regard to handling this raging bundle of fish muscle.

"Don't worry," Tuna said, looking up from his work. "We'll get the rod tip back as soon as I get the boat fixed. Just hold on."

Oh, yes, of course.

"I have it!" Tuna called in a few minutes. I watched over my shoulder as he held aloft a big square block of wood that had been whittled into a blunt point on one end. I wouldn't exactly call it a square peg, but I could see, given its irregular shape, how it had slipped out of the perfectly round hole in the transom. In any event, Tuna pounded it home and scooped out the last of the water. Then he took the tiller again, and once more we went pelting after the marlin and that portion of the fly rod which was now in its possession.

After thirty minutes of playing the fish on the stumpy butt sections, I had regained enough line to catch sight of my missing tip section, still firmly looped in place.

"How sick are you?" I asked Tennant.

"I'm better," he said. "Still a little shaky. I'm all right."

"Then I need for you to get up here in the bow and put this rod back together when I reel the tip section back in. Do you think you can do that?"

"I'm not sure. I'll try," he said.

The only problem, of course, was that Tuna had to gun the engine so I could regain line. The extra speed pushed the boat into the waves so hard that its bow was rising and falling six or eight feet at a sweep. I was sure the bucking-horse ride at the front of the boat would make Tennant spew again as soon as he got in position. On the other hand, I knew that Tuna had to be at the throttle if we were to have any chance at all. As for me, I was not about to surrender the rod. So there was nothing to do but send my ailing friend forward.

Tennant is, shall we say, an unhurried person. His father was the same way. I had learned from the old man how to extend my curiosity but not how to be patient in satisfying it. To say that Tennant took up his station in the bow deliberately is to exaggerate his speed exponentially. I passed the time by explaining how he was going to have to take the tip of the rod in hand without stressing it, then unwrap the half hitch that the fouled line had thrown around the rod's top guide. He had to perform this quickly but be all the while prepared to let the whole works go if the fish sped away. Once he had the rod tip in hand and the knot undone, he must deftly reunite the male and female sections of the rod ferrule, or joint, making sure that the guides were properly aligned. Given the lack of cooperation from the fish and the speed at which the boat was moving, this would not have been an altogether easy task in calm water.

Finally Tennant was in position and I cranked the tip within his reach. He did everything perfectly, and suddenly, we were not sinking, the tackle was in order, the line was tight and Tennant was not throwing up. Our great travail was over, but my expectations of whipping the fish by the end of the fourth hour proved illusory. Even so, in midafternoon, the wind backed around to the south and the seas flattened a bit. We were able by gunning the boat to close to within twenty feet or so of the marlin. I could see my fly plainly in the corner of its mouth. I had a solid gold hookup. Tuna was coaching me constantly, warning me not to get impatient and apply too much pressure, and his eagerness made it necessary for me to declare an intention I thought he would oppose.

"We're not going to kill this fish," I said.

"Don't worry," he said. "We'll just get the fly back and take some pictures. Isn't your yellow camera waterproof?"

It was, in fact, the popular Minolta Weathermatic that is advertised as waterproof up to depths of thirty-five feet and carried by many traveling fishermen. I had used it at the bird-killing place, and Tuna had known the camera's brand and advertised capabilities by its boxy shape and bright yellow color. Tuna moved the boat in very close to the fish. I could imagine the picture on the wall of my office.

Now the fish was swimming right beside us. Another few feet and Tuna could have touched the leader, which under the international rules of billfish tournaments meant the fish could be counted as caught and released. The rule is a conservation measure, the logic being that if a fish is that close to the boat, you could snag it with a long-handled killing gaff if you chose to. Since we were not in a tournament, had no gaff anyway and had already cast aside the holy rules of fly fishing, none of this really mattered. But I understood Tuna's reasoning immediately and bought into it. If he could get the leader in hand, we could honestly say we had fulfilled the technical requirements of "catching" this fish.

It was a matter of proof. With an underwater portrait of the fish with the fly in its jaw, no one could doubt our story. We would be able to show that we had hooked a marlin and gotten alongside it, even if we failed to boat it. Ideally we would bring the fish aboard for a full portrait, posing with it in turn, by pairs and individually. The reclaimed fly could be framed, too. But with Tuna's preliminary underwater shot, we would provide fallback documentation. People might have to take our word for it that Tuna had grabbed the leader, which was bound to happen before long. But there could be no doubt of the central fact. There is only one way to have a close encounter with a blue marlin, and we had done that with the most inadequate of tools. Such prophylactic measures in regard to evidence make sense if you want to be believed in the fishing world, which is the domain of liars.

With that, Tuna leaned over the side and thrust the camera into the water. In this clear water and bright light, the fish should show up nicely. We were so close that its dark image would stand out against a background of aquamarine. The presence of the fly would cinch the deal.

However, this was my waterproof camera's first total immersion, and it turned out to be fatal. The camera died on the spot. It was just one of those things. Luck has its limits. So, in the presence of water, does reasonably priced, mass-produced electronic technology. What do you expect for $250, insulation from the Manhattan odds on paradox and irony? For all we know, those odds govern all islands of the world and the waters around them. The camera of the same brand that I bought to replace the dead one has since been submerged many times with good results, but that day, our instrument for the accurate recording of facts had been harboring like a bad gene an undetected factory defect.

Tennant had already exposed all the film in his standard above-water snapshot camera. We spent thirty minutes or so cruising along with the fish right next to us, trying various schemes to get my unexposed film into Tennant's camera. The new plan was that, since we couldn't get the underwater shot as a fail-safe proof, we'd just bide our time until we landed the fish. Then we'd photograph it *inside* the boat instead of *beside* the boat. Perhaps it was the vibrations of our optimism that provoked the marlin into showing us what it had left.

Which turned out to be a lot.

One moment, we were going along side by side and Tuna and I were plotting how to get the leader close enough for him to grab, and the next, the marlin was tilting its nose down and playing submarine. That is to say, with me exerting maximum pressure by jamming my gloved hand against the spool of the reel, the marlin sounded.

Down and down it went, as if it had an Evinrude strapped to its butt. My two football fields of backing melted away and I could see the exposed spool. When there were about a half dozen wraps of line on the spool, I clamped down, figuring to break the fish off at the leader rather than the bitter end of the backing and thereby save my fly line. The line came tighter and tighter, the tip of my rod plunged into the water. By the fraught feel of things, I could tell that everything between me and the fish was at the breaking point. And then the last thing I expected happened. The marlin stopped its descent and began swimming horizontally again at a leisurely pace exactly 699 feet below us—600 feet of backing, 90 feet of fly line, 9 feet of leader.

At this great depth, the fish swam more slowly, with a kind of casual power. We motored along, keeping pace. The rod was bent to its most severe arc, the line pointing straight down in the piercing blue ocean, as if pinned to a peg at the center of the earth. There was no question of pumping the fish to the surface with main force. Fly rods are notoriously short on lifting power, which is why you don't use them in bottom fishing for grouper or halibut, or for that matter for winching up a sounded marlin. It would be three hours before we saw the fish again. My wish to see what it was like to fight a fish for a very, very long time was to be fully granted.

So when Tuna spoke, I thought perhaps he had some tactical advice, some ploy for us to exercise upon this willful monster for which I felt such an o'erspilling mix of love and awe.

"Howell," he said.

"Yes."

"Do you have any pliers?"

CHAPTER 17

Snapshot III:
A Great Artist Performs
in Obscurity, Burnt Mill Creek,
Circa 1951

The teller is the reader's only guide through a tale. It is a historic relationship, much abused in classical times and in our own; indeed, abused occasionally in my former profession and habitually in my favorite sport. Here, several hours into this story of a modern-day Nantucket sleigh ride, we—or at least you, reader—must confront the sensitive fact that in our culture, "fish story" is a synonym for "lie." Are you to believe what I've told you up to now and what I've yet to reveal simply because I promise here and now that everything happened just the way I'm telling it? Oh, yes, indeed, you may!

Of course, I would say that, wouldn't I? Every liar ever born will swear to his own veracity. I wish to make a larger point about the role of individual discernment when it comes to separating the sheep of truth from the goats of prevarication. The sorting is not all that complicated once you learn to identify the recreational and the pathological kinds of lying. Little did I know the decisive roles that both kinds would play in my life when as a young child I first came under the spell of Captain Frank Beddingood. His name will mean nothing to you because he lived and died in obscurity, but I'll tell you that Long John Silver was not a patch on Frank Beddingood in his prime, when he performed great works of flowing mendacity for any and all wayfarers who fetched up at his fish camp on the banks of Burnt Mill Creek in the Florida Panhandle.

You will quickly spot the commercial motivations that applied, for his business depended on hope, and hope makes us all ready targets. However, from the standpoint of an eight-year-old, he produced his works without incentive, without charge and without mercy. It appeared to me then that Captain Beddingood was simply the kind of opportunistic talker who had learned that some people lack the natural endurance he required of an audience. So he had developed a trick of cunning simplicity. Once you had rented a fishing skiff from him—the act of hope—and were preparing to cast off, he would sit on the bow of your boat, nailing it to the sandy bank and capturing the crew in their seats while he delivered his Oration of Launching. Its themes were where you should fish, what you should use and how very many fish you were certainly going to catch once you absorbed his instruction.

The process was repeated at the end of each fishing trip, when the spry, watchful old coot would come scrambling out of the shade trees and claim his perch the moment your bow scraped the beach. Anyone who wanted to take a leak was in trouble, for the Speech of Return was if anything more elaborate than the Oration of Launching. Its theme was always why you had not caught any fish, since, in fact, Burnt Mill Creek was singularly devoid of marine life. I never caught a fish there. No one in my family ever caught a fish there. None of us ever saw a fish caught there, even though the stream's waters, winding darkly from a cypress swamp into wide meadows of marsh grass, were as indisputably fishy looking as they were vacant. Captain Beddingood's fish camp was, like some marriages and certain political careers, an enterprise kept afloat entirely by the force of fiction.

In common with those other great maritime yarners Melville and Conrad, Captain Beddingood had peopled his narrative with a rich array of characters, whose role it was to act out the dreams that drive and the frustrations that hobble each and every one of us. My favorite was the Man from Ohio. The Man from Ohio is a stock character in Southern tourist-stop narratives. Being a Yankee, he is a fool. He gets fleeced in Georgia's speed traps, drunk on moonshine in Tennessee, and he buys lots in a submarine subdivision in Florida. In the Sunshine State, he appears in his distinctive motley: crepe-soled canvas shoes, knee-high black socks, remaindered Bermuda shorts and a mesh-ventilated sailfish cap.

But at Burnt Mill Creek, the fool had his day. Only a genius like Captain Beddingood could turn this court jester into a king, his sullen journey into a royal progress.

"Have you got a redheaded River Runt in that tackle box?" Captain Beddingood said one day when my brother, dad and I rented a boat. As I was in the middle seat, it fell to me to fold back the cantilevered roof of our big green tackle box and produce the requested item, a classic bass lure from the Heddon Company.

"Now, if you want to catch a big redfish," Captain Beddingood said, "you put a strip of white pork rind on the rear hook of that River Runt, then you put one dot of Mercurochrome on the end of that pork strip. A man from Ohio was in here last week, and I told him to rig up like that and sent him over there by the bridge. I went on back up to the camp and in a little while I looked down here and I saw him coming back down the creek with his rod bowed up. That redfish pulled his boat up and down this creek a half dozen times, and every time he passed the boat landing he'd wave."

All my life I've carried in my head a picture of the Man from Ohio as an image of pure joy. I see him always in the screen of memory, a man who had ventured South into an obscure and unknown place and found the blessings of luck and elation. I imagine him waving his silly cap in the air, like a bronco rider. It would be another ten years before I even saw a redfish, but the species has never lost for me the mythic aura bestowed in Beddingood's yarn. Redfish are for me as magical as King Arthur's Pendragon fish. They are all real to me, as if they were breathing the air of my library this very day—the fool from Ohio who became a panhandle king, the magical boat-towing fish and, most of all, the old captain himself, the mendacious Merlin of Burnt Mill Creek.

Little did I understand that long ago day that Captain Beddingood stood in a grand bardic tradition. In her excellent book *Lying,* Sissela Bok describes an ancient Greek tradition that regarded as truth everything rescued by storytellers from "the river of forgetfulness." Captain Beddingood could not reverse the biological or economic forces that had removed the fish from Burnt Mill Creek. Instead he had salvaged through fabrication a pioneer time when a wayfaring stranger, innocent of skill–an Ohio man on holiday from the assembly line or perhaps a small, fish-lusting boy from Alabama–could appear at Burnt Mill Creek and catch a mighty fish. The inviting waters that purled under the bridge across from his boat landing were barren by 1951, but a time of plenteous hope had existed, and Captain Beddingood had preserved it with a perfect somersault of prevarication, using recreational lying to rescue a place of recreation, a place where a work-addled, wayfaring Ohioan could learn what fun feels like. Just so have I preserved the old man from "the river of forgetfulness" through a conjuring object that recently came back into my possession and summoned him from my memories. Years ago, as it turned out, my mother had retrieved that selfsame redheaded River Runt I had produced on Beddingood's command from a pile of old lures in the house beside the pond at my parents' farm in Alabama. By coincidence she gave it to me in the year marked by the death of Alabama's archliar George Wallace, and by the impeachment of Bill Clinton.

To this day, I keep the River Runt on my desk to remind me of the old fisherman who lied for commerce and produced art, the well-intended president whose recreational lying wrecked his dreams and the governor whose malignant lying put Alabama's deadly racial virus into the mainstream of national politics. Not long ago, I'd have sworn that the three of them had taught me just about everything there was to know about lying.

CHAPTER 18

The Caught and the Uncaught

As for why Tuna needed pliers, it seems our outboard motor was attempting to escape into the roomy sea, which would leave us far from land, powerless, at the mercy of fishermen's luck or perhaps the Christmas Island Rescue Service, if such a thing existed. In thousands of hours of boating and the requisite number of mechanical failures, I had never been confronted with this precise situation. The vibration of the motor had loosened the two heavy clamping screws that hold the motor upright on the transom of the boat. As a result, the motor was jiggling slowly upward, and one of the clamps had only the barest grip on the top edge of the transom. The other screw still had a better purchase, but it, too, was migrating toward freedom. If Tuna had not detected the situation, the motor would have simply climbed up and up until it dropped kerplunk off the transom into water that we knew was at least 699 feet deep. For good measure, it would probably have jerked the gasoline tank out behind it, since the two were connected by a stout rubber fuel line.

I thought about the sounds we would have heard when the motor drowned.

Brrrrrrrrr.

A big splash.

Then silence.

I pondered, for example, the fact that losing a motor is not nearly so final as sinking. I remembered from my boyhood reading of Nordhoff and Hall that, after being forced into the *Bounty*'s lifeboats, Captain Bligh and his loyalists had survived a long drift in this part of the ocean. They had, of course, been reduced to drinking seagulls' blood and to considering the rite in extremis of eating the weakest or, preferably, lowest-ranking member of the crew. The eating of cabin boys was a British navy tradition dating back to Elizabethan times and had been upheld in the British courts. Bligh's rowboat made landfall at Timor before he was forced to begin winnowing the crew or, perhaps, facing a gustatory mutiny that was fatal for him, instead of being simply inconvenient for his naval career.

Where the hell is Timor? I wondered.

Or Pitcairn, for that matter?

In my fatigue, I was entering a new, highly personal and whimsical reality. Up until Tuna spoke of pliers, my zone of attention had shrunk to the little world in the bow of the boat and the space between me and a marlin that was sometimes near and now far, far below, his existence betrayed only by the steady pit-a-pat of energy reaching me through line, rod, cramping hand, lazy arm. Comments and events outside these areas of engagement had a slightly hallucinatory quality, like the attenuated reality portrayed in those '70s movies about acid trips, so I had not replied immediately to Tuna's query.

He amplified on his tool request. "I need a wrench or pliers," he said.

I knew without asking that a wrench would have been preferable. Tuna soon discovered that my needle-nose fishing pliers were not the ideal instrument for adjusting the clamp that had lost its handle. There was a square post where the handle had sheared off, and since needle-nose pliers open in a V, he was having a hard time getting enough purchase to tighten the screw.

In my younger days, I might have made a peevish remark about being sorry that I came to the Pacific theater without my marine repair kit. But age had calmed the temper I inherited from my hillbilly forebears and the prickly Celts who produced them. Besides, if I had wanted a captain with a full set of crescent wrenches, I could have chartered a boat on Long Island Sound.

The fact was that I was happy from my hair right down to my shoes for a very straightforward reason.

Fishing, at its essence, is the pursuit of the unpredictable. A great deal of predictability awaited me back in New York. For example, come September in every even-numbered year, I would write editorials noting that our rigged political system means that 90 percent of the sorry-ass incumbents in Congress will be reelected. Then come November, I would write an editorial bemoaning the fact that over 90 percent of the sorry-ass incumbents got reelected and expressing the vain hope that maybe they would do better in the odd-numbered year that loomed in front of our Republic.

Out here, there was nothing to bemoan. Tennant and Tuna and I had cornered the local market on unpredictability. For example, who would safely have predicted that Tuna's hands would be strong enough to achieve the impossible task of fixing the motor clamp with those misshapen dime-store pliers? Yet he did just that, thanks to the grip earned in a lifetime of heaving, hauling and stripping copra.

I was stoned on fatigue. My mood was mellow, above it all and, now that we had passed so many travails, not altogether in keeping with the facts. Tired as I was, I was experiencing a second renaissance of aspiration. When I did not lose the fish at the start, through misfortune or incompetence, and especially after Tennant put the rod back together, I began to count on catching this wonderful creature. Not so long ago, it had seemed as good as done when Tuna and I were talking about underwater snapshots and calculating how to get the leader in his hand.

Then, during the fifth hour, I entered a doldrum. I began to identify with those junior high schoolers who are made to carry ten-pound sacks of sugar everywhere they go for a week so they will understand the inescapable captivity of having a baby. I had always wanted to see what a long battle with a fish would be like, and now I understood the kind of waiting involved when you are waiting for something wonderful to happen, something that may not happen without your close attention. Simply put, there is not a moment, no matter what else you are saying, thinking or doing, when you are not alert to this demanding presence and what it will take to continue your relationship, from the pressure on the line to the exact bow in the rod to the amount of backing on the reel to the mood of your partner. With these forces in balance, the fish was always there, when I ate a waterlogged ham sandwich, relieved myself over the side, smoked one of the Marlboros I brought to Christmas Island to give my vacation a whiff of self-indulgence.

This bargain reel, I reminded myself, was the core of our problem. The Fin-Nor's mighty drag would have tired this fish by now. But the Battenkill's lighter drag, plus the pressure that I could add with my hand, did not add up to a wearying load for a two-hundred-pound fish. Our little crises about the boat were diversions from something I could not ignore much longer. The fish was wearing me out. I was fading. The marlin, having sounded, was disinclined to forsake the depths of the ocean. Then a small discovery lifted my spirit.

CHAPTER 19

The Second Editorial:
On Patience

Why, one might ask, did the waiter in *The Garden of Eden* dash down the quay to offer unsolicited advice to the young fisherman? The reason was that this waiter, like so many anglers, believed that his fellow fishermen are struck by amnesia and deafness the moment a big fish is hooked. He felt obliged, therefore, to shout over and over again, very loudly, some version of this advice: "Don't horse it! Don't horse it!" If you are the person who has hooked the big fish, this cacophony of advice can be insanely irritating, since it is all you can do to handle the nonverbal information being transmitted to you by the imposing creature on the end of your humming line. The bystanders may be irritating, but they really are trying to be helpful. They know that patience is the essential element in landing a large fish on a fly rod. In the catching of such a fish, it's hard to acquire patience or to remember to use it at the crucial time. I was patient that day in the Pacific. I have been patient with hundred-pound sailfish in Costa Rica, a thirty-two-pound trout in Patagonia and thirty-pound salmon in Quebec. Nonetheless, I can admit that of all the supposed virtues, patience is my least favorite and one for which I lack either innate ability or unalloyed admiration. That is why I felt so proud of myself upon entering the seventh hour with the marlin.

Indeed, by the time I was in my fifties, playing a fish on a line and writing were perhaps the only activities in which I could will myself into practicing patience. As for writing, Mr. McWilliams had pounded it into my head that talent is not the main thing separating published writers and would-be writers. Writers write, and they won't stop no matter how prolonged or even spectacular their lack of success. I started a novel when I was twenty-one and reworked it obsessively until it was finally published as *Whiskey Man* when I was thirty-four. It wasn't that I was so deeply committed to that particular story. I just figured there was no use starting a second novel if I couldn't make the first one publishable. For thirteen years I got up before dawn on many days and worked on it until time to go the office. All that time I had this thought about the editors at the major publishing houses in New York: Sooner or later, one of you is going to take this book, because I'm going to *make* you. I'm going to keep polishing it and refining it until someone has to take it.

Obviously, I was confused in those days about the difference between true patience and brute persistence. Impatience had served me well in newspapering at a time when the only way to get a raise was to switch jobs. Before I joined the *Times,* I never stayed anywhere longer than three years. And it was not until I got to the *Times* that I began to understand the meaning of true impatience, which can reach its zenith of torment only in an environment of enormous potential and adamantine complacency. The *Times* qualifies on both counts.

In my early years on the paper, I never met a truly talented writer or editor who wasn't driven at least a little crazy by the *Times.* Many of them dreamed of escape and traded stories of writers who had gone over the wall, like Gay Talese, David Halberstam and Neil Sheehan. The sharpest thinkers on the paper fought valiantly to keep the grayness of the *Times* from sinking into their souls, and all you had to do was look around the newsroom to see that the effort was necessary. Getting hired at the *Times* had an almost magical ability to turn young people into young fogies. Those who escaped that fate were destined to spend a lot of time trying to convince friends, family, prospective mates and colleagues on other papers that we were not as dull, as slow to respond or as literal-minded as the paper made us appear.

The dreamers thought it didn't have to be that way. For all its flaws, it was the best newspaper in the country without really trying. The *Times* was maddening precisely because it was the nation's only chance to have a newspaper that really was as good as the *Times* pretended to be. There's a big gap between being a great newspaper and simply being the best in comparison with competing rags. Even the lifers, careerists, nerds, time-servers and drones were committed to the *Times*'s values. These folks might be dull and set in their ways, but they were abundantly intelligent. They gave the paper ballast and its trademark earnestness. What if the additive energy and creativity of its "talented tenth," to use the term W. E. B. DuBois invented in another context, could be turned loose at West Forty-third Street? Then you would have a paper with the *Times*'s traditional steadiness, but it would also have the intellectual depth, vivacity, cultural acuity, wit and analytical assertiveness of its smartest journalists and its smartest readers. And the *Times* had plenty of smart people. Even at its stodgiest the place was a talent magnet, because of where it was, what it stood for, because of its hauteur and pickiness, and because it paid the highest salaries in a tight-wad industry.

But if you were a journalist of a certain sort who had been around a bit, the first thing you noticed upon being hired at the *Times* was that, on many stories, it was a churning urn of under-achievement. For a *Times* person to say this publicly would cause gales of rage within the paper. Even to say so privately over drinks was to risk being sent to Coventry if you confided in the wrong colleagues. You had to be careful. If you were a newcomer who was fascinated by how good the *Times* could be if it really tried, you soon learned that there were other animals like you in the forest, but they seldom showed themselves in plain day. Subversives who dreamed of a *Times* that was as brilliant as it was high-minded were salted away on all the building's fifteen floors, a kind of secret society. As with any underground, you could never tell who else might be a member. The defenders of the status quo, by virtue of basing their very identities on the *Times as it is,* were watchful and vengeful—a curia of careerists who knew all the tricks for tripping up newcomers who exhibited excessive energy or wanted to revise the catechism.

The *Times*'s heretic minority was disorganized and undisciplined in comparison. They had no password, no motto, no catchphrase, but the lifers did. "It's hard to turn a battleship," they would say to anyone who expressed hope of seeing the *Times* live up to its potential. The apostate, thus patronized, was put immediately on the watch list.

The paper's militant traditionalists could even manage to sound long-suffering and frustrated themselves as they spoke of our dreadnought, but you knew in your bones that they really didn't want to see the old hulk change its heading by so much as a single degree. For my part, I thought it would be great fun for everyone—especially the long-suffering readers—to take the *Times* to flank speed and adjust her rudder. In time, I would learn that the patience I was so proud of exercising in Tuna's boat that day off Christmas Island was a small thing indeed in comparison with what it would take to get to the wheelhouse of the *Times.*

CHAPTER 20

Along About Sundown

The uplifting discovery I made was in this wise. I had been looking at the bare spool of my reel for some time. This fish was two or three wraps away from freedom, so there was little I could do to make things better, and only one thing I could do to make things worse. I decided to try that. When Tuna positioned the boat directly over the fish, and I loaded the rod to its absolute maximum bend and held that pressure steadily, the fish would, after thirty seconds or so, move toward the surface enough for me to crank in a couple of inches of line. Once the fish got used to the process of responding to the pressure, it would sometimes come up six inches or even a foot. By repeating this laborious process hundreds of times, I regained perhaps half my backing. I had no illusions about what was going on. I wasn't lifting the fish so much as irritating it into a mild levitation. Then, suddenly, I felt a mighty rising far down below.

"It's coming up!" Tuna said. My line, which had been entering the water perpendicularly for hours, tilted slowly toward the front of the boat. "This fish is coming up fast," Tuna said. "Get ready."

And come it did, racing toward the surface in such a smooth, rapid surge that I could hardly keep the line tight. I cranked madly. The backing was fluorescent orange in color, and it went off into the blue like a bending beam of light that aspired to climb into strict parallel alignment with the surface. I expected the fish to break through the waves like a submarine-launched ICBM. Hubris, like a rich, waxy, white flower of the tropical night, blossomed in my chest. I remembered what Santiago had said about using the fish's leaping to exhaust and kill it. I did not want to murder this fish, only touch it and retrieve my fly. Again, I thought of the fly hanging on the wall of my office.

Framed.

In a shadow box.

Tired as I was, I believed, again, that something wonderful was going to happen. We had waited for it and it was going to happen. We were going to catch this fish. Tuna was going to grasp its bill. I was going to touch its shoulders, which would be as glossy and deeply colored as a lacquered Chinese box. Then we were going to release it. There would be no pictures, of course, because of the incompetent camera. Tennant, Tuna and I would have the one thing in angling that is better than a picture. That is a common memory of an event in which no one else quite believes. For the rest of our lives, we could all swear we caught the marlin in full knowledge that no one would ever credit our story, even if they pretended to. Fishermen, like judges, juries and lawyers, often see people line up behind a uniform lie, a rehearsed and fictional account of an alleged event. It's a sweet thing, somehow, to be telling the truth, knowing all the while that you're suspected of inventing what John Randolph, a long-dead sports columnist for the *Times,* called "a nice round lie."

When I remembered Santiago's words about the killing effect that jumping has on marlin, I would have done well to recall his thoughts on endurance: "Man is not much beside the great birds and beasts." For the fish did not jump. Instead, it came racing, racing, racing ever upward from the heart of the sea. Or so it seemed until, perhaps ten feet below the surface, the marlin simply tilted over like an airplane leveling out and began swimming away from us at great speed, ripping yard after yard of hard-won line from the reel.

I had the definite, Ahab-like feeling that it had come up not because of the pressure of the dedicated lifting and inch-by-inch cranking of which I had been so proud. Rather, the marlin had simply come up to inspect us once more. By now it had reclaimed all the line I had gained, clearing the reel right down to the spool again.

Even so, it had not sounded, allowing us to keep a modest advantage. Tuna gunned the newly reclamped motor. I reeled madly, and we closed on the fish, drawing to within thirty-five feet or so. We sped along in its wake, watching it as you would a fish in an aquarium. This fish was not as green as it had been in the morning, but like most marlin that do not burst their own hearts and die on the line, it was green enough. I began to think of strategies whereby we might bequeath a critical supplement of weariness to such a fish.

The marlin sounded yet again, as relentlessly as ever, all the way down to the spool, and yet again, Tuna put the boat directly over the fish, and I went back to the inch-at-a-time game. By the end of the seventh hour, we had been through this soar and sound business four times, and there had been an interesting shift in my physical abilities. When the fish did not sound for a fifth time, we hoped the same might be true for it.

I found I could not raise my right arm. So when I needed to pump the rod, I rested my forearm atop my thigh and lifted my leg. The leg, in turn, lifted my arm, which, in turn, lifted the rod. It was not an efficient system. I was tired as well in my left hand, which had made thousands of cranks. Yet I felt clearheaded, and deep in my chest burned a radiant core of certainty. Neither I nor my equipment had collapsed. We had shifted to a southeasterly heading. The sky along the eastern horizon was turning purple, as if night was rising from the sea. The water was blackening, too.

I looked back at Tuna, who was the picture of tireless optimism. Never once during the entire long day did he flinch or suggest that we were simply overmatched and should end it. He was a man of the southern ocean, and all he seemed to care about, aside from Baha'ist political science, was the pursuit of sea creatures. When it came to catching this fish or any other, he was in for a dime, in for a dollar.

Tuna had that singular aura you always look for in a great fisher, a great sailor, a great *anything*. You have to find the players with class, as Coach Bryant used to say when he was in one of his cryptic, walk-on-water moods. All right, maybe the Bear was not one for the original phrase, but his meaning was clear enough. To recognize quality in a person, you have to know what to look for, and you have to see it, truly see it, when it's in front of you. So I knew that above all I must avoid lumbering Tuna with any responsibility for choosing among the ways that lay before us now, for if there was ever a man with whom to ride the deep, it was he. I had pulled on enough fish in my life to know what we needed to find out. We were at close quarters now, as I said. The fish was swimming along the surface, its tail breaking regularly through the crown of the waves, a sign at last, I chose to believe, of a fatigue to match my own. Since belief feeds hope, and hope afflicts the fresh fisherman and the tired alike, I formed a plan by which we could yet prevail.

As for the task of catching the marlin, that's all I have to say right now about what happened next, the facts, the journalism of the thing, as it were. What was known to me at this point was only what had been observed or learned in Tuna's boat. A great fish had come out of the ocean. Luck had struck like lightning. We had hooked each other, and at least one of us longed to be released.

CHAPTER 21

Snapshot IV:
The Baseball Field at Avondale Park,
Birmingham, August 1954

To my surprise I was remembering baseball as I woke up on the morning after we hooked the marlin. I had slept well on the nubby, clean white sheets of the cot in our bungalow at the Captain Cook. Now, waves boomed against the crab-scuttled lava beach on Christmas Island. A fringe of dangling palm roof thatch, black against the dazzle, framed my view of the tropical morning, abrupt and businesslike in its eye-squinting palette—sand, cloud, blue water, all flattened under heavy blasts of white light.

The sun means business down here. Perhaps it was the light that brought the memories.

I flexed my right hand. It was sore from holding the rod against the strain of the marlin for so many hours. I remembered the fish swimming high in the waves at sundown, the blade of its tail carving water, then inky night on the inky ocean.

The sun means business in Birmingham, too, when you're playing ball in the middle of the day in July and August.

A specific day of heat and its own piercing light came swimming out of the past, long ago in benighted Bama's most benighted time. It was high summer of the year in which, we now know, segregation started dying.

The scene: A team of white boys playing nine other white boys.

The uniformity of color was not regarded as odd.

In those days.

In Birmingham.

Bad old Birmingham, as it was called. Not for nothing was it called that, as I was to learn in the course of my newspaper days.

Nineteen fifty-four was the year we won everything.

Almost exactly nine years later, in 1963, a neighborhood character who sometimes treated us to free Cokes at his barbecue joint after we won a big game was questioned as a suspect in the Sixteenth Street Church bombing. The FBI finally concluded that he was not at the scene. He was a Klansman all right and knew his way around dynamite, truncheons, straight razors and pistols. But when it came to the particular bundle of dynamite sticks that killed the four little girls on September 15, 1963, it turned out that his brother helped plant that one.

Forty years later, I sought out our Coca-Cola man at his favorite fishing tackle store, not far from Avondale Park. The guilty brother had died of natural causes, but Coca-Cola Man, vigorous in his eighties, was still nervous about the nonathletic events of that long ago time. "Are you FBI?" he said, when I started asking questions. He was not being sarcastic. His need to know about potential law enforcement interest in his family was still genuine, as Southern prosecutors had taken belated but strong interest in persons connected to the Sixteenth Street Church bombing, the murder of Medgar Evers and other such events in the years between 1954 and 1964.

Back then, of course, our team knew Coca-Cola Man as a benefactor, an admirer of baseball talent. In the world of childhood, everything is mundane, a given, the way it is. Or hidden and yet to come.

Our pitcher that year was a boy named Charlie Weaver, tall for his age, and a fastballer of such ferocious speed and accuracy that he sometimes struck out every batter in our six-inning games. Not only were we undefeated, but we were bound by a common faith in Charlie's invincibility, and we could score runs. But the catcher for the team we were playing at Avondale Park for the eleven-year-old championship in the Birmingham YMCA league had not heard that Charlie Weaver was invincible. He was a big kid, as big as Charlie, and in the fourth inning of our six-inning game, he hit a home run over the center field fence. It went out like a shot. I watched it go.

We had never been behind. It had not occurred to us that anyone could bang a decent line drive off Charlie, much less an authoritative homer. I'll never forget the feeling of surrender that settled over me as that galoot passed second base, where I played. They say you're whipped only when you give up. I was whipped. Looking around the diamond at my teammates, I did not feel lonely.

But in the next to the last inning, we managed to load the bases, and with two outs, it came my turn to bat. I was a good ballplayer as a kid, a sure-handed fielder and a fast base runner who scored a lot of runs. But when it came to getting on base, I had the heart of a beggar. I milked pitchers for walks by fidgeting in the batter's box and faking bunts to unnerve them. Then, once I had gotten to first on a free pass, I would steal my way into scoring position. In this situation, of course, a walk was as good as a hit, because it would push the tying run home and keep us alive. So that was my plan, I am quite sure, to beg for a walk.

As adults, we forget the extent to which childhood is a time of private strategies. We also forget the degree to which we followed those strategies unless interrupted. I was interrupted that day on the way to the plate by one of our coaches. His name was Bill Thorn. He had been my sister's classmate in high school, and now he was working his way through college on a YMCA scholarship that required him to coach our neighborhood teams in his free time. We had two such coaches, and Bill was the one who worked less often with the eleven-year-olds. Perhaps he didn't know me well enough to guess the direction of my plans.

In any event, as I approached the plate with the exhortations of my teammates ringing in my ears, Bill called to me from the first-base coaching box. We met halfway between first and home.

He bent over me and put his arm around my shoulder. Our heads were close together. I figured he was going to tell me stuff I already knew. Stay in a crouch so the umpire will shrink your strike zone in his head. Take at least one strike, maybe two, in hope of running up the count. Don't take a chance on swinging unless you have to. That is what I expected to hear. That is what I wanted to hear. That is what I would have told me, knowing how little I expected to actually hit the ball.

But Bill Thorn could not read my mind.

"Just pick out a pitch and hit it," he said.

So I did.

The very first pitch.

It was high and outside, and I had to reach up and over the plate, but I got the bat on the ball, and it made a humpbacked arc over the first baseman's head. The ball curved toward the right field foul line as it fell, since my stabbing swing had put lot of spin on it.

I am running toward first base, and the ball is plummeting toward the freshly limed foul line, a solitary, authoritative strip of white on the spongy, verdant mix of Bermuda grass and crab-grass that has been nursed through the long humid Birmingham summer to its most definitive shade of summery green.

Grass, ball, foul line all come together in a convergence of green and white before my onrushing eyes. The first baseman has turned, and he is running away from me, toward the spot where the ball is landing. The right fielder is there, too. A man in navy trousers and white short-sleeved shirt is watching these scurrying boys, and he bends low now to observe the ball as it comes at last to the sweet Birmingham ground. The ball lands precisely on the stripe, white on white, and a small cloud of alabaster dust spurts upward, unforgettably. Sometimes the fields were lined with lime and sometimes with flour. Here was a perfect blossom, like self-rising flour self-rising to the sky. The umpire thrusts his hand toward center field, a sharp jabbing stiff-handed motion, a sword thrust of virtuous truth, as he shouts out the news.

"FAIR BALL!"

Bill Thorn waves me past first base, windmilling his right arm. "Keep going, keep going," he shouts, and I do that very thing.

Just as I'm passing first base, I see that the ball is traveling away from the field of play, running like a golf shot with plenty of topspin. I know that it will go all the way to the fence before either the first baseman or the right fielder can reach it, and at that moment, I surpass speed as I have known it up to that time.

What I wish I could make you feel, sports fans, as supremely as I felt it on my tropic cot and as I feel it now in this very moment of telling, is the velocity that lived in my tiny legs that day, that released itself into wings on my heels and into a miraculous burgeoning burn of pure acceleration. I ran so fast that nothing could touch me, not fear, not failure, nor any kind of doom. I ran encased in a bubble of pure triumph, a halo of impenetrable good luck.

Ahead of me and off to my left, other boys, my boys, are rounding bases and scoring. I see the second one slide home under the throw from right field, where my hit had at last been retrieved, and their rocket-armed catcher rises from his too-late tag, throws to second, thinking to nail me for the last out even if he cannot repair the two runs that I have cost him.

I slide, and in the air above me, I see the second baseman rise and stab his glove toward the sky, and miss the throw. It zooms into center field, and I am up instantly and pumping for third. Phil English, our other coach, is windmilling his arm now. "All the way home, all the way home," he shouts.

Phil had an unpleasant saying with which he liked to ridicule players who were about to choke. That guy is so scared, he would say, you couldn't drive a needle up his butt with a sledge-hammer. But I am not scared now, and I know that after this day, Phil, a meticulous coach, will never say that about me, and I swing the turn just the way he has taught me, swerving out a little before I hit the bag and then banking off it, so I do not make one of those wide, time-burning loops outside the baseline. My body leans low to the ground, and I turn, held in the heavy centrifugal embrace of speed and gravity, and I am around the base and pumping straight again, and I see in front of me home plate and the catcher and behind him, like Jehovah in judgment, the home plate umpire.

And then, I am in the air, laid out flat and low, parallel to the earth like a swimmer making a racing start. I had read in the back of a Classics Illustrated comic book a one-page essay about a ballplayer known as the Wild Horse of the Osage. He was a man who slid headfirst. This was long before Pete Rose made the headlong slide the symbol of baseball exuberance, and all I can say about my inspiration is the fact that I had read this essay and that I am running so fast, so supremely fast that the only thing to do is to become an arrow that points toward my destination.

And I am in the air for a long time. I see the catcher, his legs astraddle the plate, lift his mitt for the throw from center field. The ball enters my circle of vision, which is collapsing now toward the catcher's knees and home plate. It is a good throw, and I know it, and I hear it strike his mitt, and I know that I am under it, roaring down to the warm dust of home. My wild horse slide has been just the thing. It cost me no time, and I had none to spare, and Jehovah said, "SAFE!"

How my teammates pound and embrace me, a swarming cluster of small boys, dancing, dancing in that long ago Birmingham summer, and Bill Thorn comes to me, smiling and shaking his head.

"I didn't mean you had to hit the first pitch," he says.

I couldn't say to him what I know now and didn't know that day.

You can't control the consequences when you change a beggar into a hitter.

The next year I hit everything they threw at me. We won the championship again. I batted .604.

Over forty years later, the marlin had done for me what Bill Thorn had done.

It ended my days as a beggar.

It made me believe I was wrapped in good luck.

Luck that would last the rest of my fishing life and invade

other parts of my life as well. I would have no need for flags of defeat or the vocabulary of disappointment known to fishers around the world.

You should have been here yesterday.

You should have seen the one that got away.

Those sentences do not even go to the most profound level of angling deprivation. We are haunted day and night by the knowledge that the amount of time we spend fishing is inconsequential in comparison with the amount of time we spend doing things we do not love. Or we worry that our stolen moments are spent in the wrong place. Or we believe that even if we could be in the right place at the right time, with enough time, the really good thing would happen to another person.

In regard to fishing, all that changed for me on Christmas Island. You can call it a gift if you want to, and I won't argue, but what I'm trying to express is that something like a new religion had moved into my heart. Here it is.

I was through with half-ass fishing.

Here was the fishing I would do from now on.

The other kind.

Like the Baha'i cops on the trail of perfect peace, I would go where I had to go.

The marlin released within me the germ of certainty. In the late innings of my life, I would always be on my way to the kind of fishing I had dreamed about but never done. Long after the marlin swam back into its sovereign existence in the illimitable womb of the Pacific, I could feel the scything pulse of that great tail, going, going, always going toward the belt of the earth, slicing through furrow and wave, always dividing the currents of my fishing life into two streams—the piddling fishing that had been and the mightier kind that was to come.

CHAPTER 22

The Third Editorial: On Exceptionalism

Later that morning at the Captain Cook, I told Howie Van Ness, the owner of a fly shop in Anchorage, about being hooked to the marlin for seven and one-half hours. "You are one crazy son of a bitch to hang on that long," Howie said. It filled me with contentment to be hailed as fanatical by a fly-fishing professional, especially one from a place noted for the lunacy of its sporting citizens.

Why did I have this reaction? Simply because it made me feel special, and there's nothing dearer to fly fishermen than the sport's carefully nourished Myth of Exceptionalism. We're talking about a belief system that reaches beyond the snobbery and elitism attributed to today's fly fishers. The Myth of Exceptionalism dates back to Elizabethan England, and the pretensions on which it rests are artistic, rather than social. The world has produced any number of outdoor pursuits—dressage, boules, cricket, Chickasaw stickball—every bit as esoteric as fly fishing. Yet no other sport has been so prone to grandiosity for so long. It's been over four hundred years since Izaak Walton invented the central conceit of all fly-fishing literature with sentences like these:

> Is it not an art to deceive a trout with an artificial fly? . . .
> Doubt not, therefore, sir, that angling is an art, and an art
> worth your learning. The question is rather, whether you be

capable of learning it? For angling is somewhat like poetry, men are to be born so . . .

This identification of fly fishing with art and with poetry in particular has been hammered home ever since, especially in modern literature by the Irish trinity: Yeats, Synge, Joyce. Yet fly fishing is nowhere near as difficult as that most rarified of literary practices, the making of poems. True, the motion of rod and line and the sport's pastoral settings can all be described as poetic. But catching a fish is hardly comparable to the accomplishment of making a poem—except in one way. That has to do with the feeling it gives the angler. Bringing a shining, perfectly formed, bespeckled, ebony-eyed fish to the hook and keeping it there is one of the few things in the mundane world that allows one to glimpse, in a milder and more transient form, the transporting interior reality that comes from artistic creation. We are not talking here about emotions so much as about a kind of glowing, synaptically complete, almost chemical pulse within one's being. It's that transcendent, addictive state described as "flow" by the psychologist Mihaly Csikszentmihalyi and other students of creativity, including Daniel Goleman, Alice Weaver Flaherty and Dianne Schilling.

For some people, fishing feels good to the brain in a way that is quite similar to what painters, writers, composers feel during the process of their work—total absorption, timelessness, concentration on the task so intense that self-consciousness disappears. The personality's yammering inner voice is stilled because all of its owner's attention is outside the self. And when the work is done, one has the sensation of emerging not from a dream or a trance but from a state of total *oneness with the task*.

This temporary sublimation of ego to the glory of one's task is the ideal spiritual state to which the Romantic poets aspired. Fly fishing is not the only doorway to the magical lower rooms of creative oneness. Journalists have their own Myth of Exceptionalism. The concentration needed to create a complex news story on deadline can be transporting. Civilians are often puzzled that journalists believe themselves superior to the wealthy, the titled, the elected and, indeed, to their readers. The reason is that those who have entered deadline world and can train themselves to do it daily if need be see themselves as a sister- and brotherhood of the credentialed, a guild of the illuminati with a sense of election very much like that of medieval secret societies.

For me, fly fishing and journalism touched the same places in my head. In comparison with that of poets, the fly fishers' and the journalists' experiences are probably pale flavors, but they carry nonetheless a hint of ambrosia. I left Christmas Island hungry for more of the feeling I had in Tuna's boat—not the funny business about drain plugs and screwdrivers but that constant prolonged feeling of being hooked to life in some deeply completing way. And I had little enough sense to think that meant something as simple as fishing more.

BOOK TWO

Why should not old men be mad?
Some have known a likely lad
That had a sound fly fisher's wrist
Turn to a drunken journalist . . .
                    —W. B. Yeats

CHAPTER 23

Epistemological Certainty
and Heavenly Intervention as
Elements of the Sensible Life Plan

I arrived back in Manhattan in the spring of 1994, my perspective clarified by the events of Christmas Island and a subsequent stopover in the People's Republic of China, where I saw that, just as Nixon had exclaimed, there really was a Great Wall, still formidable, mostly useless. In the Forbidden City, I also peered into the neglected bedroom of the last emperor. The dust-coated furniture and fading red lacquer testified that time and Chairman Mao made a powerful interior-decorating team. With these images of transience fresh in my mind, I returned to New York certain of four things relating to how I would spend my time:

First, I would be patient and politic about finding out whether, in due time, I was going to get the top job at the newspaper. That news would come in 2001, when Arthur's then freshly appointed executive editor approached retirement age. Given the prospect of a chance to wake and shake *The New York Times,* to step up its "competitive metabolism," as I put it, the job seemed worth the six-year wait. I would be turning fifty-eight by then, which meant I still had a bit of bet-hedging room if Arthur did not pick me. If passed over, I would bail out of the *Times* immediately to try to make up for the lost years of my writing career.

This attractive-sounding fallback plan presented one problem for a man hoping to be a full-time writer but not a penniless writer.

It would take money, and I was still well shy of pension eligibility of any sort. If I went over the wall, I would have to finance it myself, at least for the first few years. Even then, an early exit would deal a blow to whatever pension I got over the long haul. How heavy a blow I didn't bother to check. I already knew the necessary fact, which was that I needed individual investments with an abnormally fast growth rate. I began sending money to my brother-in-law, Herman Dean, Jr., a financial whiz who was spending his retirement years in front of a computer screen, making money by the fistful. I told Herman to put my money where he put his own and not to bother me with the details. The man loved his tech stocks.

Second, to curb my natural impatience while Arthur's new executive editor served his term, I was going to divert myself by fishing the places of which I had dreamed but could never afford until now. At fifty-one, I was in the last laps of paying college tuitions and alimony. The fact that I could now afford a certain amount of self-indulgence led directly to the third point of certainty.

I was not going to get married again and would try to avoid entangling alliances that would interfere with the second goal. On balance, my marriage was for a long time sounder than most, but I had felt confined in it. I told myself that, as you got older, the conflict between uninhibited mobility and companionship became easier to resolve in favor of the former. Anyhow, in New York, hundreds of thousands of single people of all ages were living off the land. The women's magazines insisted that these hordes of uncommitted frolickers were secretly miserable, but they looked pretty damn happy to me. Long-term relationships did not seem essential for a social life that would not only stave off bouts of loneliness but wear you out in the bargain if you wanted to play it that way.

Fourth, I was going to enjoy the job I had rather than drive myself crazy about the one I might or might not get next. There are many wonderful jobs at the *Times*–editing the *Book Review*, say, or running the Washington bureau. Yet almost no one enjoys actually doing these jobs that look like sugarplums to the outside world. I had, in fact, managed to enjoy my four years as Washington bureau chief precisely because I had watched several bureau chiefs drive themselves batty by obsessing over their next great leap. By my lights, they barely savored the main thrill that comes with the job, which consists in picking targets, matching your best people to the most promising stories, then watching them crack codes and make news and, when the planets are in alignment, raise holy hell for the sake of righteousness. A shining path lay before me. The new executive editor was an intensely traditional *Times*man who would keep the news sections on automatic pilot. That meant that if the paper was to have a pulse during the late '90s, it would have to come from the editorial page staff, and we were open for business.

You will, in the coming pages, be able to assess my prescience on all these points, including the third, where my aim fell blessedly wide of the target. I am not defensive about knowing so little as to where my heart would take me. However, I do want to say up front that, based on the evidence at hand in 1994, neither my friends nor foes would have predicted for me either obtaining a fast-track liberation from journalism or being struck by a *coup de foudre*.

For now, only the second point of certainty in my life plan, the fishing part, need concern us. After vibrating between agnosticism and atheism for many years, I have come to a late-blooming theological conviction of a highly specialized sort. Well, maybe not a conviction per se. Let's call it a providential conceit. When you decide you want to go fishing in the best way in the worst way, God will open a door.

But you better have your Mastercard ready. Neither God nor His suspected alter egos, Providence or Fate, take checks. And He/They don't worry about the cost, either. Also, if you are afraid of air travel governed by third-world safety standards, you must stare those fears in the eye and say adios. Both the Higher Powers and the low-rent deities of the House of Pisces regard transportation to be a personal matter, a detail you will handle if you really want the fishing that you have declared to be your heart's desire.

All of which is to say that one day in the dead winter of 1995, I got a letter.

The author of the letter was Nathaniel Pryor Reed of Hobe Sound, Florida. I had not heard from Reed since 1977, and his long silence was no surprise. Back then Nat was thinking about running as a Republican for governor of Florida. As a political reporter, I was an equal opportunity hatchet man, and no matter of substance or style was out of bounds when it came to giving readers a suitably warty profile of every office seeker unfortunate enough to cross my path. I ridiculed one of the Democrats for sweating too much and wearing polyester shirts that in the Florida humidity hung from his frame like wet dishrags. I poked fun at another Democrat—the fastidious Bob Graham, eventually both governor of Florida and a U.S. senator of some distinction— for still wearing at age forty the Bass Weejun loafers issued to Harvard freshmen. The lacerating style of those candidate profiles became part of the newsroom lore at the *St. Petersburg Times.* Now that I was older, the wickedly accurate but incomplete way in which I had written about Nat made me feel a bit guilty. I had been dead right about his chances of being governor, but how well had I limned the man within the would-be candidate? I had depicted him as a name-dropping elitist of the political genus known in journalese as "millionaire environmentalist." How was I to know that he was going to save the Everglades? Actually, I might have figured it out if I had listened more closely. Nat was among the small circle of Florida public figures who understood decades ago that their state would be forced to pay for its natural beauty by being turned into the New California. He dreamed of melding the green vote and the retiree vote into a statewide force that could stand up to the real-estate developers, phosphate miners and sugar-cane barons. "The retiree is deeply concerned that the fun is going out of living in South Florida," I quoted him as explaining. "He doesn't want his little bit of paradise shredded."

In the end, he skipped the gubernatorial race in favor of a self-financed crusade to preserve what was left of wild Florida. He was widely known for vigorously exposing the efforts of fellow Republicans to defile that state and many other sensitive parts of the continent, its waters and the breeding grounds of endangered creatures such as sea turtles, whooping cranes and Atlantic salmon. I doubt many readers could have predicted that from what I wrote when I was thirty-four, but hey, the young are different from you and me. For one thing, they have never been written about. In any event, Nat's letter showed he had either a bad memory or a bulletproof self-image. Betraying no hint of festering reprimand, he got down to business:

Dear Howell:

I own three rods on the Kharlovka River, July 7 through 14. Unlike the Ponoi or the other major rivers of Russia's southern Kola peninsula, the Kharlovka faces directly into the White Sea. The last glaciers left nothing but sloping rock and four or five great rivers that form inland among great lakes created by the slowly dissolving ice cubes. The Kharlovka is a big fish river; the salmon average 18 pounds. Every year there are fish hooked that exceed 40 pounds but they are very difficult to land from the shoreline as they can take off and run one out of line in minutes.

The river is alternately huge, placid, brawling, smooth, terrifying. . . . The visiting angler is dropped off at this fishing beat by helicopter daily—a few days of sheer panic, fatigue and calm, rational fear. . . . The cost from Murmansk (by helicopter) is $6,300. To that price you have to add your round trip airline ticket, NYC to Helsinki, and a fee for the special flight that departs Helsinki for Murmansk every Saturday . . . in the range of $300. . . . Take a look at your schedule, your checking account and say "yes" to a great adventure.

I prepared to toss the letter. Since the publication of *Fly Fishing Through the Midlife Crisis,* I had received a lot of tempting invitations. But I have never been much of a daredevil, and many a braver flier than I has been spooked by the words "Russian hel-icopter." I contemplated a mental picture of myself, aflame, pounding on the Plexiglas window of a Soviet-made chopper. It seemed in my imagining to be lying like a collapsed mantis alongside a "huge . . . brawling . . . terrifying" Russian river well beyond the reach of 911. I am not physically courageous, partic-ularly when you get into fiery-crash territory. Besides, this trip was pricey. By way of comparison, Christmas Island, my most expen-sive trip up to that time, had cost only a couple of thousand, plus airfare.

Then, abruptly, seditious thoughts marched across my mind. This trip was *exactly* what I was looking for to prove my dedica-tion to the financial self-indulgence clause of the Christmas Island Compact. In retrospect, that realization hardly seems sur-prising. But the next thought was. It touched on the matter of burning alive. It was: So what?

I tried it again.

Yes, indeed. So fucking what?

Most of my grandparents and great-grandparents had lived past ninety, and I was counting on that kind of run myself. But it was also true that they seemed to spend the last twenty or so years wrapped in shawls and waving their canes at dogs, suffering through pastoral visitations, trying to remember the names of their grandchildren, and reading magazines like *The Upper Room.* I was nearing fifty-two when Nat's letter arrived. In 1977, I had fulfilled the most earnest ambition of my childhood, which was to have published my novel with a major New York firm, in this case, Viking. I had raised children I liked. I had a career that, if not my first calling, was vastly rewarding. Newspapering at the *Times* was fun, a service to society, and it would, if I went the full distance, render me a financially comfortable burnt-out case. No matter if I lacked the energy to write another book under my own byline. I could at least break even with the Great Fish of the World. So what the hell difference did it make if I missed a couple of decades of shawl time?

Also, what if I croaked at sixty-two, as had Dick Blalock, who had a heart attack while driving to a pond outside Washington? Then I would have cheated myself of a salmon trip in anticipation of an old age that I would be missing anyway. Besides all that, I was living in the borough of falling cats, subway electrocutions, Jack Abbott stabbings and runaway automobiles that smash people in restaurant booths. If you wanted to play the odds, I would probably be safer on Boris's helicopter than I was standing fifteen feet from the third rail while awaiting the number 2 express train at the Fourteenth Street station.

There is no more glamorous fish in the world than the Atlantic salmon, and humankind seems to be on a march to make them extinct within a hundred years. So I faxed Nat Reed to sign me up for salmon fishing punctuated by moments of "calm, rational fear" at the helicopter pad.

On the stroke of that decision, I was filled with an infinite spirit of self-congratulation and feelings of oceanic pity for all my fellow anglers who would be plodding to dull Catskill waters while Boris the mad pilot and I roared through the grim, glacier-carved canyons of the Kharlovka. If you want to say that this sounds like the kind of shallow, masculine emotion portrayed in beer commercials, I cannot argue. If you want to suggest, more charitably, that it took me a hell of a long time to remember what Bill Thorn told me on the sideline of that baseball diamond in Birmingham forty years earlier, I cannot argue with that either. There are two kinds of ballplayers, the beggars and the hitters, and I guess if you sift through life with a net that is fine enough, you find that there are two kinds of fishermen—those who settle for known waters and those who climb on the helicopter.

I ran right home and snatched down A. J. McClane's *Encyclopedia of Fishing* to contemplate the portrait of my quarry and absorb a bit of its natural history. "The body of the Atlantic salmon is five times as long as it is deep. It has 8–10 rays on its anal fin. The dentaries become large and sharp in the spawning season and the lower jaw of the male develops a cartilaginous protuberance in the form of a hook known as the kype." You can't beat McClane for just that kind of detail. Who else thinks of the width-to-length ratio of fish or passes along this astonishing Oedipal detail from the marital bed, or redd, where the majestic kype-jawed male salmon joins the hen fish? The cock salmon lies beside the hen while she does the hard work of fanning out a depression in the gravel. After she has excavated a spot and deposited her eggs and covered them up, the cock fish swims over and commences a task of such transcendent allure that he has crossed thousands of miles of ocean, warped his way up torrential rapids and even leapt waterfalls in order to perform it. That is to say, the fish ejaculates. The part I like is what happens as the old man is all atremble in the tiny instant of hard-earned pleasure purchased by all the long months of peril in its sea-fraught life. When the moment of coming has come, swarms of baby cock salmon—little fellows called parr that have been loafing around the river living the easy minnow life for the past year—dash in, and they get off, too. It is, of course, Nature's way of enriching the gene pool in each oviposition established by the female salmon, but it also stands for me as one of the crueler facts in the annals of natural history that the salmon is so multiply cuckolded at the zenith of its migrational triumph. Being a fish, the cock salmon knows nothing of its seeming humiliation and incinerates all such human valuation in its dumb, immutable, brute magnificence.

Facts, by the way, take a beating when you talk to Atlantic salmon fishers. McClane says the average fish is twelve pounds, but around the fishing clubs and fly shops in New York, it is hard to find anyone who confesses to catching one under eighteen or twenty pounds. Its fighting abilities, its craftiness, its arbitrary moods and its strike are encased in legend. The strike, in particular, pushes angling writers to warp speed. Consider the late Lee Wulff, America's best-known chaser of salmon. "As a rule salmon are deliberate risers," he advises. "But that is not always the case and some salmon will take the dry fly on their way out of water on a clean, high leap, a rare spectacle that once seen can never be forgotten . . ." But even that pales, I learned, beside the times when the salmon comes up and doesn't quite take the fly.

"I know of no more exciting moment than the false rise of a

salmon, no moment in the sport that requires greater control and judgment." The trick is to see "whether the salmon really takes the fly or just comes up alongside and opens his mouth, missing the floating feathers by a fraction of an inch. If the fly is taken, [the fisherman] must strike; and if that great fish, suddenly appearing after hours of inactivity, does not close his jaws on the fly, he must not twitch his rod arm even a little bit but must hold steady and let the fly drift carelessly on its uninterrupted path. Such control is far from easy but it is essential to the taking of many of these curious fish."

I read such accounts with mixed feelings of ridicule and apprehension. The mythic fog surrounding this species was even thicker than that surrounding bonefish. They couldn't be that good or that difficult, I thought. In the weeks ahead, Atlantic salmon were to show me yet again that some kinds of fishing are, indeed, like making love. The activity may be greatly overrated, but there's nothing else close to it. I felt lucky to be a man who was going to lose his salmon-fishing virginity in Russia.

CHAPTER 24

A Consummation Devoutly
to Be Wished

As it happened, my virginity did not last long enough for me to take it to Russia. In June, Punch Sulzberger invited me to accompany him and his wife, Allison, to fish with some of their society friends on the Grand Cascapedia River in Quebec. The camp we inhabited was established by Queen Victoria's granddaughter Princess Louise, who with her husband, the governor general of Canada, wanted to bring British-style salmon fishing to North America. Its continued existence through several owners proved the maxim that while Atlantic salmon can be found in quite a few countries and northern oceans, the best place to look for them is around rich people. In regard to salmon, "rich" can be defined precisely as inheriting a river or a chunk thereof or as making enough money to buy or lease same.

I found the Cascapedia beautiful, the hosts charming and the martinis cold. But mainly I remember the trip because it was the last time I was to see Punch at his best although I was around him many times after. Between this first trip to the Cascapedia and our second, a year later, Parkinson's disease struck, and in a twelve-month period, he went from being a robust man in transit from late middle age to, at seventy-one, a frail old man. I remember him on the first afternoon of our first full day of our first trip. He was standing all by himself on a lush green bank high above the river, smoking a big cigar and throwing a stick for Angus, his wife's Border collie. The Canadian flag snapped in the breeze, and he was completely oblivious of those of us who were marching down the gravel drive to fish the afternoon session. For his part, Punch had already gotten what he wanted, taking a fish in the morning so that, by the tradition of the camp, he was through for the day. To Punch that was the ideal—a big salmon in the morning and cigars and naps in the afternoon.

I admired his ability to be at ease. Punch was a man of imperishable good manners. By instinct and common sense, he got two big things right in his years as publisher, 1963 to 1992. During the Vietnam War, he had published the Pentagon Papers in defiance of Richard Nixon. Then in the '70s, when the *Times* was struggling financially, he authorized Abe Rosenthal to expand the somber two-section *Times* into a livelier four-section paper. At the time, both men were accused of "cheapening" the *Times* by adding lifestyle coverage and insisting on polished writing. In fact, they were recognizing that the *Times*'s natural audience was affluent, sophisticated, well-educated people who would not be content to read the daily gruel about House agriculture subcommittees.

By the time we got to the Cascapedia, I had long since been vetted socially by Punch and both his second and third wives. He knew who he was, a personable guy who had been lucky enough to inherit a newspaper and then to outlive all the family competitors for the top job. It is no accident that Punch and Katharine Graham of *The Washington Post* were great friends. They were siblings under the skin in that neither could imagine a world in which sons and daughters of the manor did not rise. This gave each of them a kind of Whartonian grace, somewhat incongruously coupled with a severe inner toughness, that is hard to pass along to children of the modern age, even in families of privilege. In a way, Punch's approach to fishing reflected his approach to life as a whole. He was a competent but casual fisherman who accepted that it was his birthright to fish the best waters in the world.

I was a *Times*man by choice rather than birth, frustrated by the paper's stolid pace, yet committed to its journalistic values and its survival as the last best hope for the kind of newspapering the country needs. As for the fishing before us, I burned with a poacher's desire to catch an Atlantic salmon, and not just for its beauty, strength and aristocratic aura. Perhaps I sought this fish in this place for its remedial power, a way of making up for all the mundane creatures I had pursued in coarse circumstances.

When I look back on the Cascapedia, I find myself in rare disagreement with the general fly-fishing wisdom of my friend Nick Lyons. Nick, one of the best American sporting writers, gets irritated when people say, "It was the fish of a lifetime." He says fly fishing and life are too various and complex to be reduced to a single glittering event.

I sometimes feel, though, that Nick stated a great truth which may no longer apply to me. Beyond all reason, notwithstanding what passed between me and the marlin, that first Cascapedia fish shines like a diamond.

The Cascapedia is in Evangeline Country, the French-speaking area on Quebec's Gaspé Peninsula. Its history contained a surprise. Everyone knows that the area's original white settlers, the Acadians, were of French extraction. When the British took over Canada, they forcibly deported these folks to French Louisiana, where they were transformed after several generations of swamp water and filet gumbo into Cajuns. Immediately upon arriving, I understood how this miracle of adaptation had taken place. Both on the Gaspé Peninsula and down on Bayou Lafourche, the chief obstacle to civilization is the mosquito. If you can cope with the mosquitoes of either locale, everything else will work itself out.

I also noticed that the Redneck Way of Fishing—and hunting, too, for that matter—had a pretty good beachhead in both places. On the Gaspé, the local whites are making war on the coyotes because they are eating the deer that the hunters want to shoot. The Indians, for their part, are busily trying to net the migrating salmon at the mouths of the rivers so they never reach the rich toffs in the sport-fishing preserves upstream.

My biggest surprise came when I met my guides. Suddenly, I was staring into the shallows of the great hillbilly gene pool that shaped Dixie. For despite the overwhelmingly French cultural ethos of Quebec, it harbors a deeply entrenched Scottish minority, which appears to have cornered the market for salmon guides. My fellows, Ron and Glenn, would look right at home on the town square at Boaz, Alabama, or anyplace else in the cracker melting pot where the Scots, Irish, Scotch-Irish, Welsh and English got blended into one race of Anglo-Hibernian-Caledonian freckle bellies. These taciturn boys had the same compact build, the same tight-lipped, hard-eyed appraising gaze, the same genial but untalkative and slightly coiled nature that you see all across the Appalachians. With folks of the true old backcountry stock, you don't want to mistake shyness for obedience. They'd rather fight than fish or fuck. I felt right at home with Ron and Glenn. Like most country boys that wind up guiding swells, they'll have to see what you can figure out for yourself before they invest a lot of talk and attention in someone who may turn out to be a fool.

The fishing looks simple. I take the middle seat in a twenty-six-foot canoe. Ron sits in the stern and runs the ten-horsepower motor until he's got us in a position he likes. Then Glenn drops the anchor. They prop themselves up comfortably and smoke Rothmans cigarettes. I cast, first to the left, then to the right, letting the fly make a quartering drift with the current. I start with a short line and lengthen the cast about two feet with each pair of casts. Ron says to let the fly line straighten out behind the boat, because that's often where they take. After we've covered every piece of water I can reach, Glenn feeds out some anchor rope, so that we slip downstream about fifty feet. I start over—left cast, right cast, short line, long line.

In the cool midafternoon, I feel a hard nip at the fly. I pull back. Nothing.

"That was too fast, wasn't it?" I say to Ron, referring to my hook set.

"A little quick," he says, offering no instruction.

By questioning, I determine that I'm to wait until I feel the weight of the fish before striking. There is, as it turns out, no more important fact to know about hooking salmon. These lads are used to guiding a lot of nonfishing guests, and their coaching strategy is to keep their mouths shut and hope the salmon hooks itself. If necessary, they'll wind it in. For the rest of the day, I cast, and they keep their mouths shut. They smoke. Nothing pulls at my fly. It starts to get dark.

The run downriver is exhilarating, like going down a theme-park waterslide, banking through long, turbulent pools and boulder-rimmed elbows where the water is either a white froth or a deep viscous fish-harboring green. When we come plunging through a long chute that debouches into a Class III cataract, I can feel the canoe bucking and slip-sliding on the standing waves, and I am impressed enough to ask Ron the name of this rapids.

He obliges with his longest speech of the day. "Big Curly," he says. "When the water's high, it gets a lot curlier."

We pass another boat, and at the guide's urging, his client hoists a fish that Ron says will go thirty pounds. Back at the camp, I find that our group has taken fish of thirty-three and twenty-six pounds. I do not feel downcast by my lack of success but impressed with the size of these fish and a depressing fact that I put into my sketchbook. "A lot of fish are being killed here."

None, however, was killed or even touched by me through a morning of casting on the next day. I had put aside the camp's 11-weight rods in favor of my 8-weight bonefish outfit and had managed to cover a lot of empty water with less effort. On the way back downriver for lunch, we hove to along the bank at a long plateau of water called Limestone Pool. Each end was bounded by sharply descending rapids, but the pool itself was an oval-shaped table of slick, fast water maybe two hundred yards long. It sat between frothing rapids like a landing on a staircase. On the eastern side, the road swung close, and there was a launching ramp that the guides used to launch their canoes for the beats on the upper river. We stopped there as a courtesy to a canoe that was anchored along the western bank. It was crewed by a husband-wife guiding team from our camp. The husband had signaled to Ron and Glenn that they were working a fish. His wife, in the bow position, had erected a lavender umbrella to protect herself from the angler's back cast. Their clients were in the middle of the boat. The man had a decent cast and a bored wife, who was propped up amidships reading a fine book. I thought the book was fine as a matter of vanity, since I had written it. I had given it to her back at the camp as a means of possibly withstanding the rigors of being married to a fly fisher. I liked both her and her husband well enough, but I was on the edge of salmon burnout. After two fishless sessions, I had reached that stage of churlish ennui wherein I became convinced that the caster had no chance of raising the fish again.

Limestone Pool is picturesque even without a canoe and an umbrella-holding guide. I took out the sketchbook I sometimes carry. I looked up to take in the scene, then down to draw, thinking only of the picture I wanted to make and the secret hope that by drawing it I would somehow jinx them. Then I looked up to see the fellow's rod warped over in the most radical way. The woman in the bow had stashed her umbrella, snatched the anchor, and away they went after a fish that obviously knew how to pull.

There is something arresting about that moment when a fish ceases being an abstraction. It is hard to desire an abstraction, but the contact with the real thing transforms any moment. In this case, lust—salmon lust—rose in me like a bolt of lava, and it was not lost on me that I was in one of the fine places in the world to experience this particular desire. That reminded me, in turn, of the much ridiculed but nonetheless true sentiment that occurred to Scott Fitzgerald after he abandoned Minneapolis for the Big Apple. The rich are different from you and me. They have better places to fish.

Here's a question for you. Can lust, the pure force of concentrated desire, draw fish, the way that Israeli psychic claims to be able to bend spoons? Or the way, maybe once or twice when you were a kid, the radar of some unattainable princess picked up the silent, inarticulate longing being broadcast from the charged, magnetic magma of adoring, inarticulate lust that dwelled like a reactor pile, or like a new organ, in the center of your chest where your heart used to be. And shockingly, she chose you.

The answer, of course, is no. There is only one thing that

brings us into the presence of fish, and that is happening to be there. One doesn't really find fish so much as intersect with them, and desire may actually be an obstacle. Genuine, unfeigned hopelessness is much the better state of mind, and it is the state I had achieved. We had watched the other boat fight and land the salmon. They had long since returned to camp in a shower of insincere compliments from me and an entrenched silence from Ron and Glenn. I was hoping they were feeling determined. Someone in our canoe needed to be. It was now fifteen minutes until dark, and I could feel resignation settling like dusk over my soul. We had the river to ourselves after the other boat scored. We had pounded good water all afternoon to no avail, and Ron and Glenn decided we should make one final stop back at Limestone Pool, which had had plenty of time to settle down. I took the boys' willingness to fish until slam dark as a sign of approval.

We were not alone at Limestone. There was a pickup truck parked at the rocky boat ramp. A young man was aimlessly nuzzling his girlfriend while a second man watched us and stole glances at his amorous friends. The kissing was pretty desultory. Mainly they were drinking beer. There was something about the scene that took me back in time, to creek-banking days down home. I thought of country roads and mild afternoons and beer that tasted better in memory than it ever does in the here and now. I made myself smile with a mental joke. What is it about boat ramps that, north and south, attracts rednecks without boats? I guess it's the same thing that makes people buy condominiums on the backstretch at the NASCAR track in Charlotte. They like to ponder the recreational potential of the spot.

They watched us fish, which I deemed vaguely at odds with the pursuit of North America's most exclusive game fish on one of the world's most private pieces of water. Their presence made me feel reflective and vaguely horny. It often happens that when the fish are not showing I find myself thinking about fornication. In the absence of fish, my attention wanders. I begin to think that I would be better advised to spend my time in the exploration of country matters, to use the Shakespearean term.

I was snatched back from such reveries by an activity in the river.

A big fish roils the surface downstream from us, maybe seventy-five feet above the point where the pool empties into the rapids below. We move down toward the fish and reanchor. I drift the fly over the area of the rise, and the thing comes up again. The fly is drifting only an inch or so under the surface, so we can see the salmon's back as it takes a look at the fly. This is the false rise described by the great Lee Wulff, and confronted with the hardest task in all of fly fishing, I fail. That is to say, I start to strike, pulling the fly away from the fish.

"Don't move the fly," Ron says. His tone is instructional, not peevish.

His manner pleases me. A snappish guide always sets me back. I cast.

The salmon rises again. This time I am steady as I can be, but the fish refuses the fly and—oh, the heartbreak of this—disappears. Not even a half dozen fly changes will bring that fish back. What chance do we have of encountering another in the last moments of light? Next comes this, written into my sketchbook a few hours later:

> After 7:00 p.m., when we are out of fishing time and I am feeling very snakebit, fish start moving into the pool. "They're porpoising," Ron says. It looks like a head-and-tail trout rise.
>
> With activity all around, my casting goes to hell. But I settle down and start making good long casts. Finally a bathtub-size swirl around my fly raises a big oval of waves. I hold steady, not moving the fly, and suddenly the consummating weight is on my line and the reel is clicking.

I cannot contain my self-congratulation here. I waited so patiently, like a boulder in the river, while the water moved around my fly, and then while the fish moved around my fly, creating from the current a trembling arena of life. Everything about the scene, every moment of fishing I had ever done cried out for me to strike the fish. Yet I waited and, once I felt the long pull of that fish, I raised the rod and set the hook so subtly that only the language of desire suffices. It was truly the consummating moment of my life as a fly fisher.

For all that, the moments before the strike live with equal or greater force in my memory—the sight of that pod of fish coming busily over the rim of that pool, using the last light of the day to beat their way through one more staircase of rapids and find new holding water for the night. It was elemental and tragic, the way it gets late in the day when ducks come into the guns or out on the reef when the seabirds are flying home, leaving you hooked up to something big, ferocious and invisible as the sun falls into the ocean. In those moments, you feel the weight of mortality, you grasp the rushing pace, the incurable transience of all existence. The salmon have been coming over that rim of rock in the last migratory push of their particular day for thousands of years, and we are here to kiss the girl on the riverbank or throw a stick to the dog or catch the fish for less than an instant. And in that instant, what force is there in the universe to record the eucharistic mystery of the salmon's take and the solemn, tumescent blending of forearm muscle and arching rod at the moment when you come tight against the fish and feel the resistant, answering beat of another life? It's a mere click beyond nothing at all, this moment, an instant of fatal subtlety that is gone quicker than it happens. Yet it transpires with such authority—like the bat on the baseball, or like backing a country girl up against a pickup truck and feeling the hard, cooperative hump of her blue-jeaned pubic bone against your thigh—a sovereign moment gone glimmering now into the flood of indifferent time, a matter of no consequence but enduring mnemonic weight.

She came to me with all requisite ceremony, that fish, and to this day I mostly regret what happened next. This beautiful hen salmon of about twenty pounds was marred by a six-inch gash along one flank, inflicted, the boys said, by a seal or a net. It did not look that serious to me. I've seen the scars of healed-over cuts on many fish, but Ron and Glenn insisted this one would not survive to spawn. I let them whack her. My first Atlantic salmon, and there was blood on my hands. Yet I cannot tell you that it felt altogether terrible to have that gleaming silver corpse on the floor of the canoe between my feet. It is a noble thing to spare a fish, but in this sporting world, nobility cannot always be summoned to the work at hand. I felt sad all right, but also primal, victorious, and something in me needed those feelings, needed a repletion of both lust and remorse. I have released scores of salmon since, and today I'd fight you rather than kill another, no matter what wounds it carried. Maybe what I got from that first one was the simple comfort of knowing that no matter how long you live, you'll keep finding things you need to outgrow.

Then we roared down the river, those redneck Quebec boys and I, three cousins separated by two centuries, yet sprinkled into North America in the great Celtic Diaspora that sent some of our tribe south and some north, some to Southern hills, some to this subarctic sea rim. We went down, down the long, ramping slide of that river, the wind snatching cigarette smoke from our mouths, night coming down, down, rolling behind us, for we were the last boat out, held on the river long past the obligatory fishing hours by the tribal force of their desire to show me a fish and by their knowledge that sooner or later someone would see the slow-beating, humping rise of salmon coming over the lip of primordial stone down at the end of the pool, and that it might as well be us. Back at the camp, strolling out of the darkness into the dazzle of fireplace and candlelight, I announced to substantial people from several nations that New York had lost yet another virgin.

CHAPTER 25

Snapshot V:
Legion Field, in Birmingham, 1964, Enrollment Day, the Paul W. Bryant School of Journalism

At about 3:00 p.m., CST, on November 26, 1964, citizens of the great and sovereign state of Alabama gathered, thusly.

Bear Bryant stood at the fifty-yard line.

About sixty-eight thousand others arrayed themselves on the steel and concrete escarpments of the Football Capital of the South.

A scholar-athlete named Raymond Ogden stood on the north goal line awaiting the second-half kickoff.

I stood at the thirty-yard line at the opposite end of the field. Around my neck was one of the most coveted objects in that contentious land of my birth, a sideline pass to the Alabama-Auburn game. In my hand was the very first of several thousand reporter's notebooks that I was to fill in the course of my lifetime.

I knew from a female classmate who had dated Mr. Ogden that he was not a man you would look up for a discussion of *Lyrical Ballads*. On the other hand, once you put a football in his hands and got him pointed in the right direction, the result was pure Forrest Gumpian transcendence.

When the long high-arching Auburn kickoff fell out of the sweet Alabama sky into Mr. Ogden's hands on that splendidly sunny afternoon, he began running south. For a moment I lost sight of him in the fierce clot of blockers and attackers in the center of the field. Then an alley opened up as if the white-clad Auburn players had been parted by Moses, and out of that immemorial fray, that moiling melee, that hurricane of hormonal Southern mayhem came Raymond Ogden, lengthening his stride like a thoroughbred.

Behind me the Alabama stands released a gush of sound that crashed like a tsunami upon the sideline jubilation. To my left, I saw Coach Bryant disappear behind a mass of players who came off the bench like jumping jacks. I began jumping, too, and cheering Mr. Ogden as he came loping past, his head back, his feet striking the ground but four times in ten yards. I suspect life has held nothing grander for him than that moment, just as for me there has been no crisper and more seductive moment of definition than the instant in which he drew even with me on his way to the goal line.

I was actually in the air when the revelation struck me. I realized that I shouldn't be jumping and I shouldn't be cheering. I was not there as a fan. This knowledge hit me as abruptly as a slap. I remember looking at the notebook in my hand and then looking around to see if anyone had seen me. Almost thirty years later, in 1993, William Safire in his *Political Dictionary* would credit me with inventing the term "defining moment," which went on to become one of the clichés of American political reporting. I suppose if you invent a cliché it is all right to use it. This was my defining moment as a journalist. I leapt into the air as a fan, and as Raymond Ogden passed on his journey into obscurity, I came down a reporter.

It was my first assignment, earned because I had a quality greatly in demand by Scripps Howard, the penurious owners of the *Birmingham Post-Herald*. That is to say, I had volunteered to work without pay as sideline color reporter on my off day from the copydesk.

The day produced my first byline and my last cheer on company time at an event I was covering. In the hundreds of campaign rallies I was destined to attend over the next four decades with my notebook in hand, I never clapped or booed at a partisan jibe. I tried not to laugh at the jokes, which was easier with Carter than Reagan and easiest of all with the Bushes. I never joined a political party and never felt deprived when some hack politician defended himself by quoting Teddy Roosevelt on the glories of "the man who is actually in the arena, whose face is marred by dust and sweat and blood." It seemed to me then and it is still so now, for me, there was something more lasting and important than running the touchdown or making the money or winning the election or choosing a side. That is to see events wholly and coldly and try to write about them for the informational benefit of the Republic.

My almost instant conversion to the secular religion of journalism was easy for the specific reason that it came as naturally as breathing to me. I am not going to poor-mouth here. There are in the world only a few people who whip out a cast the first time they pick up a fly rod. They are naturals. I am not that kind of caster. But as a reporter, I did seem to have an inborn facility that felt like a kind of foreknowledge. I just got it from day one. I knew the instant I walked into the city room of the *Post-Herald*. *I can do this.* The thought popped into my head without announcement. I had never worked on a school paper. I didn't even know how to type. But I felt seized by an innate sense for what makes a good newspaper story and for predicting how a running story was likely to unfold. If I were kidnapped by time bandits and dropped blindfolded into that newsroom again, I'd know it just by the smell.

It took me years to figure out why that feeling came to me with such force, and I won't blame you if you don't buy it. But it's a true statement of my inner reality. It all had to do with the afternoon that Bill Thorn told me to hit the ball. There was something about the foursquare layout of that newsroom—indeed of many newsrooms in the old days—that replicated the geometry of a baseball field. It takes a little imagination to see it that way—the desks as bases anchoring the corners of a square, the lanes between them as base paths, the city editor and managing editor camped out along the side like coaches or umpires. *I know this place. I will win here.* Years later when friends asked me why I wanted to leave Southern newspapers, where I was doing pretty well, and take a shot at *The New York Times,* that old unconscious connection asserted itself. "I want to see if I can hit major-league pitching," I said.

Not that I ever wanted to be a sportswriter. That first story about the craziness and color of the Alabama-Auburn game ran as a news feature rather than on the sports pages. I never wrote about the Bear again until his retirement in 1982, and that was in *The New Republic.* Yet growing up in Alabama during the cultural hegemony of Paul William Bryant, that least introspective and most participatory of men, had an impact on how I went about my business when I became a man.

Here is what you need to understand about Coach Bryant. He had his weaknesses. He was a bit of a drunk in the off-season. He liked the ladies a little too randomly. A lot of the rich Alabamians with whom he ran—and invested—were of the coarse Snopesian stripe. But his foibles were private, and his virtues were public ones. He had a gift, rarely seen among Alabama's leading figures at that time, for dignified public behavior. He made mistakes, the most terrible being his lateness in integrating the team, but he did not shrink from grand gestures of atonement. Bryant never resorted to the NFL trick of relegating the best black athletes to the defensive secondary. His first black stars were quarterbacks, runners and receivers. The main thing I admired was this: When he walked on the field with his slow, big-cat amble, eyes squinted against the sun, the skin of his face as corrugated as a mountain range, you knew one thing. You knew that win, lose or draw, football would be played there that day.

You also knew that it would be played with passion, dignity and self-control. And there were plenty of years back in the late '50s and early '60s when it seemed like he was the only white man in Alabama who combined those qualities. I don't want to polish the man up too much. I think it's fair to say that he was ferocious about winning to the point of wanting, on some deep preconscious level, the actual physical destruction of his opponents. But he would never stoop to cheating, and he wouldn't tolerate crude public behavior or bad manners from his players, and when he lost, he did not go on national television to spew and whine like George Wallace. Coach Bryant had an idea about how a man ought to act, and if you watched him, you could figure it out. I think he was the originator of the line about not wanting his players to jump around in the end zone. He wanted them to act like they had been there before. He taught by example that early and late in life, in victory and in loss, a man ought to have some formality in his nature.

The memorable editors I have worked for all radiated that Bear Bryant thing. When they walked into the newsroom, you knew that journalism would be committed on the premises that day, with dedication and with a fierce, pure concentration that destroyed the market for excuses, whining or quitting. Yet they had a code, too, that ruled out the cutting of corners and unnecessary fierceness. For thirty-five years I've been happy that my first newspaper assignment was to cover Coach Bryant. He was long, long gone, of course, before I could balance my books with the old man, a final reckoning, a cost-benefit analysis, as it were, on the Bear Bryant Rules of Journalism, what they taught me and what they would cost me.

Summer of '46,
Birmingham:
In my first clearly
remembered encounter
with fish, I point my
popgun at the goldfish
in Vulcan Park.
(Photo: Bertha Walker Raines)

My grandfather, Hiram Howell Raines (1872–1914)

Summer of '63,
Gulf of Mexico:
During a Florida tour
that Tennant McWilliams
and I referred to as the
Great Fish, I'm at the tiller
of my family's venerable
15-horsepower Johnson
Seahorse. (Photo: Tennant
McWilliams)

Summer of '63, Carrabelle, Florida: At a stop on the tour, Tennant poses with the catch of the day, Spanish mackerel taken off Shipping Cove at Dog Island.

Spring of '65, Mountain Brook, Alabama: Professor Richebourg Gaillard McWilliams, Tennant's father and my mentor, with a large-mouth bass taken at Trail's End, my parents' farm near Chelsea, Alabama.

Fall of '91, Shenandoah National Park, Virginia: The Great Blalock, at the peak of his fly-fishing career, pursues his ruling passion, casting dry flies for native brook trout in the Rapidan River.

June 1993, Quetico National Park, Ontario, Canada: My son Ben Raines and I leave the campsite at Darky Lake where I treated ennui and a bruised shoulder with Jack Daniel's. (Photo: Patrick Tyler)

March 1994, Republic of Kiribati: Tennant and I arrive on Christmas Island with our bonefish dreams and virginal fly rods. (Photographer unknown)

March 1994, Cassidy
International Airport,
Christmas Island:
Our first glimpse of the
baggage handler from
the Captain Cook Hotel.

March 1994, Pacific Ocean
off Christmas Island:
The intrepid Tuna Smith
points at the hooked marlin
shortly before attempting
the underwater photograph
that killed the camera
hanging around his neck.
(Photo: Tennant McWilliams)

September 1990: The view of Lake Como
from the Villa Serbelloni across its
gardens and olive grove. On the shore,
at the extreme left, is the red-tiled
boathouse from which I saw
the impudent cruisers.

July 1996, Murmansk: Environmentalist and master angler Nat Reed inserts an earplug before boarding a helicopter to the Ponoi River salmon camp.

July 1996, Kola Peninsula: My fishing partner, the Maine conservationist Amos Eno (with raised thumb), and Nat celebrate a successful helicopter landing at the Ponoi.

July 1996, Ponoi River: An unintended double exposure produces a spectral image of Nat and me rigging up in the shadow of a "terrible machine." (Photographer unknown)

Autumn 2000,
New York Harbor:
My son Jeff Raines back
in the peaceful time
when you could catch
striped bass within sight
of the Twin Towers.

March 2002, Patagonia:
Krystyna Raines, on
her first fly-fishing trip,
with a sea-run brown
trout from the Rio
Grande of Argentina.

March 2002, Patagonia: Diego Motter,
guide and raconteur at the Villa Maria
Behety on the Rio Grande, weighs one
of Krystyna's trout on the day he
performed his first hook extraction.

March 2003, Patagonia: On the Rio Grande with the largest trout of my life, a 32-pound brown spotted by Alberto Molina, chief guide at Maria Behety. (Photo: Alberto Molina)

September 2003, Long Island Sound off Montauk: Krystyna with her first bluefish and Paul Dixon, the guide and fishing-tackle consultant who pioneered ocean fly fishing at Montauk.

July 2004, Kola River, Russia: The guides chat as Krystyna quietly sets the hook on her first Atlantic salmon.

July 2004, Kola River: Krystyna's freshly released salmon resting on the guide's foot, in a picture taken by the underwater camera bought to replace the one that died off Christmas Island.

Autumn 2003: Our first apple harvest at the house in Paradise Township.

CHAPTER 26

The Fourth Editorial:
On Newspapers

The editors liked my feature story on the Alabama-Auburn game. Within days I was liberated from the copydesk and made a full-time reporter. Almost immediately, I began forming the ideas that would one day get me fired. When I got that first reporting job, the conventional wisdom was that newspapers were dying because of television. From the start, it seemed obvious to me that if newspapers were dying, it was because they weren't good enough. Anyone who paid a dime and opened one of the damn things could see that.

Certainly television was a threat to movies and night baseball. Newspapers, however, had a potential audience that was larger and more affluent than ever, courtesy of those great shapers of the emerging modern nation, the G.I. Bill and the postwar job boom. From the day I first walked into a newsroom in 1964 until the day I walked out of the *Times* in 2003, the core delusion of newspaper owners and workers never changed. Nor did our inability to internalize the knowledge that the tastes and habits of America's mass audience were largely irrelevant to the future of newspapers *if* we could ride our own big wave, the proportional expansion of the quality audience composed of that portion of the population educated enough to read a sophisticated newspaper, affluent enough to afford it and smart enough to know they needed it. In other words, we didn't need to retain all the television viewers as readers, just the smart ones.

The general failure of newspapers to do this over the last fifty years can be illustrated by two lines on a graph, a rising line tracking median education or income levels and a falling line showing the circulation of daily newspapers. During this period, the pool of potential subscribers to the *Times* had expanded exponentially. Starting in the late '70s, the *Times* built a nationwide network of printing plants to reach "like-minded nonreaders" wherever they lived. Our market research said there were more than 80 million of these potential subscribers. Yet the paid circulation has bounced around at 1.1 to 1.2 million for most of the last decade, through the tenures of three executive editors. It had slipped back to just under 1.1 million daily when I took over on September 5, 2001. For two decades, we had been adding printing sites and expanding home-delivery zones with marginal circulation gains to show for the increased expense. I was convinced that stalled circulation, uneven revenues and lagging stock prices were telling us the same thing. Despite its bright reputation, the *Times* was too narrowly focused to attract the broad range of sophisticated readers within our reach. We were selling an ossified product over and over again to the same people. If you were a Manhattan resident or a Washington diplomat, it was an essential read. If you were an investment banker in Houston, a filmmaker in Hollywood or a physics professor in Oregon, you could get by without it if you had to or wanted to. I had watched as Max Frankel was unfairly pummeled for "tabloidization" when he tried to broaden the paper's appeal while staying within the framework of what he called "*Times*ian values." He was on the right track.

Although Max was a fine executive editor from whom I learned a great deal, I disagreed fundamentally with one of his favorite sayings. I'm not even sure he really believed it, given his frequent comments on the paper's stodginess and mediocrity. The saying went that the executive editor should not take credit for circulation gains, so he couldn't be blamed for the losses. In my view, it was the essence of an executive editor's job to capture a larger share of our target audience by improving the overall quality of the paper. You do that by bringing to the task the two rarest qualities in any newsroom: energy and creativity. The *Times* has hit a circulation ceiling because its content has hit a ceiling in quality, variety and vivacity. We were holding our own with Eastern corridor news junkies. But what about the millions of smart, affluent would-be readers interested in business, sports, culture, entertainment, travel, literature, food, wine, fashion, education, health care? The flat circulation numbers spoke a truth no one was eager to recognize. The days when the *Times* could grow and prosper by providing a stenographic record of government-certified news events had long since passed. The *Times* staff nurses an ingrained and outdated paranoia about the paper being "dumbed down." I thought they ought to be obsessed with what it has needed for three decades and needs today, which is to capitalize on the growth in the quality audience by smartening up.

To my amazement, the kid who detested "bidness" had grown into a man who was fascinated with the economics of newspaper survival. The base factors determining a paper's commercial health—advertising and circulation revenues—were clearly linked to the quality of the journalism that it had to sell at the retail level. Yet even on profitable papers, the newsrooms on which the quality of the paper depends are underfunded as a matter of long-standing industry traditions as to what constitutes sound management. These budgetary limitations on journalistic quality produce revenue shortfalls in advertising and circulation. The news budget is trimmed further to keep the profit margins stable despite those chronic shortfalls in revenue. Wall Street has long since cracked the code of this spiral of dwindling returns and stagnant growth. That is why the *Times* stock and many other newspaper stocks stay stuck much of the time unless there is talk of the paper being swallowed by a megacorporation. This would be a terrible fate for the *Times* and its heritage of beneficent family control. But if your circulation is continuously level-pegging or shrinking while the consumer market expands, you're going to die or be eaten sooner or later.

Sometimes such dismal outcomes are irreversible. When

you are working at one of the country's largest horse-collar factories and you see the first automobile come down the streets of
your town, as my father did in his early teens, you know that
there is nothing to be done. But the *Times* was in a very different
situation at the birth of the Information Age than was the Burton
Manufacturing Company of Jasper, Alabama, at the start of the
Automobile Age. The *Times* entered its critical epoch with one of
the finest information-processing systems in the world. It was
underfunded and undermotivated, but in regard to its intellectual
rigor and core principles, the *Times*'s information machine was the
perfect vehicle for the strategy my colleagues, our other executives and our board of directors had settled on for the first decade
of the twenty-first century. We would move from being a national
to being an international news organization, riding the formidable, if time-limited revenues from printed papers in the United
States and Europe to spread across broadcast, cable and digital
"platforms" for the delivery of news and quality information. This
was our golden moment to take advantage of the worldwide
growth in the quality-information audience by habituating them
to *The New York Times* in all its forms, on paper, on the Internet,
on television, in books.

I'm convinced the strategy would have worked at the time we
devised it. I'm worried that its time may already have passed. We
had a chance to stabilize and expand the literate, affluent minority that makes up the quality-information marketplace. Now we
may be seeing a coarsening of our society's information tastes that
is reducing the audience for impartial news and acute analysis.
Our strategy for growing and protecting the *Times* franchise was
built around delivering high-quality, fact-based information and
analysis, around news that is found out rather than imagined.
Now, the United States is moving toward a journalism of assertion
and allegation, if indeed we dare call it journalism. The growth of
blogs and the Fox network suggests that the quality audience once
so proudly and confidently measured by *Times* pollsters may
be settling for, even demanding, a less refined product. The
unedited, uneditable outpourings of the bloggers consist of infor-

mation that has gone through none of the conventional screens associated with American journalism in the last half of the twentieth century: screens for ideological bias, political cheerleading, religious or racial special pleading, financial conflict of interest, factuality. Fox, by its mere existence, undercuts the argument that the public is starved for "fair" news, and not just because Fox shills for the Republican Party and panders to the latest of America's periodic religious manias. The key to understanding Fox News is to grasp the anomalous fact that its consumers know its "news" is made up. It matters not when critics point this out to Foxite consumers because they've understood it from the outset. That's *why* they're there. Its chief fictioneer, Roger Ailes, had been making up news in plain sight for a half century. Originally what he made up was spoken publicly by his political clients. Now it's voiced over the air by hirelings placed in visual environments designed to make the audience comfortable with a willing suspension of disbelief about what is journalism and what is flapdoodle. The process by which pseudonews is produced has become so open and public that it ought to be easy to combat. Even so, it is fashionable in mainstream journalism to believe that the disenchanted newspaper subscribers who now consume cable news have been duped by big-lie techniques and that our brainless bloggers have been seduced by the phony freedom of a normless technology. The sad fact is that traditional journalists let these audiences drift away by failing to explain that we believed in—and the nation deserved—journalism based on time-proven principles rather than the ideological fads and amoral commerciality of Rupert's World. As a result, a majority of Americans now really do believe the big lie that journalists in traditional venues have abandoned—indeed, never tried to follow—the guiding ideal of impartiality. In fact, my generation of journalists was trained in an intellectually rigorous process of fact-finding and analysis that evolved in the country's newsrooms after World War II. For fifty years or so, that training produced the most factually reliable and politically balanced journalism the world has seen. History may record it as a failing on our part that we were too proud to respond to the propaganda campaign that led millions of Americans to believe we were yellow journalists of the antique American sort or partisan sensationalists of the modern British sort.

It's nicer to think our audience was tricked, seduced, kidnapped away from us by a process that was devilishly subtle. An equally cogent case can be made that mainstream journalism is slipping in influence because it failed to capture and habituate the quality audience it once took for granted. A few short years ago, I thought we had a chance to stabilize and then expand that audience while there was still time on the clock. If I were in the business today, that clock is something I would worry about.

CHAPTER 27

Mother Russia,
Her Drunken Populists,
Her Fish-Shaped Objects,
Her Rednecks

Boris Yeltsin actually looks a little like Big Jim Folsom, and in the 1996 Russian presidential election, damned if he didn't do the same thing Big Jim did in the Alabama gubernatorial campaign of 1962. He got drunk. Yeltsin at least had the good sense to go to bed. Poor old Jim went on statewide television, where he forgot, among other things, the names of his children.

By the time I landed in Moscow five days before the vote, that old devil vodka had laid Boris out flat, and he was not to rise again. The journalistic rationale for my visit, to see Yeltsin on the campaign trail, was dashed. So I hit the shops in the Arbat in search of items to add to my international collection of fish-shaped objects, a collection that might be described in an auction catalog as eclectic or, more accurately, as idiosyncratic or, most unkindly, as worthless.

I was just biding my time for Sunday, when I was to meet Nat Reed in Murmansk. A couple of American reporters had promised to take me to the mother of all flea markets. I prepared for the journey by acquiring a Yeltsin-scale hangover at the annual summer-solstice party held in the courtyard of the government apartment complex that the Soviets, in the interest of efficient eavesdropping surveillance, had provided for the foreign press corps. It was festive. One could join Russian girls dancing to "Twist and Shout" and, on the morning after, feel empathy for bedridden politicians of all nations.

Despite my wounded state, my friends drove me to a vast plaza marked by weedy parking lots and blocks of high-rises in the requisite stages of post-Commie dilapidation. I knew right away that my Disappearing Flea-Market Theory, based on the assumption that someday all the worthless crap in the world would find its intended home, was doomed.

The New Russians had seventy years of shopping locked up inside them. Thousands of them prowled five hundred acres of booths and kiosks. It looked like a joint project of the Ministry of Trade, Wal-Mart and the Psychic Friends Network.

We are talking the heaped, uncataloged detritus of Soviet decay and Cowboy Capitalism, a confluence of bad taste and people whose pockets bulged with loose, untaxed change. They had whatever you didn't want—carved amber, fake carved amber, nesting dolls shaped like Dennis Rodman, a three-thousand-dollar Stalin rug, a KGB T-shirt, a high-strung Irish setter with those crazy Dan Quayle eyes. In other words, it was just the place to add to my inventory of carved-fish-of-many-nations.

My favorite genres are high-tourist kitsch, such as the orange carp with articulated joints that I found on sale at the Seven Star Cave in Guilin, China; the truly primitive, like the crude soapstone fish I found in Kenya; or the irresistibly elegant, like the antique koi-shaped opium bottle of carved bone that I snagged in Hong Kong. A really good fish object should not be cute. It must have the authority of unadorned beauty, the aura of stupidity or naïveté or be ugly in an original way. The last category was certain to be the best bet in this setting. I told my friends to watch out for "objects that are hard to like."

They led me to the dick-headed fish—small carved minnows with tails raised like flags and heads that were anatomically correct replicas of the business end of a penis. I wondered if reverse mermaids were a folk-art motif.

"Pure ivory," boasted the Russian in charge. You can get arrested, of course, for bringing ivory into the United States. I envisioned a *New York Post* headline that said "*Times* Editor Nabbed for Dildo Smuggling." My lack of enthusiasm must have vibrated through the language barrier.

"You want bigger?" the Russian shouted. He produced fish dildos of escalating sizes. The championship models were as imposing as anything you can find at the sex-toy boutiques in Greenwich Village.

Later, a weather-beaten man with an acute tooth shortage displayed a garishly painted ceramic fish with bugle lips and an abruptly pointed tail. The man put the tail in his mouth and blew. The thing whistled. He moved his fingers, and the pitch changed. It was a fish flute. Its mouthpiece still shined unhealthily with his spittle when I handed over fifteen dollars in rubles. In time I was to discover that even the czars had fish-shaped flutes. It's a venerable folk motif, but neither the Hermitage nor the gift shop at Catherine the Great's palace could produce a fish flute as ugly as mine.

I would be in St. Petersburg on election day. With Yeltsin still abed, I thought I'd check out the has-beens and thugs running for president as they campaigned around Moscow. Mikhail Gorbachev, revered in America and hated by his countrymen, was hopelessly behind. Aleksandr Lebed, a Red Army general, was running on his reputation as a barracks brawler who enforced his orders with one-punch knockouts. Gennady Zyuganov, the Spiritual Heritage, or retreaded Communist, candidate for president was by this time running on the fact that, unlike Yeltsin, he could stand upright. Of his own relationship with strong drink, he said, "I am fine. I drink a bit more than Gorbachev and a bit less than Lebed." As for the current political situation, he said, "Russia is dying."

Not since Big Jim's heyday in Alabama had I been near a campaign that so reeked of strong drink and sour populism. None of the Russians could match the humor of old Big Jim, of course. I recalled the more or less true story about the time when Jim, well sauced, joined some other Southern governors for a demonstration cruise aboard the then-new *Nimitz* aircraft carrier.

The navy wanted to show off the steam catapult used to launch its fighter planes. The commanding officer told the governors they were about to see "the world's greatest air show." With a mighty roar, a jet was catapulted into flight. It caught fire on takeoff and crashed into the sea, the pilot narrowly escaping death by ejecting at five hundred feet. Rescue boats with blaring sirens raced to the pilot. Sailors rushed to and fro on the flight deck. Big Jim's state of exhilaration was such that he thought both the crash and the rescue had been choreographed. He clapped an admiral on the back and bellowed, "If that ain't a show, I'll kiss your ass!"

It's been said that Russia is a country only a fool can love. My guide in St. Petersburg, a well-informed young woman named Paulina, argued that it was also a country only a drunk can save.

"I don't know what will happen to this country if Yeltsin doesn't win," said Paulina as she drove me from the airport to the polling place. She wanted to cast her vote before we started our tour of czarist relics. Her grandfather was a Red Army general who helped shell the Reichstag. Her parents were high-ranking scientists in the Soviet defense establishment. Paulina and her lawyer fiancé, still in their twenties, were surfing along on a wave of American money. She guided corporate clients for U.S. travel agencies. Her future husband worked in the St. Petersburg office of an American company. The whole family—three generations of nomenklatura—was voting for reform candidates. "We are all New Russians. I am a child of perestroika. If Yeltsin loses, what would happen to my husband's job?"

The polling place was in the dim corridor of a school. The babushkas who were supposed to be in charge gossiped among themselves. There was not a uniform in sight. Paulina let me mark her ballot for Yeltsin. I folded it and dropped it in the ballot box.

In St. Petersburg in those days, free enterprise in all its legal and underground variations was on the march. The Russian mafia regarded murder as the management tool of first resort. The week before I arrived a don in his mid-fifties was shot alfresco in a sidewalk café. The local papers noted, drolly, that the widow was twenty-six. The bars at the four-star hotels were packed with these potential widows, long-legged girls from Ukraine who had figured out that tight jeans, spike heels and hooking beat marriage to a vodka-addled prole. Given the high mortality rate of their tourist customers, only an idiot would hire one of these truly fetching entrepreneurs of the night, but in the New Russia, the quick, the dumb, the occasionally dead and the newly prosperous all fit under the umbrella of a market economy.

In our two days of touring, Paulina had explained that defeat of the neo-Communists was needed to protect commerce at all levels. When we went to a long lunch at the D'Angleterre Hotel, where the American journalist John Reed stayed during the Revolution, she took the tutorial to a more detailed level. Economics aside, Paulina explained, there were also reasons of taste for avoiding Zyuganov. He had a "peasant face," embarrassing neckties from the '70s, and he was depending on the "the Sovok vote."

My radar went up. It did not take a lot of heavy parallel analysis to see Zyuganov as a Russian George Wallace and the Sovok vote as the redneck vote. I tried this out on Paulina as our distinctly un-Sovok waiter was sweeping in with the sturgeon.

"'Sovok' cannot be called the exact synonym of the word 'redneck,'" she said. "It is becoming the Russian synonym for 'a fool.' We use that term when we're extremely irritated. To call a person a Sovok is to insult. You see them on Sunday driving an old unfashionable car. They are crazy about gardening. You see them in their old cars hauling firewood or stumps or seedlings. They still manage to find shops that have the worst goods and to queue for them.

"Sometimes they're young as well—youngsters who work at state factories who are very badly dressed or who have bad haircuts or if they try to dress expensively they buy the wrong things—made in India or China." These young Sovoks, she believed, were polluting the newly freed marketplace with socialist work habits. "Those who are used to this relaxed way of working cannot get used to the new way of working and the idea that their amount of pay is directly related to how much work they do. They're going to vote for Zyuganov, of course."

I thought of Paulina as a sweet little Russian Valley Girl, a child of the clandestine aristocracy that prospered within the classless society. Her class prejudices took me back to my own youth in Birmingham. City boys like me used to ridicule the country folk, behind their backs, never mind the fact that our families were only a generation removed from their hick towns. Now I'm inclined to believe that Scotch-Irish borderers, the Sovoks and the modern American rednecks are all members of a vast international undertribe, despised perhaps but necessary. Every modern civilization has to define its own rednecks, the class that is its emblem of backwardness but also endures as the receptacle of its primal energy and has to be called into service whenever the plutocrats start a war. Hitler, after all, had bombed and starved Leningrad into a forlorn heap of frozen rubble. Now, a half century later, the Sovoks are still there, making jam and chopping firewood and happily driving their loose-fendered, smoke-belching cars.

With hindsight, we know that Yeltsin presided over the greatest looting of a national economy in modern history, at least up to that time. Vladimir Putin may edge him out in the final reckoning of history, but in his day, Yeltsin was the champ. Not even the Bush-Cheney-Halliburton combine could match it. The rules were simple. Everyone who would have gone to prison in a normal country got rich. Russia now has more billionaires than any other country. But if I had it to do over, I'd still vote for Yeltsin because of the high hopes the world's fishermen had for him and the New Russia that Paulina saw on the horizon. We believed Yeltsin and the New Russians would guard the precious Kola Peninsula and thereby save the Atlantic salmon—this fish of kings, this monarch of the homewaters of the Soviet nuclear submarine fleet—from extinction. For my part, such a belief fit nicely with the mind-sets required by the activities in which I've invested so much time. As in fishing, we must be optimists in our expectations. As in journalism, we must be realists in assessing the gap between the Imagined Ideal and the mess in which we find ourselves.

CHAPTER 28

Dans le Zone à l'Ombre

The leftover helicopters of the Soviet empire make a deep impression on everyone who survives them. Allan M. "Pinky" Pinkerton, a well-traveled fisherman from Ventura, California, swore off Russian salmon fishing forever when his pilot left him alone in the aircraft as it sat idling on a bar in the river. Spontaneously, the machine rose thirty feet in the air. It made a slow 360-degree rotation as Pinky was trying to decide whether to grab the controls, jump out or simply kiss his ass good-bye. Then it slowly settled back to the ground, dead level the entire time. Later, Pinky lodged complaints with the management. "What really upset me," he said, "other than the fact that it could have easily proven quite disastrous, was that the pilot absolutely denied ever leaving the aircraft."

Our copter, sitting on the tarmac at Murmansk, looked not so much dangerous as tired—a lassoed Communist dinosaur. In a change of plans, we were now headed for the Ponoi River instead of the Kharlovka, but we anticipated the same level of aeronautical thrills. Before us was a twin-engine, military-style transport, newly painted in Aeroflot white and blue. Some anglers have reported seeing the faint outline of the Red Army star under new paint jobs, but that was not the case with our beast. However, even the bright paint could not hide the dents and general decrepitude of the craft. Next, one's attention was drawn forcefully to the most notorious feature of Soviet design: exterior fuel tanks hanging like saddlebags alongside the passenger compartment. These tanks were painted red as if to punctuate the agree-

197

ment of the global aeronautical community that no nation has invented a more efficient set-up for roasting passengers in the event of a crash.

The helicopter was about the right size for an infantry platoon, and that is how we sat in the damn thing, infantry-style, on benches down each side of the fuselage. The floor space between the two benches was filled entirely by a midden of luggage, rod cases and wader bags. Not long after we lifted off, Nat Reed nudged me and pointed through one of the portholes at what was, obviously, a hydroelectric plant on the outskirts of Murmansk. I removed my earplugs long enough to hear him shout that the plant had been "triple-targeted" by the United States in Cold War military planning. That is to say, in the event of war, it was to be hit with one set of nuclear bombs dropped from planes, another set launched from submarines and another lobbed over from the States on intercontinental missiles. Unbeknownst to the Soviets, U.S. Navy submarines had planted listening devices on the floor of the sea near Murmansk. The Americans learned that this particular hydro plant supplied the power for the electric cranes used to lift the nuclear missiles into position aboard the Soviets' main submarine base on the White Sea. The American strategic doctrine was classic Cold War gunslinger logic. Knock out the plant, and the Reds can't reload their pistols.

Nat, I should say here, is a powerful and habitual explainer, and I have always had a soft spot for big talkers with style and that essential redeeming dash of self-awareness. It is that last quality, that winking sense of "Let me entertain you," that separates marathon conversationalists from the fish-camp windbags encountered on waters around the world. Readers of *Fly Fishing Through the Midlife Crisis* may remember that it recorded the words and adventures of my dearly missed friend Dick Blalock, a diplomat–fly fisher–gourmand–autodidact–conservationist–gadfly–raconteur who died in 1992. The Great Blalock, as I always thought of him, was the duly elected president and self-appointed guru of Trout Unlimited in Washington, D.C., and an unforgettably Falstaffian character. Nat was the most formidable and fascinating talker I've met since Dick, with one quality that Dick, rest his bones, wholly lacked. When they could get a word in, Nat regarded other people's stories as interesting in their own right, rather than mere interruptions of his own Grand Narration.

Nat stands about six and a half feet tall with the deceptively skinny build of an old-time tennis pro. I soon learned that, even at sixty-six, he was a maniacal wader of fast currents. He was also a prodigious caster and has caught just about every kind of fish from giant tuna in Nova Scotia to grass carp from golf-course ponds at Hobe Sound. He had been in air force intelligence, hence his discourse on nuclear targeting, and also a deputy secretary of the interior under Presidents Nixon and Ford. He was a hero to bird-watchers for preserving the breeding grounds used by whooping cranes in Texas. In 1977, he had abandoned his trial-balloon candidacy for governor of Florida, shortly after and for all I know partly because of my acerbic campaign profile of him in the *St. Petersburg Times.* He can tell you about condor nesting and wowed the Russian government ichthyologist stationed at our fishing camp on the Ponoi River with his knowledge of the microscopic growth rings on salmon scales.

In the days ahead, I was to discover that Nat has a quality often attributed in print to various Americans of patrician birth but seldom encountered in the flesh. With curiosity and easy sincerity, he can talk to anyone—a fishing guide, a carpenter, a scientist, a corporation president—about *what they know* and seem perfectly content. I regard him as the second most voraciously curious man I have ever known, the first being Tennant's father, Richebourg McWilliams, the scholarly professor I once caught interviewing a concrete pourer on a hot Birmingham street about the importance of joints in a sidewalk.

The subarctic landscape below our helicopter was low and monotonous, but not trackless. It was crisscrossed with trails. When I noticed Nat shouting in my direction, I removed an earplug and heard him say, "Reindeer trails."

"Where are the reindeer?" I shouted back.

"This time of year they've all migrated down to the coast.

The mosquitoes drive them crazy if they stay in the middle of the peninsula during warm weather."

"Isn't that where we're going?" I asked.

"Yes," said Nat, pulling a head net from the pocket of his shirt. "That's why I always carry this."

The fishing gods are so perverse. From the Arctic Circle to Belize, everywhere there are fish, they have conspired to plant mosquitoes by the billions. Mosquitoes school up with particular intensity along shorelines hospitable to salmon and bonefish. The mosquito, like the hedgehog, knows one big thing. To complete the reproductive task that is the sole mission of its short life, it must drink mammal blood. Human skin, needless to say, is easier to penetrate than reindeer or jaguar hide. So any *Homo sapiens* traipsing through the tundra or the aptly named Mosquito Coast of Central America is assured of a speedy welcome. There are some humans, of course, whose body chemistry serves to repel mosquitoes. I, by contrast, appear to strike mosquitoes of all continents as the buggy equivalent of beluga caviar. I dilate on mosquitoes by way of passing along a tip to fellow blood donors. Before this trip, another uptown doctor, Albert Lefkovitz, Dermatologist to the Supermodels and Somewhat Older Upper East Side Ladies Who Lunch, started me on vitamin B1. It causes a skin odor that moved me from a solid ten to a six or seven in terms of desirability to flying bloodsuckers.

Our helicopter rattled down to a landing pad on a gray sandy plateau that overlooked the river from a height of 150 feet or so. Below us, along the outside of a slow curve of river, lay a tidy camp arrayed in bright northern colors—white tents, green treetops, red fire barrels, red outhouses, red mess hall, red supply shed. All the salmon veterans, including two massive Scots who lacked only blue war paint to qualify as extras in *Braveheart,* headed for the home pool to cast until supper. Home Pool at the Ponoi camp is generally regarded as one of the best places on the globe for salmon. Guests who don't get enough fishing during the day can stay up all night wading the home pool if they choose, and some do.

After the various levels of decadence and decay on display in Moscow, St. Petersburg and Murmansk, this looked like good country for being alone. Of all the things sought by an angler in modern times, the hardest to find—more elusive than the shyest fish—is the enchantment of solitude. The company of anglers is the salt of the sport. Solitude is its pepper, needed in smaller amounts, to be sure, but essential to its sum and substance. As to what it is we seek on the solitary stream, for years I've liked these lines from an otherwise forgettable poem by William Herrick about fly fishing in the Catskills.

> *Down by the River*
> *a man and a boy*
> *down among the bones of the old years,*
> *looking for each other*
> *in the ruins of a river's time*

As a man moves through his mid-fifties, he comes to see that the gray-haired fly fisher and the boy who seek each other along time's stony, flowing river are one and the same being. Even if the river is in Russia, you must enter it alone to visit the boy you used to be. I was sure I would find him in *le zone à l'ombre*. My plan to venture across its subarctic borders brought me into almost immediate conflict with the sporting protocols of Mother Russia.

After dumping my gear in my tent and pulling on my waders, I strolled down the sandy main street of our tent camp, my trout rod in my hand and my heart full of unsociable hope. I couldn't tell if the sky was overcast or if the sun was simply riding below the ridges that girded the low, bowl-like basin where the camp lay. Up on top of the globe in the summer, the sun doesn't arc over so much as swing around you, like the pendulum of a great clock. In keeping with my age, I had commenced trying of late to affect the deliberative calm of those fishermen who avoid the frothing herd in the pursuit of some idiosyncratic pleasure. I had read somewhere that grayling fishing on the Ponoi and its tributaries was an unexplored resource. So this was a rare chance to up my lifetime grayling count from its present modest status—none—and also avoid the competitive slashing that I envisioned on Home Pool. Near the rod rack outside the dining tent, I ran into the head guide, Alex Kojajev, a compact fellow with the impassive expression of a Red Army fire-control officer. I asked him the way to the best grayling water.

"But we are here for salmon!" he said fiercely, hitting the last words like a drum in a Russian symphony—sahllll-mahhhhnn.

The Russians, it turns out, have quickly adapted to the evangelical attitude perfected by snobbier members of the Atlantic Salmon Federation. There is only one fish worth pursuing. It is *Salmo salar.* Only a dolt cares for anything else.

But in my new way of walking—the seasoned fisherman calmly following my own aesthetic map—I resolved to stand up to the guy. I was not about to be intimidated. Hey, I'm the one paying six thousand dollars a week and risking death by helicopter.

"I intend to catch a grayling today," I said firmly. "Salmon tomorrow."

"Up the tributary there are grayling," he said in the international intonation of a guide who, having been disobeyed, is offering minimal information.

So be it, I thought. We can play it that way. I persisted until I found out that a half mile up the road I'd find a hill. It was more a hump than a hill, but the tributary, called the Purnach, was an east-running stream that tumbled along with the promising look of a medium-size Montana trout river. The Purnach joins the larger Ponoi on the perpendicular, defining one leg of the wedge of land that holds the camp. The Purnach has cut its course through bedrock that stands in angular bluffs at some points and has been reduced in other places to descending fields of jumbled boulders. In color, the water reminded me of streams in Florida. It was clear but tannin-stained, like Burnt Mill Creek. No fish were splashing, another reminder of Burnt Mill; this river was a blank blackboard daring me to write a formula that made sense. Relying on a core tactic of the world's far-flung fly-

fishing tribe (and on a little reading I had done back home), I tied
on a Royal Wulff and began casting to likely runs and pockets.

I fished a long, tubular slide of uncommunicative water along
a grassy bank. I took a brown trout of about twelve inches, a silvery fish with none of the yellow and red custom touches of its
North American cousins. This was a no-nonsense gray-and-silver
fish in a gray-and-silver world of rock, birch bark, stone and ice.
I was not impressed, for I was in the throes of grayling hype, a
promotional mode that reaches its grandest expression in Clive
Gammon's splendid book, *I Know a Good Place*:

> The grayling is a fish romantic enough to make you lose
> your head—a member of the salmonidae, an ancient, ice-
> haunting species left behind twelve thousand years ago
> when the glaciers of the Pleistocene retreated after gouging
> out lakes and river valleys. It is a clean, cold fish that is less
> tolerant of pollution than any other member of the salmon
> family. French ecologists classify the uppermost reaches of a
> river, where the water is unpolluted, as *le zone à l'ombre*, the
> grayling region, and the first sign of deterioration in a stream
> is the disappearance of grayling from the fast water they
> favor. There are not many around these days.

Even in the worshipful state induced by Gammon's tribute, I
could not get it out of my mind that this mythic ice-haunting
salmonid would look like the humble creek chub save for the
rainbow-hued dorsal fin that waves like a banner above its back.
Granted, it was a mysterious minnow, but I think the appeal of
the mission lay in the habitat, the uppermost reaches, *le zone à
l'ombre* itself.

For it came to me there, as I fished without event up the boul-
dered bed of the Purnach, that I had been fishing in crowds all my
life. Even in big places, from the Gulf of Mexico to the Rockies,
"having it to myself" was a rare experience. At any moment
another boat would zoom into view or another fisherman come
ambling out of the forest. The water is crowded everywhere

these days. I'm not one of those fly fishers who bitch about the legions of Orvis-clad, Sage-waving neophytes flooding into the sport. In the States, our unifying mission has to be saving rivers, and anywhere on the globe, the only way to save a river, in the political sense, is to share it.

Still, a dose of Wordsworthian solitude is good for the soul, not to mention a temporary balm to the genetic selfishness that is our lost heritage as territorial primates. As a matter of theory and actual practice, I'm generous when it comes to sharing water. But like most trout fishermen in the Eastern United States, I'm always secretly gratified when I find my favorite hole vacant and a little irritated when another angler sticks his head out of the bushes. So in this mosquito-humming wilderness, I had something almost impossible to find in the land of the free. I had an entire river system to myself. Search as I might, I could not find another footprint on my river's marshy rim. I could not spy a beer can or even a single cigarette filter lodged among the stones. There was zero chance that the salmon-crazed Americans, English, Scots and Russians down on the home pool of the Ponoi were going to contest my title to the Purnach.

There was just me, the river, which presumably harbored these lusted-for salmonid minnows, and, suddenly, the caddis flies. On any continent, a caddis hatch is unmistakable. The little brown buggers skitter along the surface, popping up, then down, flailing their four wings in accidental imitation of those pedal-driven biplanes you see in the history-of-flight documentaries. Everywhere I've ever been, if a caddis fly skitters too slowly, it gets eaten, and this global ritual was taking place when I arrived at what turned out to be the stream's best pool. A modest waterfall plunged there into a cliff-wrapped basin. Fish rose. I traded in my Royal Wulff for a *cul de canard* caddis and cast. A number of eighteen-inch grayling bit and came to hand. I inspected their ostentatious, bespeckled, sail-like dorsal fins, their purpled flanks, their slightly carplike mouths, their deeply astounded eyes. I caught a half dozen bingo-bango. Then, just like that, the bite was over. The caddis flies were still skittering, but the fish were down. I rested the pool, thinking they were a little spooked. But there was something else going on. I had fished enough in the last half of the twentieth century to know that these fish were finished.

So I hiked through the crepuscular light and the vast Russian emptiness toward my tidy tent, a contented man who had defied the head guide and fished according to his own desires. I recalled the self-help book I had picked up during a miserable London winter ten years before. "Try to figure out what you want to do and do it." Following the advice had led to a divorce and other disruptions. I had found a modest, calmer kind of self-indulgence here. Upon rereading Clive Gammon, I would even recall the reason the fish quit hitting so promptly at 11:00 p.m. He reported that the same thing happened to him on a Finnish river at about the same latitude. His guide said that grayling "have to sleep even though the sun never sets."

On most rivers in the world, of course, the sun rises and the sun sets. There is nothing new under it, and one of the few things you can control is the number of casts you make in the years that lie between the boy you will always be in the mirror of memory, and the surprising and surprised gray-haired man who peers back from the shaving mirror.

He's a shy one, the remembered boy who lives down among the bones of old years, and comes out when there are only the two of you and the fish and the water, the earth's clear blood, which runs toward you, around you, binding you back into one, then goes on, bearing all things away, without malice or relent, carrying alike the dry fly that lands lightly on the water, the fish rising in the current and the fisherman's years, the numerate weight of a given life, one life, your one life, rushing by. How can we make ourselves grasp this, my brothers and sisters? It is all and always *rushing by*.

CHAPTER 29

Four Aspects
of Russian Salmon Fishing

I. CALM, RATIONAL FEAR

Before our first full day on the river, there was to be an orientation in the dining tent by Mariusz Wróblewski, the genial and handsome trilingual fly-fishing Pole who managed the Ponoi camp for its American owners. He started by revealing the conditions under which we were to be strewn up and down the river in pairs, sometimes by boat and sometimes by air. Afloat, we were safely in the hands of Dogpatch technology, cruising up and down the river in big aluminum johnboats made in Arkansas. Russian technology ruled the air, and Mariusz didn't hide what he really thought.

"Russian helicopter is really dangerous," he said. "Try to leave it and enter it with your guide. Make eye contact with the pilot, and he will direct you. Never walk around the rear, where the rotor is, because that is where most accidents occur with this terrible machine."

There, in the umbrageous light of the white canvas dining tent, I made myself a solemn promise that while I would fly up and down the river, I would never under any circumstances go near the rotor. I would try at all times to maintain eye contact with the pilot. I had no further questions because, luckily, at this time I had not yet heard the story of Pinky's levitation. Also, at the time Mariusz spoke, I was several weeks away from meeting the

207

beautiful Communist princess from Silesia and therefore had no reason to suspect that his view of the terrible machines may have been colored by a generalized, inbred Polish loathing for all things Soviet and, in particular, for anything Russians describe as safe or reliable.

It is true that, on our flight from Murmansk, I had observed during a refueling stop at a remote reindeer camp that the pump attendant held a burning cigarette in his lips and fanned his face with a leafy branch while he filled the tanks. I was, as it happened, sitting directly inboard from the saddle tank he was filling. I observed him through the scratch-hazed Plexiglas window. Only after bolting from the helicopter did I learn that the combination of cigarette smoke and the waving branch was a standard operating procedure for keeping the mosquitoes away from one's eyes. I stood far from the plane and let the mosquitoes gnaw on me while the gentleman completed his task.

There was no explosion that day, and it would be another eight years before I heard the tale of two fly fishers from Alabama who came to Ponoi for the salmon. Supposedly, they won general praise for, first, bolting from the helicopter just before the explosion and, second, chasing down the pump guy and rolling him in the tundra until his clothing and hair were extinguished. I heard this on the fly-fishing grapevine and cannot therefore vouch that it is correct in every detail, but believe me, it could have happened.

One thing I did learn on my own in the course of flying up and down the river during the next week, and I'm happy to share it. Your pilot is not in interested in eye contact if he knows what he's doing. His eyes are on the engine-heat gauge that is the best indicator of whether you are going to stay airborne. If he lifts off before that gauge hits 85 or 90 percent of optimum engine temperature, you can probably kiss *your* ass good-bye.

II. The Economics of Optimism

Western fly fishers discovered the Kola Peninsula during the heady days of glasnost, when Mikhail Gorbachev's regime eased travel restrictions in the area around Murmansk, since World War II a strategic and highly restricted city in the Soviet defense system. The peninsula takes its name from the Kola River, the first of several streams found to have heavy runs of salmon each summer. These fish were discovered just as the salmon runs on the storied rivers of Canada and Scotland were being wiped out by offshore commercial fishing. In addition, the healthier rivers of Norway and Iceland were becoming expensive, even by the extreme standards of the global fly-fishing community. Soon word circulated that other rivers on the peninsula—the Kharlovka, the Varzuga, the Ponoi—were even better than the Kola. The Soviet government recognized that these rivers could be turned into a source of currency brought in by a breed of hard-spending tourists who arrived with fly rods, American dollars and British pounds sterling. Moscow closed the rivers to commercial fishing, and Soviet game wardens appeared to be making headway against the traditional poaching by hungry inhabitants of the thinly populated peninsula. Then the government began awarding franchises for fishing camps along the rivers. This led, quickly, to the salmon wars of the '80s and '90s.

Western investors, local politicians and the Russian mafia began competing for fishing rights. People and places were bought that wouldn't stay bought. Lawsuits were filed, and sometimes more direct action took place. American fishermen as eminent as the late Jack Hemingway, Tom Brokaw and Nat Reed were chased from some rivers at gunpoint as the contending parties, foreign and indigenous, asserted their rights to fleece the richest tourists seen in that part of Russia since the Revolution.

Confusion reigned during this period of transition as Russians perfected their system of armed kleptocapitalism. Then things got sorted out. Money found the places it needed to go, in both Moscow and Murmansk. Local pride and international fiscal principles found a balance point. Americans got some rivers. Brits, Finns and Scandinavians got some, and Russians got some, too.

By the mid-'90s, it looked as if this last best stronghold of the Atlantic salmon was going to be protected by a new, money-driven environmental consciousness that had taken tender root in the cold soil of one of history's most remorseless polluter nations. By the time I arrived, optimism abounded. Some of the world's best guides—notably young Americans and weathered Scots—were spending two or three months a year guiding sports along the Kola rivers. As a matter of community relations, the American owners of the camp where I fished made a special effort to recruit and train Russian guides. Soon these young Russians could meet the exacting standards of clients who fish everywhere from New Zealand to Bimini.

Mariusz Wróblewski and his guides beamed as he told our assembled group about the dawning of a new day in environmental protection. It was part of "changing Russia to an entirely different country, making Russia part of the world community that is trying to save the unique places in the world. We believe Ponoi is one of the most unique."

III. THE INTERNATIONAL CODE OF FISH WEIGHTS

My guide for the first day was the star of the new Russian guiding crew, Max Mamayev, a tall, blond guy in his twenties with rough-hewn English, considerable charm and a knowledge of fly fishing approaching that of the imported guides. His feel for the local rivers surpassed theirs since they had been his training ground. Max made it clear that a kid wanting to learn fly fishing in the old USSR had to be a bootstrapper.

"There are maybe thirty fly fishermen in St. Petersburg," he said of his hometown. "I know them all."

He anchored our boat in the Purnach beat, at the junction of my grayling river and the larger Ponoi. He explained that the camp owners had spotted him when he was in the area on vacation. They saw him ripping out long, furling casts on the public water near Murmansk and hired him more or less on the spot.

Max rummaged in my fly box and came out with a big, dumb-looking Mickey Finn, the Model A Ford of all salmon flies and the last one I would have picked in this exotic place of yellow-streaked cliffs and thermal-hopping gyrfalcons.

"Big male salmon hit big flies, like territory defending," Max said.

Damned if he wasn't right. My boat partner, Amos Eno of Freeport, Maine, and I were high rods for the day, with nine and eight fish respectively. This was a smashing day of salmon fishing, and Max demonstrated an intuitive grasp of the most fundamental rule of client management.

"Twelve pounds," he said after my best fish of the morning.

I caught another a little later on and asked about its size.

"I'd say about twelve pounds also," Max said.

Then near the end of the day, we anchored where a nook in the shoreline and a big boulder at the edge of the main current protected a flat piece of holding water that proved to be stacked with fish. Amos and I had already caught several there when I had a long hard pull. I waited the proper time, then struck, had the fish for the briefest moment, then it was off. I left the fly in the water, and the creature came back and loaded up for good this time.

The first of four leaps showed it clearly to be the fish of the day. In the midst of the salmon's thrashing, the drag of my sturdy but worn Orvis DXR reel quit dragging. I compensated by palming the rim of the spool, and after ten minutes or so we had the salmon in the net. It was an exceptionally hard-fighting fish and bigger than anything we had caught so far on this very good day.

Max was hanging over the side of the boat, reviving the salmon by pushing it back and forth in the water. When I guessed the fish at fifteen, he turned his face up to me with a broad, knowing smile.

"No, but this fish really would weigh twelve pounds," he said.

Together we watched the salmon swim away in the truthful brown current. As good a fisherman as he was, I decided, Max still had a lot to learn.

I began casting again. In a few minutes, as if to himself, Max said softly, "Maybe thirteen, fourteen pounds."

I looked at him with expanded admiration. He puttered innocently with some flies, not meeting my glance. After only a few weeks of collecting tips from American anglers, he had discovered that the relationship between fact and fiction in fishing is capitalistic. That is why salmon grow so fast when you interrupt their swimming in the river of forgetfulness.

IV. THE CENTRALITY OF MANNERS

Dick Blalock had been dead over three years by the time I got to the Ponoi, and to tell you the truth, I was only just starting to really miss him. It was not because I wanted to share the fishing with him. He liked smaller fish, closer to home. Alaska had offended him with its brawling rivers and big rainbows that gorged on the eggs and flesh of dying salmon. Russian fishing had some of those same raw qualities. I think I started missing Dick in Russia because he was becoming ever more dim in my memory. Right after someone dies, his presence remains very strong in your mind. You can still summon the feeling of being in that person's company, the way he looked or laughed. But after a few years, the sounds and pictures fade. Perhaps it was fishing with Nat Reed—a somewhat older man who had fished longer than I and done it better—that set me to thinking of Dick. I enjoyed fishing with both men for the same reason. Each had impeccable manners on the stream.

The twentieth century ended and the twenty-first announced itself with a savage decline in civility, at least in the city I was forced to think about most in my line of work, that being Washington, D.C. It saddened me as a Southerner to say that the aspect of manners most identified with the region, gallantry, reached its nadir in the Clinton White House. George W. Bush and various presidents have misused the FBI, NSA and IRS, but never before have White House defamation experts been turned loose to do their worst to women suspected of rendering random sexual kindnesses to the president over a period of thirty years. Of course, Arkansas has always been the most inelegant corner of the South. I can't believe an Alabamian and even a Mississippian would have behaved so badly toward the various Paulas, Monicas, beauty queens and personal assistants to be found around any campaign that's likely to win. The aforementioned James Elisha Folsom well deserved the nickname Kissin' Jim. But when aides wanted him to expose a woman of low degree hired by opponents to catch him in flagrante, Governor Folsom knew where to place the blame. "Boys," he said, "if they use that bait, they'll catch old Jim every time."

The Clintons may have lacked social graces, but they did have a social conscience. The dazzling commonness of the Bushes in this regard beats anything I ever expected to see. If generations of wealth and education in the best schools cannot produce a smidgen of nobility in a family, what's the point? The elder Bush was simply myopic when it came to less fortunate citizens. This younger Bush and his minions meet a needful world with a combination of Eastern snobbery and Texas brutality. Their response to the poor, the lame, the dark of skin is to ignore them, as Hurricane Katrina showed, or otherwise to tax them, convert them, enlist them or electrocute them.

Thinking such thoughts is, of course, one of the ways you know you're getting older. Older people always think civility is in decline. Sometimes they may even be right. What made Dick's civility as a fisherman so striking was his lack of competitiveness. With Nat, it was the absence of greed. I became aware of this when he told me a surprising thing. Although he was the strongest wader of fast water with whom I had ever fished, Nat said he didn't have much time left to fish the big, dangerous waters in places like Russia and Argentina. He was cramming in as much hard fishing as he could before his body failed him. Yet his sense of urgency had, if anything, sharpened his observance of angling protocols.

Take the day our guide pulled the boat ashore where a little trout stream bounced out of a small canyon to join the big river. At the confluence there was a pretty green glen in which to have lunch. Amos and I were fishing that day with Alexei, formerly a Lada mechanic in St. Petersburg. He was a man who knew how to pick his specialities. If Russia has more of anything than salmon, it is broken Ladas. Alexei was building a fire for tea outside a tent that the lodge had erected in this pleasant spot. We were waiting for Nat and his guide to join us. It was developing into a good day for a tent, as a morning mist began congealing into a fine rain. While we were waiting for the other boat, I spotted a salmon moving in the shallows just below where the creek entered the river. The fish appeared no more than seventy-five feet down the stream from our picnic spot. I fetched my rod from the boat and walked downstream to work the fish. One of my first casts moved the fish, but it turned away from the fly. This happened just before Nat and his guide, a personable young fellow from Chattanooga named Mac McGee, came around the bend and grounded their boat beside ours.

Nat comes down to chat, and he amiably takes my rod to show me how to mend line more effectively. He knows that I am new to salmon fishing. Being unusually generous for a fly fisher of his attainments, he means to help. He has no way of knowing about the fish resting downstream. Being a Southerner cornered by his good intentions, I am, of course, too polite to tell him that he has interrupted me while I was working a fish.

Nat makes a demonstration cast, and suddenly, a fish—*my fish*—appears again. It comes at my fly, which is attached to my rod, which ought to be but is not in my hand. The fish misses the fly but leaves a finely tied question of etiquette bobbing in its ripples.

Under accepted rules, this is my fish, since I raised it first. Unfortunately, I am the only one in possession of the full facts, which I had not declared. To invoke my rightful primacy now would look like an effort to chisel Nat out of a fish he thinks *he* raised.

"Here, you catch him," Nat says, offering me the rod.

"No," I say, "you raised it."

"You were here first. It's your spot," he says.

"No, go ahead. I insist. You moved the fish," I say.

"Really, *I* insist. I would rather watch you catch him."

So it went, back and forth. Finally Nat's superior generosity, along with the fact that I knew I had found the fish before his arrival, wore me down. I took the rod, and twice more the fish rushed the fly without striking.

"What fly do you have?" asked Mac the guide.

Salmon flies have elaborate histories and formal names: the Jock Scott, the Highlander, the Alley Shrimp. I hadn't a clue about the fly the guide had attached to my line.

"A blue-and-white one," I said. "The same shade of blue that came on the nineteen sixty-nine Chevrolet Impala."

"At last, Alabama's gift to salmon fishing," Nat said, laughing. "The Impala fly."

Mac gave me a white muddler minnow with a lot of silver sparkle wrapped around the shank of the hook. "A guy in Pennsylvania ties these especially for the Ponoi," he said.

Then, to my surprise, Mac overruled Nat as to where I should be standing for the next cast. He moved me closer to the fish, so that the fly would sweep across its nose from a different angle. Nat and I were chatting, and I did not have my eye on the fly when the fish came again and, in the way of the species, hooked itself. The fish raced out of the shoaly flat along the shore, hit the center current of the river and did a to-the-right march toward the distant sea. Line whizzed from the reel. The fish went deeply into the backing and seemed unstoppable.

"A very hot fish," Nat said. "If I were you, I would move about fifty yards downstream as fast as you can."

I was dubious but obedient. Nat had spotted a current nook and calculated that, by changing the direction of the line pressure, I would be able to lead the fish toward this deep eddy.

Once it hit that spot, the fish settled down for a tough but manageable fight. I remember thinking specifically that this was the sort of moment I had envisioned without being able to visualize precisely when I decided to get as much of the world's good fishing as possible in whatever time I have left on this earth. So here I was, on one of the world's best salmon rivers, being coached by one of the world's best salmon fishermen.

As the fish came into Mac's net, I thought of how much the moment told about the underlying tension of difficult fishing. In our tales we exalt the fish that does the extreme or unexpected thing. Yet all our guile—like Nat's recommendation to dash down the bank—is directed toward getting these powerful creatures to follow the predictable, instinctive habits that will defeat them.

I felt for the dumb salmon as it lunged and circled, lunged and circled in its desire to escape. In the deep, slow water along the rocky verge of the river, each effortful lunge brought it closer to the landing net. If the fish had kept riding the powerful main current down the center of the stream, it could have spooled me. Instead, it opted to swing into what looked like safer water, just as Nat had known it would. A similar phenomenon may be observed among the more cunning creatures who indulge in war or politics. Victories in life may be shaped by strategy, by plans or even by dreams, but what looks promising can mutate into defeat when our instinctive strategies lead us toward the net.

Mac had the fish out of the net and held it up to be photographed.

"Ten pounds?" I said.

"Eight or nine," Mac said. Then he adjusted upward as he lifted the fish to be photographed. "Maybe ten."

We took some pictures and he had the fish in the water, making sure it was ready to swim on its own again.

"This fish feels heavier than I thought," he said. "Could go eleven." This smoothly calibrated expansion of truth was reassuring. Good Tennessean that he was, Mac, too, had remembered his manners.

CHAPTER 30

Snapshot VI:
A First Sighting of the Great Blalock
and His Expandable Fly Box,
March 1989

Dick Blalock had gotten fat in the way of former athletes, which is to say that he had become rotund without becoming clumsy. His belly preceded him through the world like those wave-breaking bulbs on the prows of ocean freighters. His balding head was wreathed around with puffs of white hair. For a man of his age, he had surprisingly smooth skin and rosy cheeks. You could picture him as an inflated cherub on a Renaissance ceiling or as someone who could have done quite well as the Santa Claus at Bloomingdale's. Now that I think about it, if you put him in Bermuda shorts and crepe-soled shoes, he could also have passed for the Man from Ohio. But in full battle dress for a day of fly fishing—voluminous waders, vest bedangled with hemostats, thermometer and spools of tippet, Patagonia sweatshirt, wading staff and tweed tam-o'-shanter—he was an arresting sight, which I first beheld on a cold, sunny day in March when we journeyed north from Washington to fish the Yellow Breeches near Boiling Springs, Pennsylvania.

As Blalock glided toward the stream with the stride of the agile fat man, his fly rod, clasped in a meaty fist, looked like a splinter. And there, perched atop that plateau of a belly, was what appeared to be a small accordion, held in place by a web of elastic straps and shiny steel snaps. It was, in fact, a six-layer fly box. The box opened to form a succession of trays, horizontal to the ground, every tray rimmed and lined with black material like a portable magician's table. Each tray held several hundred tiny flies, arranged in the frank rows of a military formation. All had been personally tied by Dick Blalock. In a world where time is money, my new fishing friend was clearly a man with time to burn.

I remember the day quite distinctly, both for what I learned and for the unaccustomed feeling that came to me as we drove across the Monocacy plains to Frederick, Maryland, whence we took Highway 15 north toward Gettysburg. The surprising feeling I had was one of sympathy for Robert E. Lee. We were following the very road that carried him to years of sullen retirement, brooding about what might have been if Jeb Stuart's cavalry had been on time and Longstreet had not let him down among all those damnably well-tended fields around Gettysburg, fields where the stolid generations of rock-stacking Germans built fence rows for connivers to hide behind. This is the Lee for whom one could feel a twinge of sorrow, his heart failing, finishing out his years as a mere college president. He must have been exactly as Donald Davidson portrayed him in the poem "Lee in the Mountains," surrounded now by rich schoolboys in the place of the raggedy soldiers who worshipped him in fierce denial of the logic that might have saved their lives. "The young have time to wait," this Lee mutters to himself. "And I am spent with old wars and new sorrow. . . . Was it for this / That on an April day we stacked our arms . . . And was I then betrayed? Did I betray?" This, as I say, was the Lee for whom I could summon some pity, but only a little bit.

He was, after all, a man who owned flat fields of cotton and cannon, and I am a hillbilly boy, bred in the bone and in the blood of those lads upon whom those cannons were meant to feed. In my day, starting in the first grade, the white schoolchildren of Alabama were asked each year to venerate an ever more

grandiose retelling of Lee's life. For my part, I took him as a political idiot the moment I heard the teachers say, in praise, that he
regarded loyalty to his home state, Virginia, as more important
than loyalty to the American nation. By simply looking around
Alabama, I could tell that a state was a piddling thing. Later, we
were told that Lee's battle plans were still studied at West Point.
Why, I wondered. He lost. All these thoughts were appropriate
for a descendant of the outlier Hiram Raines and the loud-
mouthed Lincolnite Hial Abbott, who received $178 from the fed-
eral government in 1872 for providing recruits and fodder to the
Union Army during the war. But I did not know the details of
Hiram's life or Hial's at the time I decided, based on my private
analysis of historical facts as related in the state-approved text-
books of Alabama, not to worship Robert E. Lee.

Yet even for me, the manicured pastures and orchards and
flowing turnpikes of northern Maryland invited a less hateful
understanding of what seduced Marse Robert. It was perfect
terrain for an army driven by honor and led by a general with
absolute faith in cataclysmic offensive warfare to pick a fight.
Given his nature, there was no way for Lee to resist crossing the
Potomac into such a country, first for Antietam and then for Gettysburg. The land itself pulled him in. Lee might have won at
Antietam if a carelessly discarded copy of his battle plan had not
fallen into Union hands. With an advantage like that, even
McClellan, the Union commander renowned for staying in
camp, was willing to fight. I once worked with a reporter who was
a lineal descendant of Lee's aide-de-camp. I used to torment him
by speculating that it was his great-grandpappy who dropped
Bobby Lee's battle plan on the dusty Maryland road where the
blue skirmishers found it. After Antietam, McClellan enraged
Lincoln by refusing to pursue Lee's retreating army into Virginia.
A year later, Lee came across the Potomac again, and the favor-
able terrain led him all the way to Gettysburg.

There he met, in Meade, a general who was less fond of staying in camp and who knew how to position his boys behind
fences and ditches and hilltops. *C'est la guerre,* say the old folks. It

goes to show you never could tell Robert E. Lee a damn thing about charging across open ground.

My ruminations on the war that day were private. This was the first of many fishing trips we were to make together over the next few years, and what I was hearing from Dick was a nonstop narrative of the purported facts of his life. I learned that Dick, as a freshman, played football for Bud Wilkinson at Oklahoma, back in the time when there were 180-pound guards on major college teams. After dropping out of college, he had been an infantryman in the Korean War and then stayed on in the army to attend OCS. Then, like many a fly fisherman of his generation, he may or may not have been a spy while serving as an officer in army intelligence in Germany and later as a foreign service officer at American embassies in the Middle East. He was thirty-seven when the State Department insisted on retiring him with full benefits after he contracted an intestinal disorder in South Yemen. He protested the truncation of his career to no avail.

"So I decided that if they were so determined to pay me not to work, I'd take advantage of the opportunity and go fishing for a while," Dick said. Therein was the key to the life of leisure that enabled Dick to pursue fly fishing with the dedication of an artisan. For the past seventeen years, he had lived the life of 3-weight rods, razor-blade line splices and feathers twirled onto hooks smaller than a surgeon's stitch. It was a rich man's life based on a poor man's luck. At a time when ten to twelve hours in the Washington bureau was a short day, having that kind of leisure seemed an impossible luxury. In his place, I would have spent less of that time obsessively tying flies and arranging them in rows, but that's a matter of taste. For a work-haunted man in his mid-forties, Dick's example raised a couple of questions. Why did so few people approaching retirement look forward to having time on their hands? And why did so very few, once they had it, use it to do what Dick Blalock did, which was what he damn well pleased for as long as he wanted to?

CHAPTER 31

The Feeling We Seek on All Waters

Even nowadays down South and out West, you'll hear older people talk about "carrying the difference." It means having a gun concealed on one's person. In rough old days, the saying underscored the importance of distinguishing between a man who could be trifled with and one who couldn't, and the abrupt difference—arbitrary, irreducible and surprising—between success and failure in certain circumstances.

Fishing, as it happens, is full of categorical divisions.

There is nothing more sharply divided than catching fish and not catching them. As the British writer Arthur Ransome said back in the days of relentless fish killing, "The difference between a basket containing a brace of fish and a basket containing none at all in it is an absolute, not a relative difference."

In fishing, what makes the difference between success and failure so maddening is that its cause takes an infinitude of forms. Sometimes the difference has to do with location, whether you are trying too close to shore when you should be out in the middle of a stream, for example. Sometimes it has to do with equipment— say, a sinking line over a floating line. Sometimes it has to do with technique, fishing your fly dead-drift rather than manipulating it.

Here's the killing part. Every location, every piece of equipment, every technique is right sometime, somewhere. There are even certain golden days when several approaches work. But on many days, there is only one right approach and an endless selection of perfectly reasonable alternatives that will not produce, no matter how earnestly or artistically you apply them.

This part of fishing is mystifying to novices. "What's the difference?" they demand when you tell them they must fish in one place, not another or with one fly and not another. After all, on most streams and lakes, one spot looks as good as another, and all flies and lures look equally implausible. There is no sensible answer to the perfectly reasonable question of why A and not B, beyond what everyone who fishes must learn. These creatures we seek may not be smart, but they are picky.

This fact brings out my obsessive side. When I'm not catching fish, I'm constantly thinking about what would make a difference, what tiny adjustment I could make that would alter my fishlessness. I know that the universe contains a single fact of singular, unmitigated potency for this situation, and that until I discover it, my state of plenary deprivation will continue unabated. Now that I think about it, maybe this turn of mind is another of the reasons I stuck with newspapering so long. You can rock along following the routine of surface events or you can make each day a quest for causation, a chance to discover what's really happening and to divine what's really needed.

I dwell on the frustration of being on the dark side of the difference in fishing by way of defining the soaring, shuddering, climactic, altogether illogical perfection one feels on figuring out the solution on any given day. At the moment of discovery, what a feeling of pure triumph! Part of the sweetness is the transience of the feeling. Today's discovery counts for nothing toward what tomorrow might bring. For the moment, the answer is here, wrapped all around you, then gone aglimmering, rushing into your past as rivers rush to sea and a falling tide to the remote, unknowable center of the ocean.

Or something like that.

Anyway, I encountered the difference on what was to be my favorite day on the Ponoi. I was fishing alone with Ned Bowler, a young Californian who was guiding his last season before going home to marry his girlfriend and teach English at a prep school in

Ojai. We had a pleasant day of book talk, but after taking an eight-pound fish at around eleven in the morning, things went dead until almost three o'clock. Ned was changing my flies constantly. As a result, he had to replace my tippet. I had been using a transparent colorless Maxima monofilament. I have always had a bias in favor of clear, untinted leaders. Ned had Maxima as well, but in the brown-tinted version the company designed for stained water. He put the brown tippet on my leader.

Within minutes, I had a strike, and it turned out to be the fish of the trip in every way. We hooked it in the center of a magnificent sweep of river, and it ran upstream against the current, ripping a long, current-bent skein of line from the reel and then shattering the glazed surface in a leap that let us see its size and freshness. It was the biggest fish I had hooked on the Ponoi and by far the strongest.

The struggle lasted thirty minutes, and finally Ned decided to beach the boat, so that we could follow the fish on foot along a series of shoreline rapids. At last, I was able to pull it close in a deep, still, boulder-rimmed eddy, and Ned stretched full length on the shore and plunged his arms deep into the water, well past the elbows, and cradled the fish ashore. We measured this one so there'd be no guessing. According to the formula for converting length and girth into a reasonably accurate weight estimate, it went eighteen pounds.

Afterward, I needed to replace the tippet again, since the fish had frayed it badly. I asked Ned if I should use the clear Maxima that I had in my vest.

"I don't think it makes any difference," he said.

But we fished for a half hour with no luck, which was my just dessert. I had violated the most fundamental of all rules about fishing. Never change something that works, even in a small detail, for in making the change, you may be destroying the difference that, in this case, is operating in your advantage.

"Ned," I said after a while, "I've gotten superstitious about this clear leader. Let's go back to your brown leader."

We both agreed that the leader color should not really matter, given the color of the water and what our experience had been with these fish all week. Then we made the change, and within minutes, I had another strike, a fish that showed itself in two magnificent leaps to be as big as or bigger than the first. It fought just as adamantly as the first fish, but after twenty-five minutes, it was tired enough for the slow, close pulling the outdoor magazine hacks call "slugging it out." Indeed, salmon do have a head-shaking motion that, when telegraphed up the line and into the rod, calls to mind the ponderous but dangerous blows that weary heavyweights throw in the late rounds. You can see a big salmon sort of hump up when it shakes its head against the pull of the leader. There is something slow, monarchic and altogether somber about this movement. The creature is fighting for its life, and that fact is shaming to the other beings who are there merely for fun.

Many fish are lost at such moments. This one was. Ned and I were alone in the supreme beat of the Ponoi. There are usually big fish in it, and you can watch peregrine falcons in the cliffs along the northern side of this beat. It is called the Tomba Beat after a river that stair-steps into the Ponoi from the north. The Tomba looks like the sort of stream where a man could do serious brown trout business. But as Alex, the chief guide, said on the first day, "We are here for sahllll-mahhhhnn."

So we were. In switching the color of the tippets, Ned and I had cracked the difference the way Willie Sutton would crack a safe. We talked about the American novels he would be teaching, and as I thought of those books that I had known for so long and of this young man giving up the vagabond life for home and hearth and of the fishing we had just completed, I felt for no reason I could nail as if I would never die.

Not old.

Not young.

Timeless.

It is an illusion that comes to me sometimes when I am fishing, always fleeting, always in some beautiful place, always late in the day. It happens more often as I get older, a feeling unpredictable and exhilarating and levitational, even though you know it cannot last or change the course of mortality. I remember a description by the Mississippi writer Barry Hannah of catching a bass in the company of his father and sons, "You could cut the joy with a knife."

I was still under the thrall of that moment the next day when I told Misha, a surly Russian guide, about the experience we had with the leaders, how the brown was taken and the clear refused.

"It doesn't matter on this river," Misha said. "You can use orange if you want to. You can drive the motor over them, and they'll still take—these fish."

It tells you something about the fall of the Soviet empire, I think. Russians just don't believe in the difference, unless there's a gun involved.

CHAPTER 32

Newspaper Days: A Hierarchy of Worthy Dreams

I never expected my love of newspapering to last so long, to grow so strong. It was a real love, but it was, after all, the kind of love that grows in the second chamber of the heart, worthy but practical. I turned thirty at *The Atlanta Constitution,* where my peer group included several reporters with remarkably similar ambitions. My friends and I wanted to write books, and fuck-you money was our holy grail. We dreamed of the day when the advance check from a book publisher arrived, and we could walk into the managing editor's office and tell him exactly what kind of son of a bitch he was. Dog-cussing the managing editor was a universal fantasy among the newsroom's frustrated litterateurs. As a breed, Southern managing editors were notably hostile to reporters who daydreamed about writing books. We all knew that Cox Newspapers had a secret "scab school" in Oklahoma, where reporters were taught to run the presses in case the printers' union went on strike. The joke was they must have an asshole school for managing editors out there, too.

Newsrooms are tribal, and every newspaper tribe I ever saw contained two clans separated by an invisible line. On one side of the line were those who had majored in journalism and thought of newspapers as a life destination. On the other side were those who rose at dawn to work on the Book, a big-canvas novel or nonfiction epic with which we could buy our freedom. Newspapering was honorable work that paid the bills. When it came to bill-

227

paying, early marriage, the birth of two children and a thirty-year mortgage had concentrated my attention mightily. I was proud of our little family and our trim house on a leafy Buckhead street. I was determined not to be one of those one-of-these-days "writers" whose families live grubbily while they pile up bar tabs and pink slips. But I never gave up the Dream of Escape, even as I became ever more idealistic about the role of newspapers in a fair, humane democratic society.

As long as there have been newsrooms, rumbling presses and ink-stained wretches with a need to comfort the afflicted, otherwise sane people have fallen in love with newspapers. Paul Hemphill, who escaped *The Atlanta Journal* at thirty-three by writing *The Nashville Sound,* a fine history of country music, had as good a general explanation as I've found. "The newspaper is a monster. You fall in love with it, it's so big and strong, and you promise you're going to feed it every day. But what you feed it is you."

Personal tastes also figured in my becoming addicted to newspapers. My father was a builder. I had grown up around cabinet shops and construction sites. I was fascinated by the intricacy and velocity with which a good news story and the newspaper itself come together. It was like seeing a spanking new house built from foundation stone to weather vane in a day, every day, for time everlasting, amen.

Then there was the matter of my political education. My parents were civic-minded and moderate. They voted without fail, supported the least racist candidate available for governor of Alabama, and sometimes gave contributions to the most honest-looking seekers of local offices. But my political education really began at Britling's Cafeteria in downtown Birmingham, where we went to dinner each night after the first edition of the *Post-Herald* closed at 7:00 p.m. I listened with fascination as two bosses I admired, Duard Le Grand and Clarke J. Stallworth, Jr., the news editor and city editor, held forth. Sometimes the discussion was literary, for Duard was a formidable Faulkner scholar. Other times, they dissected segregationist politicians (and the segregationist policies of our newspaper) and the gaudy corruption of the state

legislature. Clarke would tell how the "reform" governor who preceded Wallace had evaded the competitive bid law by writing up
$100,000 road graders as disassembled collections of parts worth
$500 or less per part. Even as we spoke, Wallace was buying leg-
islators at $10,000 a pop by declaring them official insurance
agents to the state.

Clarke and Duard were uncloseted liberals on race and social
issues, or as close to uncloseted as you were likely to find among
white men of their age in Birmingham in those days. In 1964, the
South was gripped with Goldwater fever. One fall night I was
walking back from Britling's with Duard, and he looked up at the
Goldwater billboard catty-cornered from our office. "In your
heart, you know he's right," I heard Duard say. Then he mur-
mured sotto voce, as if the thought police might be listening,
"But in your guts, you know he's nuts."

All around us, Southern newspapers were reporting dishon-
estly on the civil rights movement when they were not simply
ignoring it. Debased journalism and the silence of the white
establishment added up to community endorsements of the verbal violence that Wallace used to trigger the Klan's physical violence. For truthful reports on race, the best work was being done
by outsiders, principally the television networks and writers like
Harrison Salisbury of *The New York Times.* In 1960, Alabama
law enforcement officials responded to Salisbury's damningly
accurate article "Fear and Hatred Grip Birmingham" by forming
a grand jury to identify and prosecute residents who had "slan-
dered" the city by talking to Salisbury.

My political awareness and journalistic education continued
apace. I began to understand the damage or benefit that a newspaper could do for its community. Alabama in those days was
like a reverse Jeffersonian laboratory, in which you could see
how timid journalism produced wicked politicians and bad government. Jefferson's conviction that a vigorous, free press is the
most essential element of democratic government became for me
an article of faith. I came of age as a journalist during a time of
tremendous optimism about the possibilities of news reporting

that was creative, aggressive, independent, fearless, nonpartisan, analytical and truthful. Glenn McCutcheon, a news editor at the *Constitution,* and I used to joke about founding a no-holds-barred Southern newspaper called *The Vindicator-Astounder* with the motto "You can't hold back the dawn."

If journalistic writing was of a lower order than "real" writing, it was still a noble enterprise with lofty civic potential. Plus, a press pass in those days in the South was a ticket to witness a revolution, the death of an old order and the birth of a new dispensation. I loved the color and clash of politics, the rascality or doomed idealism of its practitioners, and above all contact with the courageous generals and foot soldiers of the civil rights movement.

I made a discovery about newspaper writing. You could get high on it, if you went at it passionately, and you could attract readers and their praise if you did it stylishly. That kind of newspaper writing brought the gratification of instant publication. It was also safer and easier than private, creative writing, where you try to write something wonderful at the risk of utter failure. In journalism, the theater of life provided the subject matter much more reliably than could an individual's imagination. Another risk-reducing aspect of newspaper writing is that you have to let it go at a time certain, and even if you go loco on deadline and turn in gibberish, the copydesk will fix it. If it's irretrievably bad, someone along the chain of command will spike it. In serious prose, as in poetry, there is no one but you to make the risky decision that something may be good enough to send into the world. If you fail, the loneliness deepens. Measured against that prospect, the warmth of the newsroom, the mad wit of newspaper people, and the camaraderie of worthy, joint enterprise look very inviting.

As much as I loved newspapering, though, the Dream of Escape that first touched me on those childhood trips to Panama City was always there to remind me. While newspapering was essential civic work, every day spent in a newsroom burned up a day that could never be reclaimed for making books. The days quickly turned to years. The newspaper jobs kept getting better and better. The world you were paid good money to travel and watch became ever more weirdly fascinating. In the space of eight years, I had the fine duty of trying to explain the rise of two of the most unlikely presidents in American history, Jimmy Carter and Ronald Reagan. Quotidian America seemed to want to put an end to novelists. Who could make up personalities as strange or campaigns as unlikely as theirs? Still, every now and then it would come back to me, like a stab of angina—this full-blown fantasy of deliverance from the daily newspapers that so consumed my thoughts, energy and patriotic conviction.

A sleeping dream you can blame on misfiring synapses, but a lingering, elaborated daydream has to have a willing host, and at the level of the unconscious mind, it also has a raison d'être. In this fantasy, I would be fired in some sort of showdown with my bosses. Instead of pushing on to yet another newspaper—I went through five of them in thirteen years—I would summon the courage to embrace my sudden liberation from feeding the rumbling beast in the basement of every newspaper building. I would drift away to life as a free man, usually to New Orleans or Key West because of their literary associations. There I'd live the boho life and measure my success by the amount of time spent indulging the three genres of bliss most important to me—writing the books I hoped to create, fishing whenever I liked for as long as I liked and pursuing the pleasure of romance wherever it might lead. I could just picture myself in the early mornings taking café au lait and beignets at the Café du Monde in New Orleans or snatching yellowtail snappers from the reef at Key West or contemplating country matters with an unconflicted heart.

All this was possible in the world of daydream, because in that invented place, the book publishers of New York had finally wised up and sent me my fuck-you money. In reality, they repeatedly failed to do so. All that changed, abruptly, in 1977, when my novel *Whiskey Man,* and an oral history of the civil rights movement, *My Soul Is Rested,* were published in the same month to good reviews and briefly promising sales. Together they brought what seemed a huge infusion of cash, over fifty thousand dollars for paperback rights and a movie option. My bosses at the *St. Petersburg Times* were congenial toward my idea of taking book leaves when I got an advance and returning to the paper when I needed a monthly paycheck. I had a house payment of less than two hundred dollars a month and a twenty-two-foot boat that I bought with the first installment of the *Whiskey Man* money.

Just then, as luck would have it, the Good Gray Lady invited me to dance, and I figured just one whirl around the floor couldn't hurt. Plus, the *Times* was offering the sole newspaper job cherished by me and my cronies at the *Constitution.* That was to be based in Atlanta and roam the South, filing in-depth stories written in the colorful style demanded by Abe Rosenthal. The *Times* had always had smart correspondents. In the '70s, Abe was shaking the place up by decreeing that he was looking for smart correspondents who could also write with flair. Abe's ukase was the culmination of an amazing turnaround in newspaper thinking that had taken place in the fourteen years I had been in the business. The old, J-school dogma that readers didn't care about good writing was withering. The new wisdom was that smart readers demanded it. The chance to roam the outback South with a license to write vividly about it for the smartest newspaper readers in the country was irresistible. I shelved my plans about being a book writer on the Gulf coast and moved back to Atlanta from St. Pete.

It was not to be the last time that what I would come to know as the Manhattan Deathbed Principle—will I be happy if I pass this up? why not have it, at least for a little while?—got me in deeper and deeper with the *Times.* I can't say I wasn't forewarned about the old gal. Blackstone Drummond Ayres, one of the *Times*'s captive poets and a traveling correspondent of notable endurance, warned all who would listen: "The Good Gray Lady wants it every day."

CHAPTER 33

Confabulators I Have Known

Like any fisherman, I've been tempted to lie on land and sea. Yet I've always fought the impulse to say, for example, that I caught a twelve-inch trout when the tape said eleven and a half inches. It's not my fault when the guides exaggerate, like Max and Mac in Russia. Once on the Big Hole River I watched a guide put the tape on a brown trout that was exactly seventeen inches long. "Eighteen," he said as I looked over his shoulder. (I'm not going to name the guide, by the way, because after you live in New York for a while, you like to see a good deed go unpunished, just every now and then.) Now, there was no way I could unsee what I had seen in the full light of a bright and sparkling day under a cloudless Montana sky. The point is that when I think of that particular trout and its flawless rise to a dry fly on one of my better casts, I lean toward accepting the rhetorical truth of my guide as opposed to the metric truth that passed before my eyes. Perhaps that's what Mark Twain meant when he spoke of "stretchers." Mark Twain also said, "Some people lie when they tell the truth. I tell the truth lying." I guess he was talking about the difference between journalistic and novelistic truths, but I could be wrong. Twain could be pretty Delphic when he wasn't simply being prankish.

The thing of which I'm trying to convince you is that I've always been touchy about telling the truth in all aspects of my life, except of course until I became a manager of people. Let's face it, to manage is to lie, especially if you're trying to manage soldiers, voters or journalists. One of the first things I discovered after joining *The New York Times* was that anything written by the executive editor and labeled as Memo to the Staff was almost always openly and hilariously mendacious. It's an odd trait of *Times* culture that people joked about the clumsy, euphemism-laden memos, but they almost invariably got mad when someone slipped up and posted a true memo or a boss said a true thing in a verbal or written evaluation. Such slip-ups never happened, by the way, in memos regarding changes of assignment. Business historians who mine the paper's personnel archives in future years will find that, whenever anyone got demoted at the *Times,* the official reason was excessive competence. Frankly, I think I can claim to have written a higher proportion of mostly true memos than any executive editor, for the simple reason that the staff performed so brilliantly in the year following 9/11.

Given my high regard for factual and moral truth, it's interesting to think what a decisive role liars have played in my life in the years beginning with Captain Beddingood and ending with the twit who shall not be named again until a later chapter. It's also interesting to note that, when I got back from Russia, I felt no need for stretchers. The fishing had been so good the facts sufficed. Yet I plunged right away into the most flagrant intentional lie of my life in the summer of 1996.

Not all grand lying is intentional. What psychiatrists call "provoked confabulation" is a transient condition over which the liar has no control and is innocent of any motive to deceive. This kind of lying is a neurological disorder that can be caused by a thiamine deficiency. For my part, I was right up to par on thiamine, niacin, riboflavin and beta carotene when I committed "spontaneous confabulation," as it is described by Dr. Charles V. Ford, M.D., in his valuable book, *Lies! Lies!! Lies!!! The Psychology of Deceit.*

I do not take it as coincidence or mere synchronicity that Dr. Ford published his book while on the faculty of the medical school of the University of Alabama in Birmingham. From the time I reached the age of reason, I regarded the city of my birth as an epicenter of lying, at least insofar as politics, family reunions, race relations, amatory fidelity and religion are concerned. But I cannot blame bad old Birmingham for my venture into "spontaneous confabulation," described as a condition in which the practitioner "impulsively" provides "spectacular and spontaneous false information" and does it absolutely on purpose. My only excuse was that I began to confabulate spontaneously upon meeting, unexpectedly, the love of my life.

Let me set the scene. It was all decorous enough in the beginning. My colleagues and I were sitting in the editorial board room of *The New York Times* with the president of Poland, who was expounding on the superiority of black athletes. Because Africans were equipped by birth to run in the heat, he said, the poor Polish track team did not have much of a chance in the Olympic Games in Atlanta, his next destination.

A few minutes before the meeting, I had met Krystyna Stachowiak, a member of the official party who was sitting in the row of chairs along the wall behind the president. I had positioned my own chair so as to keep an eye on this striking woman, so it was possible for me to catch her gaze at this exact moment. I expected to see the frozen look of horror one sees on the faces of American press secretaries and political aides as the boss inserts his foot deeply into his mouth. Instead, she gave me a look of knowing amusement that seemed to say, "Impossibly thick, isn't he?"

As it happened, neither my colleagues nor I was in the mood to torture our guest. He'd be put in his place soon enough if he continued his speculations in the presence of Atlanta's black leadership. As the meeting broke up, I rose briskly, and in the throes of an unaccustomed surge of Manhattan hospitality, I carried out my hastily concocted plan to accost Ms. Stachowiak at the door as the presidential party gathered to depart. I asked how long she was going to be in New York. I was thinking of my civic duty to make sure that slender brunettes representing newly democratic governments got a fair chance to dine at, say, the Four Seasons. She really should sample the pleasures of New York while she and the presidential party were in the United States.

"I live here," she said. She didn't need to say verbally the amused message delivered by her expression, which was "and I know I'm being hit upon, rather transparently, in the sanctum sanctorum of *The New York Times*." As a Polish citizen employed by a New York City public relations firm, she had advanced the president's trip to the *Times* pro bono as a patriotic favor to the Polish embassy. I had been wrong-footed, as the Brits say, and did not recover with my accustomed savoir faire. The lovely creature let me off the hook, so to speak.

"I liked your book on fly fishing," she said.

I recovered my wits, and this is where the high-velocity confabulation set in. I told her that I was working on a new book in which I hoped to cover fly fishing in Eastern Europe. I had heard of good trout fishing in the mountainous Czech Republic. Perhaps she could find out about the trout fishing in Poland.

"You want to go fly fishing for trout in Poland?" she said.

I vowed that was the case. I asked for her card. She produced it somewhat reluctantly and with an expression of amusement very much like that with which she had greeted the president's discourse on eugenics.

I stuck with my story when I called the next day. We met a few days later for drinks at the Algonquin. She gave me a coffee table book on the Polish lake district, where Lech Walesa liked to cane-pole fish for carp and perch. She said that was as close as she could come to finding anything on fishing of any sort in Poland. At least there were pictures of water in this book.

After ordering drinks, I was able to use the conversational methods of the trained investigative journalist to learn more about her and to raise the subtle point that perhaps I was more interested in her than in the angling possibilities of former Communist nations applying to join NATO. I learned that she had come to Washington a few years earlier as a correspondent for a Polish newspaper. I observed that hers seemed a most interesting career. So tell me, I continued, what you've done year by year since you left college.

"I could do that," she said, "or I could just tell you what you're trying to figure out. I'm thirty-two."

That meant she was born the year I finished college, which in my beloved Manhattan meant we were an entirely plausible couple. On our first date, she gave me some news when I began asking about her likes and dislikes, which were precisely defined and boldly stated as a consequence of her upbringing. "I'm a Communist Princess," she said. "At least, that's what my friends call me when I set my mind to something." Her father was the former governor of Silesia, Poland's southern province. She had majored in and taught English literature at the university where she did her master's thesis on W. B. Yeats, the patron poet of fly fishers. She and her family had traveled: England, Italy, Russia, where they stayed in Stalin's villa on the Black Sea. I was able to piece together the implications of this information on my own. She was a child of the nomenklatura and used to being catered to. Since I grew up in the land of belles, I had good training in catering, and I did my best.

The summer of 2000 found us in Southeast Harbor, Maine, in a fine old inn with a big breezy room looking toward the sea. We were laying plans for what was to be her first serious fishing trip. We would be going after smallmouth bass, and I offered to give Krystyna a casting lesson on the day before we were to meet a guide at a boat landing on the Penobscot River near the Old Town Canoe factory. Krystyna said she'd rather spend the day reading in the window chair of our lofty room.

"You're right," I said. "Casting can't be all that hard. Men from Alabama do it." She laughed and I laughed with her. She was wicked smart and wickedly funny. After a few lessons with the spinning rod from the guide at the launch ramp, she also had a wickedly accurate cast, zinging her lure within inches of the rocks and pockets he pointed to along the shoreline. She had been a fencer in high school, once defeating a steroid-charged woman from the East German Olympic team. Being skilled with the foil had apparently endowed her with the ability to meet the exacting Alabama standards for hand-eye coordination. She caught the biggest fish of the day, half again larger than anything I took on the fly rod. I deny her recollection that the guide thereupon became nervous because I got testy. It was on balance the most important fishing trip of my life, more significant in the long run than anything that happened at South Sauty or Panama City or Palatka or on the breast of the Pacific. I had simply never enjoyed a day of fishing more, anywhere, anytime, with anyone.

For a while, the world was our oyster. Unfortunately, one of us had the brain of an oyster. Having vowed to live single for the rest of my days, I would not allow myself to consider the possibility that I had met my other half. What with my myopia and her company's decision to post her to London for a year, it was to be a prolonged courtship and one not entirely free from complications.

I figured that the year apart would restore my resolve as a romantic freelancer. Still, no matter how hard I tried, I couldn't consign Krystyna to the river of forgetfulness. Instead, I remembered her as she was during the Olympian summer and, later, on the river in Maine, the way she laughed, the way she kissed. I admired her razor wit, her subtle but unshakeable hauteur in the presence of pretension and the pretentious. Her carriage was that of a dancer or a fine-blooded colt, and I never tired of looking at that slender figure, elegant as a knife blade. My close friends were crazy about her, and of course, they realized long before I did the proper name for my condition.

The trip to Maine's cool waters was also memorable as a time of contrast and new directions. We went there immediately after the Republican National Convention in Philadelphia. It was hot, glary and politically oppressive, and I needed to rest in the shade, having witnessed, in the guise of "compassionate conservatism," a historic and triumphant revival of H. L. Mencken's booboisie. Only this time, the Protestant fundamentalists would not be haring after the papists and Bolsheviks, as they had in Mencken's day. Indeed, conservative Roman Catholics had been absorbed into a pan-Christian alliance of a sort I would never have predicted back in the days when I thought the South was recovering from its monkey-trial fundamentalism. Instead, that Old-Time Religion was mutating, all the way from the suburbs of

Atlanta to the industrial ruins of Cleveland, into the New Redneck Church Militant that would, in a few months, deliver us into the Land of W, where the monkey trial gives way to the monkey grin.

Maybe I shouldn't be so hard on President Bush. All men belong to the brotherhood of the obtuse. I had known Krystyna for over four years before it dawned on me that the feeling I had in that boat was a revelation, directly connected to the most important quest we face in pursuit of a successful life. That is the task of finding the one and only person in all the world with whom we are meant to be until we die.

Of course, many novels, poems, charming films and mindless sitcoms have built their plot lines around the glacial pace with which the male gender realizes that dreamland is within our reach if only we can wake up. In *Blink,* Malcolm Gladwell contends that we know in the first two seconds if we are attracted to someone. For me, that moment came when Krystyna appeared at *The New York Times* with that wild and crazy guy, the president of Poland. As for the time lapse between that moment and the Penobscot revelation, I can attribute only one reason more detailed than general male obliviousness. I was pursuing exactly the wrong life plan. My earlier book contained a chapter entitled "Amare o Pescare," about the tension between domestic bliss and the desire to fish whenever, wherever and for as long as one wants to. With Krystyna, I entered the world of "amare et pescare," and that required, shall we say, a period of adjustment.

For her part, Krystyna possessed greater clarity. "I don't want to have another romance with Howell Raines," she told me over lunch at Barbetta when she moved back to New York after her sojourn in London. I was jolted that she now referred to me in the third person, the way Bob Dole had referred to himself in his hapless 1996 presidential campaign.

We had by that time been through a couple of romances and I had visited her in London, but my pursuit had been confused and desultory, due I now realize to the misguided nature of my life plan. Of course, Krystyna had figured this out before I had, said realization rendering my continued attentions absolutely expendable as far as she was concerned. By this time, I did know her well enough to know that she was not being coy. She had thought things through with her accustomed clarity and decisiveness. I was history.

Remember, however, that this was in the little nation of Manhattan, where the social and the personal connect in ritualized ways. There began, as is the custom of broken-up lovers in that city-state, a slow trickle of Friendly Dinners. This was in February 2001. In a few weeks, I was to undertake a series of dinners with Arthur involving a courtship of a different manner. I would be trying to convince him that he should appoint me executive editor instead of giving the job to my main competitor. I had been rehearsing my presentation, but without much enthusiasm or conviction.

Not that I didn't need the job. My career as a dot-com millionaire-on-paper had been brief. As I contemplated how to protect the money my brother-in-law Herman had made for me, I followed the counsel of *The Wall Street Journal* and several television commentators I knew to be barking mad in real life. But they sounded sensible to me when they urged the legions of irrationally exuberant newly rich investors like me to be patient. The bubble had lost air, but surely it could not burst. Then one day I read in the *Times* business section that a famous billionaire had converted all his stocks to treasury notes. He was out of the equities market. I had snorkeled enough reefs to know that when the sharks take off, it's past time for the minnows to hide. Something big and ugly is on the way. But if I bailed now, I would lose a third or more of what I had gained. I waited for the bounce back. I waited until Phil Taubman, one of my deputies on the editorial page, told me he was selling his AIM Aggressive Fund, of which I had a load. By the time I got through dumping my high-tech mutual funds, I was back to where I started. I saved what I had put in, but I was no longer a man whose seven-figure F.U. money would guarantee the option of early retirement no matter what happened at work. I was going to need to work until sixty-five, and if I was going to stay, I wanted a new job. Eight years of editorial writing is a long time, even when you've got the Clintons and the religious right providing your targets.

I began sharing with Krystyna my thoughts about the news-paper and the decline in vitality that was especially apparent in the Sunday paper, which is the *Times*'s biggest moneymaker. What I really needed to communicate, Krystyna said, was my passion for journalism and the *Times*. I should be bold in stating my theories about how the *Times*'s journalistic weaknesses were a threat to the paper's economic health and eventually to its tra-dition of independent family ownership. She helped me see that it was a genuine and intense passion, my thwarted literary ambi-tions notwithstanding. My conviction about the place of truth telling in American life was, in fact, my real religion. In Alabama, I had seen how constitutional democracy withers unless newspa-pers are willing to take on a society's most sensitive issues, probe its darkest secrets and stand up to the wealthy and powerful. I was passionate about journalism because I was passionate about social and economic justice in America and the world. I was pas-sionate about the *Times* because it was the last, best hope for an American journalism that was clearly in decline.

As bright as my hopes were for the *Times,* my vision of the last decade in American life was dark and influenced by the deca-dence I had observed in British journalism while living in London during the Thatcher years. I jokingly told friends that you could trace the deterioration of standards in the New York magazine world to the moment Tina Brown arrived in the city bearing the journalistic equivalent of mad cow disease. The increasing pres-ence of Rupert Murdoch was a far more serious threat to the stan-dards of impartial, nonpartisan journalism that had evolved in the United States after World War II. Starting with the 1979 elections in the United Kingdom, he used his newspapers to promote Margaret Thatcher's political career; over the next decade, her government supported the regulatory changes that allowed him to take over much of British television and build a global satellite broadcasting system. He was using the *New York Post* and *The Weekly Standard* in the same amoral way to advance his political friends in the United States. The print campaign was aimed, of course, at the goal of a deregulated and debased American television that would travel around the world on Rupert's cables and satellites. Fox Television showed us the future—outright lies and paranoid opinions packaged as news under the oversight of Rupert, a flagrant pirate, and Roger Ailes, an unprincipled Nixon thug who had assumed a journalistic disguise in much the same way that the intergalactic insect in *Men in Black* shrugged into the borrowed skin of a hapless hillbilly.

I believed then as I believe now that the *Times* ought to be leading the handful of newspapers capable of preserving ethical journalism in America. What I had to make Arthur see was that the *Times* was like a eutrophic lake. At first glance, such lakes have beautiful shorelines, clear water and enough healthy-looking trout to divert the angler. But scientists can predict with certainty that, as such a lake ages, the bottom clogs with layer after layer of silt until the oxygen is depleted, the lake dies and the beautiful shoreline becomes a mudflat fit only for tadpoles and turtles.

As I laid out my vision for a daily journalism that was more vibrant and more stimulating intellectually, several notable things happened. For the first time in my life, my guilty regret over abandoning my literary dreams began to moderate. Trying to fix *The New York Times* was honorable work, every bit as essential to a viable moral and intellectual culture as a literature that explored, in Faulkner's term, the human heart in conflict with itself.

In the course of these discussions, my standing with Krystyna gradually improved. We were inseparable. Like a hunter home from the hill, I felt a calm certainty that a long search was, at long last, properly ended. In May 2001, I got the job, and Krystyna and I began to plan another fishing trip.

CHAPTER 34

The Fifth Editorial: On Sinking

One of the things to be learned from events in Tuna Smith's boat on a certain day he spent guiding two North Americans out on the blue Pacific was that sinking, when it begins to happen in a serious way, is apt to feel more like an event than a process. You're sailing along. Maybe there's a little problem here and there on the boat, but nothing that can't be fixed when you get around to it. On balance, everything looks fine. Then, suddenly, you are sinking. At this moment, you will be sore tempted to think that the thing we call luck is playing a positive or a negative role. You will want to curse it or reverse it. But luck is like the physics of buoyancy. It simply acts in the one and only way it can. One of the many things it can't or won't do, no matter how hard you conjure, is care about consequences.

The circumstances under study here do not mean you are out of business, in the sense of being without recourse. Maybe you'll get a chance to reverse the event. Maybe you won't. Maybe you can find the plug and get it back in the hole. Maybe you'll do exactly the right thing, then another event will neutralize the right or even virtuous thing you did by instinct or design. At this point, surprises may advance upon you much as waves move toward a beach. You're now in a situation where the first good remedy is irrelevant to the new event that's going to sink you. As observed above, it's not an orderly process.

In a book having but one author, the "we" of newspaper editorials sounds inappropriate or even lacking in firmness. Hence this declaration of a personal rather than an institutional sort seems in order. When the small, amiable, brown-skinned young man known as Jayson Blair was exposed for publishing lies that damaged the *Times*'s reputation, I knew exactly what to do. I did what I had always done, which was to rely on radical applications of truth and the intelligence of our readers. I had long disdained the Editors' Note and the Correction Page as instruments of obfuscation that insult the readers' intelligence. For the commission of error in a newspaper, unlike the sinking of a boat, is most often not simply an event but the result of a long, complicated and embarrassingly preventable process involving many well-meaning people. A book may have one author. A newspaper has many. Moreover, a newspaper in trouble has the same institutional instinct as a government in crisis, which is to make a de minimus confession of error, long on contrition and short on facts, and depend on the river of forgetfulness to do its work. The last thing most newspapers are willing to do in such situations is to publish good journalism—replete with facts the reader can judge in their raw, multifarious complexity—about how the bad journalism got into the newspaper in the first place. In regard to providing that kind of disclosure about what really happened, the Correction or Editors' Note, even in a newspaper as well-intended and truly high-minded as the *Times,* often ranks, as a vehicle of truth, right along with the average government press release. No one still employed in the business is likely to tell you that, but there it is.

As for me, I loved being executive editor of the *Times.* I couldn't wait to get to work each day. I revered its traditions, its values and even the very eccentricities it needed to shed. I believed I had learned through long study what needed to be fixed to guarantee its noble existence into future generations. Yet there were limits to how much I loved that job. I had not come so far from gritty, mendacious old B'ham, nor worked so hard for so many years, nor denied one dear and worthy dream to pursue another, nor come to believe so fiercely in the worth, indeed, the nobility of the *Times*'s mission and that of all honest newspapers, to start, so late in the day, faking it with our readers.

BOOK THREE

Capt. Beddingood's
Magic Dot →

He had found the great river. He was gone.
—JAMES SALTER, *Solo Faces*

CHAPTER 35

In the Foothills
of the Prelapsarian Range

It was by the neutral agencies of luck and precipitation, rather than a purposeful act of Dempewolffian guile, that Krystyna and I found what Nat Reed would have called our little piece of paradise, and it was there, in keeping with the Edenic traditions of every faith known to have been practiced by civilized and savage members of our species since the first day that the ages of sidereal time began to roll across the face of the earth, that an old way of life was to end and a new one begin. Which would be the better of the two? We did not find the answer to be so obvious in real life as it is made out to be in the creation parables, in which lovers fall from the garden, not into it.

For the nonce, *mis amigos,* suffice it to say that we found by the side of the road a house that seemed full of promise. The date was Sunday, May 12, 2002. Krystyna and I were not yet married, but we knew that no body of water wider than a trout stream would ever come between us again. In the morning of this particular day, rain had driven us from the trout stream. The main mayfly hatches of the spring trout season in the Northeast were over, the Quill Gordons and the Hendricksons, but we were hoping to catch the first of the *Stenonema vicariums,* big mayflies whose popular name, March browns, always puts me in mind of comically mad pursuits. You see the symmetry: March brown, fishing, March Hare, craziness. Fishing in a steady cold spring rain is too much craziness, so we shed our gear and went for an aimless drive on unfamiliar country roads. Like many New Yorkers in that first shaky spring after 9/11, we had been thinking about getting a country place, a haven against what might come your way at any moment. Manhattan was beginning to regain its swagger, but it did not feel safe anymore, and with George W. finishing up the first of his wars, the one in Afghanistan, neither did the world.

When you follow the winding forest lane that leads to the house Krystyna and I found that day, you will pass, before you reach the house, a sign that seems out of place in such a world as ours. The sign marks the western limit of our local governmental unit. It has white letters on a blue field, saying:

PARADISE
TOWNSHIP

Immediately across the road from the sign is the driveway to a low cedar-and-glass house. From its perch on the Pocono Escarpment at a place called Sunset Hill, the house looks northwest across several intervening valleys to Kittatinny Mountain, a high, reclining, slightly undulating blue hump that stretches from horizon to horizon, like a giant's body. Its recumbent mass reminds me of Sleeping Indian Mountain, which faces the Tetons on the highway between Jackson Hole and the south gate of Yellowstone Park. But our mountain is longer and lower, and it is cut into two frank pieces at the Delaware Water Gap by the fine, fast river of the same first name.

This house with its supernal perch and its lyrical view of the blue-lapped ridges on the far side of the river is not our house and never will be. It is, however, the first house on the western edge of Paradise Township, and in that role, it has something to do with this tale, which is in some sense about the yearning within all of us for a place to say, as does the state motto of Alabama, "Here we rest." The house was built by an earlier refugee from journalism, the late Richard F. Dempewolff, a retired editor of that 1950s bible of practical knowledge *Popular Mechanics*. Back in *PM*'s heyday, wistful lads all over America pondered the magazine's plans for, say, taking the engine from Dad's lawn mower and the chain from your own bicycle and building a miniature jeep that would run seven miles per hour and get 180 miles to the gallon. At the ends of such articles would be footnotes soberly warning us to check with local authorities about traffic regulations before using these magical contraptions on local streets.

I'm sure there were boys in America who did just that, but my personal role model in the matter of driving small cars on the streets of suburban America was Doyle Sessions, Jr., and he had a different attitude toward instructions, both civic and parental. It was Kiss my ass! Doyle Junior, the wild son of my father's hunting buddy, Doyle Sessions, Sr., was a couple of years my elder and, by my lights, both popular and mechanical. He was also lucky, having escaped without paralysis or a punctured lung when the flywheel on the souped-up Tecumseh engine of his handmade car, going far in excess of seven miles per hour, responded to Doyle's demand for a few more rpms by disintegrating and shooting shrapnel into the back of the driver's seat. Doyle Junior had the foresight to build a metal plate into that seat. Its dents and damaged ridges were the emblems of his survival.

So far as I can learn, Dick Dempewolff never built a car, but he did pull off a neat bit of political mechanics, according to the patrician retiree whose land abuts the Dempewolff acreage on Sunset Hill. Andy Hunter was a Greenwich Country Day School classmate of George H. W. Bush, and at eighty-one, he is the living history book for several Pocono tracts acquired by his father in 1916 as part of his dealings with a vaguely utopian vacation community called the Mountain Crest Colony. The place was to be a "little Chautauqua" until the Swedish professor who was to lead the educational program was dismissed for providing lodgings for a vacationing pack of nudist, syndicalist free lovers from St. Louis. You can still see the spot where the building, known locally as Old College, in honor of the supposed credentials of the vanished professor, burned down.

I have always been drawn to neighborhoods with stories, and I'd like to tell you more of them, as I've picked up quite a few in my short time in these hills. But let us return to our main interest, the late Mr. Dempewolff, the Manhattan magazine editor who first visited these parts as a small boy around 1918. When he became a man, he purchased the property on Sunset Hill, but he was dissatisfied with its superb location in one respect. He hired surveyors and wrangled local officials into moving the township line a hundred feet or so farther to the west, so that the house he built was no longer in Pocono Township. He made no secret of his aspirations. "He wanted to be able to say he lived in Paradise," Andy Hunter told me.

So did Krystyna and I when we saw, a half mile or so deeper into the township from Dempewolff's survey line, a house with a For Sale sign. It was advertising the availability of an upright, steep-roofed gray house that looked down a hill toward an orchard of ancient apple trees and a meadow dotted with maples every bit as tall as the lofty chimney of boulder-size rocks. So we said to ourselves, Why not have it? We closed on the place two weeks later, even before we found out our house, too, had a journalistic pedigree.

The seller informed us the property had once been owned by Merriman Smith, the famous UPI White House correspondent who covered the Kennedy assassination and many historic moments of the Cold War. Our friend Gene Patterson, the chairman emeritus of the *St. Petersburg Times,* as a young UPI correspondent in Europe, knew him well. Together they covered the 1955 Geneva Summit of Eisenhower and, on the Soviet side, Khrushchev and Bulganin. Well, not exactly together, said Gene. Smith, in addition to being a famous reporter, was a famous drunk. Pulling rank, he stayed in his room, tippling, while Gene and other underpaid UPI knaves were made to file reams of copy about Ike and the Russians, round the clock, all under the byline of the renowned Merriman Smith. The house had less obvious journalistic resonances. It was originally built around 1925 for a spinster schoolteacher from Nutley, New Jersey, named Margaret Spinning.

As mountain ranges go, the Poconos are extremely modest

but interestingly carved by the glaciers and rocks of the last Ice Age. Our house sits precisely at an elevation of 1,100 feet on the ridge separating the Swiftwater Valley from Paradise Valley. The valleys are named for the creeks that flow through them. By some accounts, General Phil Sheridan, who came to the area to rest after the Civil War, named Paradise Creek, which had formerly been known as the West or Henryville Branch of the Brodhead. In their day, Presidents Benjamin Harrison, Grover Cleveland, Chester Arthur, Teddy Roosevelt and Calvin Coolidge all fished Paradise Creek. So did Arnold Gingrich, the redoubtable fly fisher who edited *Esquire* and commuted from the city in a Stutz Bearcat convertible. Early in the twentieth century, there was a touch of show business connected with the place. Joe Jefferson, an actor famous for portraying Rip van Winkle, was a regular. Buffalo Bill Cody signed the registration book. Where the meadow in front of the old Henryville House hotel ran down to the stream, Annie Oakley staged a shooting demonstration that stunned the local nimrods. Nothing comparably jaw-dropping was seen in these parts until Andy Hunter's father, William T. Hunter, allowed a fellow to land a gyrocopter in the topmost pasture at Hunter Farm about seventy years ago. It was a test. The Hunter patriarch was thinking of commuting by air to his factory in Brooklyn, but he wisely decided that the buzzard-wafting thermals over the Delaware Water Gap would probably kill him.

Before his death in 1951, William Hunter provided lots for summer cottages to be built by Hunter sons and daughters and cousins, Hunter in-laws, family friends, friends of friends and multiple generations of their offspring. The result is a neighborhood in which toddlers splash in the lake where their great-great-grandmothers learned to swim. Over the years, a number of non-Hunters like us have acquired houses and benefited from the patriarch's decision to keep most of his property as a woodland preserve rather than surrender our—well, actually the Hunters'—lovely woods to the subdividers marching west from New York.

There's a special way you love a house you think you cannot live without when you discover it with a person you know you cannot live without. Krystyna and I couldn't get enough of our new retreat from the ceaseless drumming of Manhattan and the controlled chaos of the *Times* newsroom as the paper's staff followed up its acclaimed coverage of the September 11 catastrophe by pelting from one big story to another—anthrax, Afghanistan, Enron, Iraq. Every Friday night, Krystyna would pick me up at Forty-third Street, and we'd light out for Paradise.

My father, Wattie Simeon Raines, died in September 2002, a few months after we bought the place in Pennsylvania. He was ninety-five. When we told my mother that the perdurable Mr. Wattie had passed over, she took to her bed. We had supposed she would live on. Bertha Estelle Walker Raines, the stylish and indomitable little flapper who had owned the first high heels ever seen in Arley, Alabama, made another choice. If ever there was a self-willed death, she showed us one. She was gone, too, before the fall was over.

When we went down to Alabama for the second funeral, my brother and sister generously insisted that I should inherit one of our father's dearest possessions, the rabbit-eared double-barreled shotgun that had belonged to the first Howell Raines. Mr. Wattie had wanted me to have the man's name, they said, and he would want me to have his gun and, in my time, pass it on to the next generation.

The gun would be coming to Pennsylvania in an insured shipment. I was given title to another treasure so dear that I carried it back on the airplane to Newark in my own hands. It was a carved wooden sign that I had given my parents in 1962. I was in college at the time, and their glorious little hobby farm south of Birmingham was at its peak. Its eighty tidy acres were jammed with bass ponds, catfish creeks, scores of hand-tame Angus cattle belly deep in pastures of crimson clover, woodlots for the wild animals, pens for the bird dogs, grapes on their arbors, beans in rows, orchards with limb-breaking loads of plums, bees that buzzed you but would not sting when my father pulled the honey from the hive. You may think that bit about bees an exaggeration, but any beekeeper can tell you there are mean bees and peaceful bees. My father had one hive of bees with the mean gene, but he got rid of them. It was the very last house on a long country road. Beyond it lay thousands of acres of pine forest crossed here and there by rocky ridges of scrub oak and blackjack. I paid a wood-carver to carve into a cedar plank the words they always said when they reached the farm: Trail's End.

Krystyna and I hung the sign on the high front porch that faces, across blue-hazed miles, Kittatinny's recumbent mass and its neighbor, the Delaware River, mighty of constitution but not to be seen at this distance, its waters below our line of sight but constantly magnetic in their pull as the river winds its way through history, flowing green, clear and militant with hope at Valley Forge, tan and clouded with commerce and wisdom at Philadelphia.

On March 8, 2003, friends from two continents and all points of the Cherokee compass gathered at the Merriman Smith fireplace to toast the first Silesia-Alabama nuptials in anyone's memory. Krystyna and I had our wedding portrait made on the porch, and I was resting there, in May, during March brown time and a delayed honeymoon timed to a lull in the Iraq war, when the telephone started ringing.

I could hear Krystyna trading pleasantries with Gerald Boyd, the managing editor of the *Times,* who was in charge in my absence, as she brought the phone out to the porch. He was on a speakerphone, our colleagues around him, a significant fact but up until the next moment a neutral one. There were two pieces of news he wanted to share. A Texas newspaper had accused Jayson Blair of plagiarizing its stories. Jayson, under interrogation, had proclaimed his innocence, but a preliminary check by his editors suggested it was Jayson, instead of the Texans, who was lying.

The other bit of news, added to lighten the mood, came from Tuscaloosa. The wires were reporting that Alabama's newly hired football coach had spent the night in a Florida motel with a woman he met in a strip club under circumstances that indicated heavy drinking, heavy spending and the possibility of sporting exertions not involving the coach's wife. He was gone in a matter of days. Here, I thought, was a man who had not been properly briefed on the map of Dixie. Someone forgot to show him where America buckles the Bible Belt.

Here on my porch sat a man whose honeymoon had been interrupted, and some folks said he looked a lot like me. Did that call mean the honeymoon was over or just beginning? The answer might be a surprise, even to me, a fan of the Crimson Tide. My first twenty months as editor of the *Times* had been a winning season, with the paper's staff earning seven Pulitzers for 2001. After that beginning, I had the political capital to rework the paper top to bottom, taking on one after another those creaky, dust-covered sections that were supposed to tell our readers about culture, travel, sports, books, the life of the mind. With such a start, how could anything stop us?

In the three years since, I've thought often of the day the phone rang. It had been a fine week up until then, Krystyna and I alone every hour of every day, the only entry in my fishing log written from an easy chair on the front porch: "First humming-bird of the season on azalea." The ringing phone, the whir of bird wings. What would those sounds come to signify in our life, this life, this sweet, sweet life, this sweet and fishy life? Was it the plan-gent, yet impersonal sound of the Manhattan Luck Warp, bend-ing like a whipsaw panel of pure energy suspended in space, passing through time, flexing indifferently back and forth as it goes, as it forever must? Was it the whisper of another cat falling? Was it a sound specifically appropriate to a Spinning house in Par-adise, the sound of my coattails' first catching in the blades of that spinning machine I had served so long, with such devotion, without cause for complaint? You can take your pick if you like, just as I did, and you might be right or you might be wrong, just like me. You never can tell. It's a trick I practiced on the editorial page, picking a clear line and sticking to it.

CHAPTER 36

The Sixth Editorial:
On Remediation

In the matter of Jayson Blair, I knew one thing from the first instant I got the news. On this point, there could be no doubt. However disgusting Jayson's behavior, it was all going to be news that was fit to print. We would track down his every sin and our every mistake and put them in the paper. That was the sovereign antidote for the damage he had sought to do to the *Times*'s reputation, and in the new age of information hurricanes, it was more important than ever that the *Times* be transparent in regard to its internal operations if we wanted to hold and expand a sophisticated readership. Whatever happened to any individual did not matter. Wherever there had been mendacity or incompetence, our readers would find us responding with institutional candor. Only that would protect the paper. Only that would be in keeping with the spirit of the traditions we claimed to honor. I was convinced, and remain convinced, that it was impossible to give the readers too much information about the affair. They might forgive or even admire us for a detailed admission of our mistakes that was comprehensive to the point of being tedious. They would not forgive an effort to hide or minimize them. I believed, moreover, that it was beneath the dignity of the *Times* to address our problems by bantering back and forth with television news hosts. We would communicate with our readers the way we should—directly, through unblinkingly self-critical news and analytical stories, prominently displayed in our newspaper.

My resolution only hardened as I read the memos charting the little man's journey through my *Times*. Salient details of those documents shall be revealed to you, but first let me say this. Fellow citizens, fellow laborers in the modern workplace, take care when you enter the land of memos, for whether they are analog or digital, you may come to know the feeling that came to Pinky Pinkerton as that footloose Russian helicopter moved, pilotless, into the sky.

When I returned to the office that first Friday after Gerald's phone call, Arthur chided me affectionately for coming back early. I told him this had the feeling of something that needed to be attended to. For on that day I had a chance to do something an executive editor seldom does under ordinary circumstances, and that is to read the entire personnel file of a junior reporter. I worked backward through time, starting with the initial accusation from the *San Antonio Express-News*. Its editor had politely protested that Jayson Blair had plagiarized their story about a poor Hispanic woman whose son was killed in action in Iraq. The story was full of heartrending quotes that Jayson, according to the accusation, may not have heard with his own ears. There were also colorful descriptions of rooms he may not have entered. The author of the Texas story was a gifted young woman who had interned with Jayson at the *Times* and then returned to San Antonio to take care of her ailing father. Jayson, a ceaseless cruiser of the Internet, had no trouble finding her byline. If he was a plagiarist, he was a reckless one.

Challenged by the national editor to address these accusations, Jayson had produced a minute-by-minute written account of his trip to San Antonio. Never before had a dog eaten so much homework. Jayson didn't have a hotel receipt because he had slept in his rental car after the flight got in around midnight. Our fact-checkers had discovered a problem. The rental agency at San Antonio International Airport was closed at the time Jayson claimed to have picked up the car. A layperson might call this memo, which describes a visit to a house with "an orange/dark tan roof with ruffle-like shingles" and "yellow ribbons on the flagpole," a masterpiece of spontaneous confabulation, but that person would be wrong. A close reading of Dr. Charles Ford confirms that this was *provoked* confabulation. That is to say, we asked Jayson a question—the provocation—and he answered it in admirable detail. I do not think I overstate when I say that Jayson's memo was positively Beddingoodian in scope, in tone, in vigor of language, in richness of detail and in its general aura of optimism.

There was no question that Jayson was a liar. The question that had to be answered for our readers was how many times he had lied. I plunged into his personnel file. This one was two inches thick, astonishing for what it included and provocative in what it omitted. Its hundreds of pages described a troubled internship that began on June 1, 1999, and culminated in a puzzling promotion to full reporter status on January 21, 2001, seven months before my appointment as executive editor. In his best periods, Jayson had produced a steady flow of enterprising stories. At his worst, he produced fewer stories and even those were laden with errors that had to be corrected in print. He had been reprimanded and threatened with dismissal, then applauded when he got on track, sometimes for months at a time. Two patterns were clear. Whatever his performance, he received promotions and pay raises along with peers who performed more consistently. Indeed, several novice reporters who showed more promise and had better track records were washed out of the trainee program as Jayson advanced. This was in keeping with the affirmative-action policies followed by me and every executive editor back to the 1960s. All along the way, he was also defended and cosseted by the Newspaper Guild, the reporters' union. When the copydesk cracked down on Jayson's errors, the president of the guild issued an official communiqué, a "Shop Paper," complaining that one of its members, unnamed, was being harassed and that the union wouldn't stand for it.

Even given all that, what were the details of the process by which the *Times* promoted a guy with such a patchy record? Since the editorial page occupies a different floor and a different world within the *Times,* I had no way of knowing and no reason to be consulted at the time Jayson went on the staff. If the files ever contained an official sign-off from the executive editor, as required when anyone is promoted from trainee to full reporter status, it was missing from the sheaf of papers before me. The missing records didn't prove anything. Record keeping at the paper has always been slipshod. Much of the decision making at the *Times* is verbal and collective. Sometimes people get behind on their paperwork. Sometimes they forget about it, by accident or by way of self-protection or by way of helping a young protégé avoid trouble with the boss. Like most seasoned executives at most organizations, I had over the years seen it go both ways.

I still wanted to know what happened. By Monday, the *Times*'s lawyers and I had in hand a report from the associate managing editor for personnel that filled in some missing bits of the picture. Jayson and three other trainee-reporters had been up for promotion during December 2000. Jayson's promotion was put "on hold" for reasons obvious to all. On the Sunday night before Christmas, at 1:00 a.m., he took an astonishing gamble. He sent an e-mail to his mentor on the personnel staff saying he didn't want his troubles to hold back the other three candidates, two of whom were white and one Asian-American. The wee-hours e-mail might have been taken as a sign that Jayson was drunk or crazy. Or he might have been seen as setting up the *Times* for a racial-discrimination lawsuit. By asking around among the editors, I satisfied myself that the latter interpretation prevailed. The report put it more blandly: "Ultimately the decision was made to promote Jayson with the others."

By whom precisely? I considered that an interesting academic question and a valid journalistic one if you were writing a ticktock on the Blair affair. But I knew that questions of personal responsibility at various points in the chain of command were irrelevant for someone in my job. What mattered was accountability. Like every executive editor before me, I was accountable for all messes, including inherited ones. That's the rule, and I knew it when I asked for the job. If you're not willing to play by that rule, you shouldn't take the job. I knew the rule. I took the job. Selah.

In that first reading of the file, I found a print copy of an e-mail from Jayson's immediate supervisor during one of his screwup periods. It said, "We have to stop Jayson from writing for the *Times*. Right now." It went to two editors in the personnel office. It was not copied to me either electronically or on paper, nor was it copied to anyone else in the paper's high command, the seven "masthead editors" who reported directly to me. It never occurred to me that a memo I never saw could become a smoking gun. It did occur to me immediately that we had to share it with our readers, along with an explanation of the ramshackle personnel system that had produced and, apparently, buried it.

It was axiomatic among *Times* editors and executives that someday our Dickensian bureaucracy would "bite us in the ass." Fixing it was not high on my list of priorities. An executive editor has only five years or so to shape the paper. I had come to do the journalism, not the bookkeeping. It was an eyes-wide-open gamble. After we lifted the news report to a uniform level of quality, I'd get around to fixing the other stuff, if there was time, in year four or five. As old-timers, both Arthur and I knew immediately what had happened. Jayson had sneaked through the system or leaked through it or gamed it or benefited from well-intended supervisors who protected him. Anyone who has ever been a company clerk in the army can explain it to you. The point was, ass-biting time had arrived. Arthur was steady. "Attention is on you now, but these are problems that affected all previous executive editors and were not addressed," he said. He also used one of his favorite sayings: "It's not your fault. It's just your turn."

I made the decision of what to do on the basis of the instinct that had guided me since my first day at the *Birmingham Post-Herald*. Tell the truth. Write it as clearly and elegantly as possible, and trust in the judgment of your readers. We had to tell the truth, all of it, using whatever investigative effort and newsprint it took. A standard "mistakes were made" correction would not do, even if it ran on the front page. A more expansive Editors' Note would not do, as the *Times* had used such notes in the past as damage-control devices. I had distrusted the format ever since Abe Rosenthal invented it in 1983, during the last, sad, crazed years of what had been a brilliant editorship. Those of us who were reporters at the time saw it as a vehicle Abe needed to placate powerful people with whom he had taken up in his late-blooming career as a socialite. An artfully written Editors' Note looked on the surface to be explaining the bureaucratic natural history of an error of fact by reporters or judgment by editors. But the *Times* is so complicated in its structure and so human in its foibles that a detailed Editors' Note becomes the journalistic equivalent of a congressional committee report. It can be used to give an individual reporter or editor sole title to an embarrassing institutional lapse. Or it can blur the lines of individual responsibility by wrapping a fog of words around the critical decision points. Only a lengthy front-page story about Jayson's career and our failure to catch him, about our porous personnel system and our multilayered editing system, would give the readers the information they needed to make a balanced judgment about our reliability. We had to report our own cock-ups with the same detail and dispassionate analysis we would apply to a government or corporate scandal. For me it was not a risk-free strategy. My political calculation was that I would get enough credit for openly addressing our mistakes to survive as executive editor. As a personal matter, it was the only strategy available if I wanted my life to continue to make sense and if I regarded, as I did, the credibility of the *Times* to be more important than my career or reputation.

Before leaving work that Friday, I called a halt to an in-house investigation in which a group of the editors who supervised Jayson were to dissect the reporting and editing of Jayson's stories. An enterprise so riddled with conflict of interest was unfair to the people we were calling on to investigate themselves and to our readers. I ordered the assembly of an independent team that ultimately would include five reporters and three editors. They were to compose a lengthy article on the Blair affair and put it in the paper without interference from me or anyone involved in supervising Jayson's performance. Neither Gerald nor I would read the article before publication, to prevent any possibility of a cover-up at the top or the appearance thereof. I did put my thumb on the scales in one way. I made sure that the team included two reporters I regarded as the smartest on the paper, one an investigator and the other a legal authority. I was not close to either man and did not expect them to go easy on me or anyone else. It was simply a matter of going with the best talent you've got.

I left work that day as I had left work every day for thirty-seven years—with a clear conscience, with an absolute conviction that I had made the right decision ethically, and without worry about my future, let it come rough or smooth. There are a lot of things you can't get from newspapering, but a satisfied mind is something you can have each and every day if you follow the compass of honor.

CHAPTER 37

Fly Fishing the Wudacudashuda

The things I carried when I went fishing on the Delaware River on Sunday, May 11, 2003, were one 4-weight Sage fly rod with an Orvis reel, one six-foot Cabela's spinning rod with a Pflueger reel, one bright yellow Bass Pro Shops dry bag containing my Patagonia rain suit, Banana Boat 50 sunscreen, a spool of Seaguar fluorocarbon line in case my reel needed replenishing, Imitrex nasal spray in case of migraine and a folded A-section of *The New York Times*. In other words, I was surrounded by some of the most reliable and venerable brand names America has to offer when I found out that, in all probability, in a professional sense, my ass was grass. The news came from the paper. I put it back in the dry bag. There was no point letting that ruin a day I had long awaited, inasmuch as the McKenzie River drift boat being rowed by Michael Padua, an able guide from Tyler Hill, Pennsylvania, carried in its bow seat one of the finest brand names in contemporary American letters, John McPhee.

John and his wife, Yolanda, had spent the night with Krystyna and me in Henryville. We had a voluble twilight dinner in our dining room, its French doors open to our dreamy blue-green meadow speckled with fireflies. At daybreak John and I drove up the lush, foggy Delaware River Valley, passing such riverine landmarks as the Roebling Bridge, named for that John Augustus Roebling whose greatest work, the Brooklyn Bridge, was also his last, and Dingmans Ferry, named for that barefooted Judge Daniel Dingman who around 1820 sentenced a miscreant to New Jersey in lieu of hanging.

Those are the kinds of details you would typically find in a McPhee book, of which there are almost thirty. I have been reading him for forty years and doing so with an admiration widely shared in the journalistic, literary and academic worlds. In many ways, he had lived the life for which I had aimed. He had escaped from salaried toil at *Time* and supported himself by teaching at Princeton and contributing to *The New Yorker*. His prose is lapidary, and his appetite for information is as fathomless as that of a white shark for elephant seals. He is a fisherman who "can feel the adrenaline when I fill a glass of water." I beamed the day he told me that he counts me among the fishingest people he knows. On this day, we are floating down the Delaware in quest of the most efficient ram ventilator among the American sports fish, the American shad, whose habits are described in detail in John's book *The Founding Fish*. Young ones gain weight by swimming with their mouths open, combing out oxygen and plankton with their gills. Big ones, on their spawning run up the Delaware, open their mouths for flies, darts and spoons, but nobody knows if they want to eat them or simply bite them. They pull. They jump. The flesh is bony. The roe is manna.

Krystyna and I have come to love the Delaware so much that I usually think of it as "our Delaware." It is the longest undammed river east of the Mississippi. It may support sport fishing for more blue-ribbon species—shad and striped bass swimming upriver from the sea, smallmouth bass, largemouth bass, brown trout, rainbow trout, brook trout, muskellunge, pickerel, walleye— than any other river on the continent. "I've been fishing this river since I was a kid," said Michael Padua, "and when I think you can still catch so many species from it in this day and age, it gives me chills." The water is clean enough to drink, as do folks in New York and Philadelphia. It comes within sixty miles of the Lincoln Tunnel, yet is wild enough to be one of the best places in the country to watch bald eagles. You can also see mink, deer, bear and turkey on the shore and, in the clear waters, rough fish like catfish, carp, chub and suckers, as well as rough customers like snapping turtles and lamprey eels. Krystyna and I bought a new jet-outboard boat expressly for fishing in it, swimming in it, motoring up it and floating down it. But on this day I was forced to recognize that our Delaware had the potential to become my Wudacudashuda if I let it.

That is to say, I realized I could spend the rest of my life thinking about ways I might have handled the Jayson Blair scandal rather than ordering the publication of the 7,400-word story that I read while John McPhee cast his fly tirelessly from the bow of Mike Padua's boat. The published story and sidebars listing Jayson's fabrications took up four pages, but it was less complex than I had expected. I understood immediately the process by which it was produced. One of the smartest reporters had formed what lawyers call a "theory of the case." I knew this from questions he had asked me in an interview. His theory had become the spine of a key section in the finished article. There was nothing unusual in this. I had done the same thing hundreds of times in pursuing investigative or political stories. The approach, like much of journalism itself, is inevitably reductionist, but it can also lead to the truth or an honestly derived version thereof. The theory of this case was that the *Times* would have been spared the Jayson Blair scandal if Gerald Boyd and I had paid more attention to complaints from the U.S. attorney in Baltimore and other prosecutors about stories Jayson had written on the arrest and questioning of the two suspects, John Muhammad and Lee Malvo, who were charged in 2002 with the Washington, D.C., sniper killings. If I had been writing the story, I would have gone for an approach of layered complexity, placing our failure to catch Jayson into the context of the *Times*'s long-standing editing and personnel practices and dissecting the turf battle among state and federal officials involved in the sniper case. But that was exactly the point, wasn't it? That I not write or edit the story, so we could tell the readers there would be no special pleading about my tardiness in spotting Jayson.

Were there complexities? It appeared so to me at the time. A U.S. attorney whose warnings we were supposed to have heeded was one of several Washington-area prosecutors vying for control of the case. Among the voice mails left on Jayson's answering machine was one from a rival prosecutor saying his stories about the infighting over the defendants were right. The person assigned to comb through Jayson's e-mails, phone messages and personnel records was under orders to tell the reporting team anything they wanted to know. He told me later that he was asked to clear up some details but was never extensively interviewed about his overview of Jayson's entire history on the paper. For my part, I also realized that perhaps I had not been explicit or emphatic enough with the three reporters who interviewed me. I had not wanted them to feel intimidated or lobbied. In what seemed an odd twist to yours truly, one could read the story closely and come away with the mistaken impression that I had ignored the stop-Jayson memo and all the other warnings that did not reach the top of the pyramid.

There has never been a news story written that did not have such ambiguities or omissions of detail. They are seldom malicious and seldom matter, unless through a process of accretion that, if uncorrected, undermines the central theory or blurs a critical point. Reporters don't have the time to make a news story into a nonfiction novel, and Jayson left behind enough leads to stump a fleet of detective writers about what information he stole, what he made up, and what he acquired during spurts of apparently conventional reporting. The eternal problem of journalists is to find the thematic truth—the dispositive explanation—among a cluster of lesser and greater truths, synchronistic facts, quasi-facts, irrelevant proto-facts and those anti-facts we may think of as lies or mistakes. It's a messy process, but if journalists thought of it that way, it would never be finished. "Go with what you've got" is both a deadline exhortation and a recognition of epistemological reality. During the course of an inquiry, there is a sharp line between those who write and those who are written about. The fact that I am a person who stood at a very high level on one side of that line and who stood in a very bright spotlight on the other side is something you may choose to regard as fiercely symmetrical or ironic or paradoxical or as simple justice. At any rate, it's

all interventionist. Think of the Sinus Doctor to the Stars, an innocent marlin swimming in the remotest of oceans, the strollers of
Manhattan on that inevitable day when the terminal velocity of
cats becomes a divisional factor in determining what label we put
to the indifferent fact of luck. When caught in intersecting force
fields, the sentient being can claim a certain dignity in understanding how easily the flip of salvation becomes the flop of doom, and
that's about all you'd better expect in the category of consolation.

A Washington writer named Eric Pianin once wrote a deftly
instructional, intricately detailed article about a lung surgeon in
the capital of our nation who refused to quit smoking. One day,
late in his highly successful career, the surgeon looked at his own
chest X-ray and saw his death warrant. The moment illumi-
nated, for him and for us, the question of what replaces hope
when hope begins to wither. The answer is duty, endurance and
honor. The ailing physician behaved admirably, but in a different
way. He played golf on mild Saturday afternoons and sometimes drank as many as four Miller Lites afterward. Always the
physician, he understood that he would not be exempt from the
process of decline he had observed so many times in his patients.
Inescapably a human being, he also began to ponder as his own
decline advanced more radical kinds of chemotherapy, radiation
and surgical treatments that the physician treating him might try.
That doctor, a friend, told him no. They were beyond that point
now. Even in his extreme condition, the physician-patient recognized the medical aptness of his friend's decision. Don't worry, the
doctor's doctor said, I'll take care of you until the end.

That final mercy was nice, but beside the point. What matters
is that a spot small as a pinhead recorded by a silver halide
process on a piece of celluloid had intervened in that man's life
and, for that matter, in the life of his brother physician, and had
changed both the nature and the duration of their relationship.
What matters most of all, it seems to me, is the professionalism of
the thing, the fact that he read his own X-ray correctly in the first
place, that he struggled to act on what he knew to be valid even
as hope faded.

CHAPTER 38

The Seventh Editorial:
On Prescriptions

The suspicion that I might not always be a newspaperman did not rob me of that most indispensable tool for any writer of any kind, curiosity. I had my first look at the Roebling Bridge on the day I fished for shad with John and Michael. In due course, I turned to *Bridges over the Delaware River: A History of Crossings* by Frank T. Dale, *Natural Lives, Modern Times: People and Places of the Delaware River* by Bruce Stutz and *The Encyclopedia of New York City,* Kenneth T. Jackson, ed., to find out how the great John Augustus Roebling had come to build a laced span of timbers between the Pennsylvania and New York shores of an out-of-the-way part of the Delaware River. It was an elegant bridge and, Stutz reports, "the oldest of Roebling's remaining bridges" in the United States, but modest in size, location and renown compared with the Brooklyn Bridge.

I found the smaller one had started life in 1848 as the Delaware Aqueduct. The aqueduct rested on piers of hewn stone, each pier tapering ever so slightly upward so that it looked balletic rather than massive. The aqueduct was an early work of Roebling but by no means an apprentice work. He was forty-two years old at the time and, having not left Germany until 1831, was in a hurry to get rich by making sure that the commerce of his new country was not inhibited by rivers. He had invented the twisted wire cable that replaced hemp rope for the suspension elements of the aqueduct. Its central trough was eight feet deep and twenty feet wide, and it carried the waters of the Delaware and Hudson Canal over the Delaware River at a place called Minisink after the Leni Lenape subtribe driven from the area by the Treaty of Easton in 1758. It was all part of that same process by which England's Lord De La Warre, owner of a river he had never seen, changed the name of the Lenape people to the Delawares.

By Roebling's time, there were traffic jams at the Minisink shoals, where the Delaware and Hudson Canal flowed into and then out of the main river. At low water, the canal boats got hung on the rocks. At high water, timber barges roaring downriver from the New York mountains splintered the smaller, more fragile canal boats as they navigated the rapids separating the western and eastern arms of the canal. When the aqueduct opened, all that travail came to an end. Commerce continued in all seasons, in flood or drought, the canal's waters carried nobly aloft like the waters of ancient Rome. Mule teams on a path beside the trough pulled barges and boatmen that were lifted into and out of the aqueduct on a series of locks. As they crossed, the boatmen on the D and H Canal could look over the edge of the trough at the river running at right angles thirty-five feet below their aerial artificial river. In the proper seasons, they could see shad, striped bass, et cetera, in the clear water.

By 1867, Roebling owned a cable factory in Trenton and, like many rich men of his time and ours, had learned how to get the New York legislature to appropriate millions to assure the profitability of his work in the metropolis. *The Encyclopedia of New York City* tells that construction of the Brooklyn Bridge, the world's first steel-cable suspension bridge, experienced a "severe setback" in June 1869, when John Augustus Roebling "was fatally injured by a ferry that toppled him from a waterfront piling." That's true, but so incomplete as to cheat Roebling of the distinction of having engineered his own death in the assertive style of the island to which he built a bridge from Brooklyn. Long before anyone had heard of Malcolm Gladwell, Roebling was a *Blink* man and also a bellower. So on a June day in 1869, Roebling was clumping around the massive timbers at the waterfront construction site, shouting orders to beat the band, when a ferry hit the dock. Roebling may or may not have "toppled." The important point is that the timbers slammed together, crushing his toes. Soon he was bellowing orders at a physician in lower Manhattan, ordering the amputation, sans anesthetic, of the useless toes. He also ordered the doctor not to treat his wounds with antiseptic. Roebling believed that bathing a wound in warm water was the quickest way to heal it, and he was eager to get back to bellowing orders. The foot soaking led to gangrene, and that, in thirty days, led to a funeral attended by many of the officeholders who voted to give him the money.

Among educated people, knowledge begets empathy. That is why, learned readers, you might identify, as I do in some ways, with Roebling's impatience and his decisiveness. Another lesson comes to mind in contemplating the parable of Roebling's toes. Unlike the Sinus Doctor to the Stars, he had the consolation, such as it is, of dying from following his own prescription instead of ignoring it.

CHAPTER 39

Snapshot VII:
The Pacific Ocean, March 1994,
a Night Passage

As of this time, I have not seen Tuna Smith in eleven years, yet when I think about him, these are the words that come to mind. What is so admirable in life as a man who is both mannerly and undaunted? There was no rudeness in him and no quit in him, either. He was not quite young enough to be my son, yet my feelings were protective. Whatever happened in regard to the marlin, I wanted him to think of it as a stroke of luck, rather than an action he might have influenced or prevented. For he had done, I do believe, the best that anyone could with his fish and his fisherman and with the tools at hand.

My plan for the endgame was not fancy. I wanted to see whether with steady low rod pressure on its left side, I could make the marlin swing in that direction. If I could do that, just turn its head one time, we could make it start swimming around and around the boat, like a horse on a tether. It might run again, it might sound, it might even leap again, but we would know and the fish would know that it had been turned, and if our gear, boat, crew held up for a few more minutes as it had for hours, there could be only one ending to our story. The fish could make what demonstrations it chose. We would abide them and then bring it to hand by small but relentless shortenings of the line. Once the circling started, it would not even matter when or if we lost the light. Tuna could bill the fish in the dark. He would not lose his grip no matter how hard the fish struggled at the side of the boat. I imagined it all, me slumped over the unburdened rod, Tuna holding fast to the whipping fish, Tennant leaning over the gunwale to unhook it amid showering banderoles of plankton light threshed from Mother Ocean.

The water was inky now, the fish a moving bruise under a dorsal fin and tail that sliced the water like knives. We were close, thirty-five feet or so, and being tolerated. What I felt through the rod was the steady, breasting pace of a displacement cruiser instead of the bursting, speedboat energy with which it usually responded to our proximity.

"The fish is still strong," I told Tuna.

"Yes," he said, "but he's staying on top."

I did not tell Tuna that I thought a time for summing up had come. Even a big fish, if you bend hard into it at just the right time, can suddenly acquiesce, like a heavyweight who has been hit twenty times with no discernible damage but falls like a stone on the twenty-first blow. Unless it was susceptible, why would it allow us to stay so close for so long? There was another factor known but to me, and it related to the dialogue that the smart part of my brain was having with the fishing part.

"You are over fifty years old. You are in fair condition, but you have not trained for this level of exertion. It is possible for you to kill yourself doing this. It is only a fish."

"But a damn nice one," said the fishing part of my brain. "The best ever in every way."

"Of course it is," the smart part said, "but there's no mystery left in the enterprise. If you stick with it and if you don't croak, what you will see will not be surprising in regard to what happens to this fish. You can do what you need to do now or you can hang on and continue to pester it. It will turn at midnight or it will turn at daybreak. We know that. The only thing left that we don't know is whether you can turn it *now*. That's where the suspense is. If you had tried at any time before now, it would have broken off because it was too fresh. If you wait and wait and wait, it will be so tired that you've proved nothing. But now, to turn it now, as tired as you are, as fresh as it is, that would be something. The point is to understand this day. You've already had the best of it. The best part is over and it will never leave you."

The marlin was pulling with the line positioned over its left shoulder, a position ideal for the turning of its head. Tenderly, I increased the pressure on the twenty-pound leader that the Orvis Company had made so well. We had a solid gold hookup. The hook was not going to pull no matter how much we increased the load on it. Other misfortunes might occur if I rushed things, but not that one. The fish needed only a little more coaxing. Strong as it was, I knew that after seven and a half hours of pulling against the pressure in the left jaw, it wanted to do what a horse wants to do when you pull on its rein. It wants to turn in the direction of the urging. Every corpuscle up and down the fish's left flank would welcome a turn. Only one thing, the instinct to flee something bigger, a boat hull, which probably registered on its lateral line as some kind of shark, kept it pulling straight ahead. If only I could bring that little bit of pressure that would teach the fish how sweet it would be, how good for both of us, if it just came around to the left and rested for a bit by circling our boat. If I wanted to dress this up with a nice round lie, I could write at this point about how this creature's great fighting heart had through all the long day kept it from quitting. But you know and I know that what kept it going was its lack of a sizable brain and its fear of staying in the same part of the ocean with something it couldn't comprehend.

Once the fish turned, I would keep it calm by backing off on the steering pressure. No need to be impatient then. Just keep a tight line and maintain its steady encouragement for the marlin to keep swimming in easeful, imperceptibly smaller circles that would draw it by and by within Tuna's reach.

I knew what Tuna was thinking, of course. He was thinking that, thanks to all his coaching about going gently, gently, I had not done anything abrupt or stupid. Soon, night would crash down the way it does in the tropics. The astonishing stars of the equatorial sky would pop out. I thought about what kind of sight the fly would become, a faint white slash being carried through inky water, invisible to us in the boat, visible only to the eyes of the creatured sea. Once that kind of night came, very soon now, we would be able to see the fabulous glow of disrupted plankton where the line cut through the water, then a shower of light, great plumes of organic radiance when we had the fish thrashing beside the boat.

It had been a long time since either Tennant or Tuna had asked how I felt. There was no point. Only I knew how much longer I could go on. I remember the mystification I felt as a small boy when Grady was reading to me about Santiago cursing his hands and denouncing the left one in particular as a traitor. No part of a boy's body is untrue to the mission of living. So he cannot understand a betrayal in the physical realm of the self.

As for the fighting of the marlin, I guess that's about all there is to say about the facts right now, the journalism of the thing, as it were. A great fish had come out of the ocean. I had been caught by it, and then . . .

"It's off," I said.

"What? What's wrong?" Tuna said.

"The leader broke," I said, which was true as far as it went, but may not be the whole story. Look at it this way. Once upon a time, there were redfish in Burnt Mill Creek, which flows into St. Andrews Bay, north of Panama City, Florida. If you don't believe so, you could ask the Man from Ohio. I wouldn't be surprised if he was living still. He can tell the tale. So could Captain Beddingood. In matters of fishing, he was opposed to forgetfulness in its many forms, hence his ceaseless iterations of tales of hope and wonder for all who inquired about what might happen if you rented one of his boats and followed precisely his instructions as to the selection and decoration of lures. But our captain speaks no more. He has entered that river which will take us all one day, that larger river into which flow both the rivers of forgetfulness and remembrance, the great river which will take us and everything except the words, true or false, that we write down.

For a long time after the marlin left us, taking my wonderful five-dollar fly into the far ocean, no one spoke. For the first time that day, Tuna let the motor idle for a bit. I cranked in until both line and broken leader were onto the spool of the tireless Battenkill 10/11, the choice of budget-conscious traveling fishermen around the world. I propped the rod, a 10-weight Sage, in the bow of the boat.

I still have that Battenkill reel, too, and will until I die. The Fin-Nor was waiting in my mailbox in Manhattan when I got back from Christmas Island. I gave it to my son Ben, since for me it had no sentimental value, no link to the fish that came out of the ocean and stayed until I no longer needed to possess it. I thought of the Dylan lyric: "I shall be released." So may we all be released, fellow travelers, in our hour of darkness, in our time of need.

Darkness was upon us now in the sweet situation that enveloped us at every point of the Cherokee compass—the diamonded sky above, the sea below and roundabout, and the place where we were, in a hardy boat with quite a good chance of surviving our plunging navigation through the churning combers that rise, curl and crash luminously night upon night all across the very pass that admitted Captain Bligh on that Christmas Day so long ago to the island that had become, despite the intervention of guns, personalized devils, contrary religions and thermonuclear flashes, just what the sign at the airport promised, a paradise of fish and birds.

Tuna spoke. "Do you have a flashlight? The plug has come out again and I can't see it."

"Do not worry," I said. "I have one in my bag."

It was a Maglite, another brand-name product that in my experience you can trust without stint at land or sea. But it counted for less than a firefly under the great meadows of the equatorial night. So once his work was done, Tuna snapped it off and away we went without running lights or spotlights toward home. Another boat, the first we had seen in many hours, was running that night without lights toward Captain Cook's pass. We overtook it on our port side, passing close enough to see that it was a motor launch, laden, as heavily as any refugee boat, with men and women and children. Its gunwales barely cleared the waters whitened by its passage. Tuna, in answer to my question, said the passengers had nothing to fear from the booming waters ahead. It was a taxi boat whose driver knew how to surf it through the pass. These people were not refugees but citizens of the happy isles on their way in a slow boat to seek friends and fun or perhaps a bit of religious recruitment or amorous contentment in the town of Banana or up the beach at Poland.

CHAPTER 40

Four Aspects
of Reaching Terminal Velocity

I. AN INQUIRY FROM A SUPPORTIVE SOUTHERNER

"Dad, is Jayson Blair a dwarf?"

This question came over the telephone from my son Ben, a reporter on the *Mobile Register*. He had been following the Blair scandal on the Web sites devoted to media news and commentary. I was being blog-flogged to a fare-thee-well.

"No, he's not a dwarf," I said. "Why?"

Ben explained that a friend of his who worked at Christie's had met Jayson at a party in Manhattan and took him for someone with genetic dwarfism.

"Jayson is very short," I said, "but he's not a dwarf, at least not a physical dwarf."

We laughed. The idea of Jayson as an evil gremlin was a terrible insult to the political sensitivities of Little People but was hilariously apt to my situation. He had cast a spell over the *Times* newsroom that had to be lifted quickly or I would be swimming with the frogs. And at that point, I did want to survive out of a duty-driven determination to finish renovating the *Times*. As for my own future, however, I understood the implications of the X-rays I read on the Delaware. I might not be beyond treatment, but my situation was very grave. Already, I was suffering from that sudden de-escalation of adjectives I had observed as a sign of morbidity in the central figures in many a political scandal. In my case, "gregarious" and "charismatic" were giving way to "autocratic" and "heavy-handed." Whatever successes I had seemed irrelevant, possibly accidental and certainly secondary to the fact that I was a mean son of a bitch. Maybe I had been a "larger than life" figure at the *Times,* but I was terminally infected with "arrogance" and "hubris." At this point in the narrative, I will comment on only one feature of the critique. When was the last time they handed out important jobs in New York on the basis of humility? If hubris was going to take me home, so be it. At least I'd be leaving on the horse I rode in on.

Arthur and I adopted the strategy that LBJ called "hunkering down like a jackass in a hailstorm." I would listen and consult more. I had no problem with that. I'm a sociable person. The downside was that it would take three years of management psychobabble, focus groups and sensitivity training to accomplish the reforms we could have installed in the next six months. By the time we finished, I'd be near the end of my tenure. I believed in the destination so strongly, I was willing to go by any road. All it would cost me in the end was the time I had planned to spend on fixing the ass-biting bureaucracy and, of course, my joie de vivre.

On the upside, the strategy was pragmatic. For decades the *Times* had hired mid-career journalists who were confident of their ability to meet the performance threshold at the paper. Now the newsroom was packed with much younger reporters and editors, brought in as "trainees" and promoted to full-time status while they were still cubs. All but the toughest of them were terrified they would not be able to make it in a "star system." Calming them down would be good for the paper in the long run. Anyway, most of the outright losers would eventually be driven away by meritocratic competition, and the earnest but less gifted would find a useful level of mediocrity. The only problem with our pragmatic strategy was that it was ignoble. It involved pandering to those on the staff who wanted the *Times* to live in the past or creep uncertainly toward the future. We decided to give them a chance to ventilate by following one of the *Times*'s more dubious traditions—the town hall meeting.

II. A Last-Minute Instruction
I Definitely Needed

"You can do this," Krystyna was saying. "Don't get impatient. Don't lose your temper. If someone says something outrageous, just say 'I'm sorry you feel that way.' And no matter how much you're tempted, don't quote Bear Bryant." That would only provide regional fodder for the caricaturists, she said.

We were sitting at a quiet window table at Charlotte, a white-tablecloth place in the Millennium Hotel. We were having the kind of meal you have in the planning sessions before a big meeting—salade niçoise and sparkling water for her, rare hamburger and Coca-Cola for me. Around the corner, a thousand or so *Times* employees were gathering in a theater on Times Square. The buzz had shifted a bit. Our readers and many of my longtime acquaintances in the professional journalism community agreed that the Sunday story disclosing Jayson's antics and our mistakes was in keeping with the *Times*'s tradition of stainless-steel integrity. The buzz in the newsroom indicated that a new obsession had set in. Did Jayson Blair get a break because he was black?

Pop quiz: Does everyone remember we work for *The New York Times*? Around 1990, Max Frankel declared as formal policy of the *Times* news department that we would hire one reporter of color for every white reporter hired. Over the years, the *Times*'s affirmative-action formula had varied from fifty-fifty and become less arbitrary, but the formal, publicly acknowledged principle was firm. The *Times* would make every effort to find, train and hire minority journalists and bend over backward to keep them. I followed those practices as a midlevel editor, enforced them as executive editor and believed in them personally. "Where I come from you have to pick a ditch to die in on race," I said. "I made up my mind a long time ago I would die in the ditch for justice." That meant in my view going the extra mile to pay the historical debts of racial discrimination.

For what felt like the hundredth time, I also explained in detail what I had hoped to have documented in the Sunday story. Jayson Blair did not get a second chance on lying. The second chance that Jayson got—appointment to the team of reporters covering the Washington sniper story—had nothing to do with his history of making errors in his stories. The record of his up-and-down accuracy, which ought to have been our first tip-off that we had a confabulator on our hands, had disappeared into the bottom sediment of the *Times*'s personnel files. Jayson's second chance had to do with his claims of addiction. He had volunteered for treatment for alcohol and cocaine abuse. He came back, stayed clean and sober for several months, was cleared for duty by Human Resources, and in keeping with *Times* practice and my own inclinations, I gave him his shot.

One editor lambasted me for not heeding the warning of the U.S. attorney in Baltimore. He had me there, and once again the subject was lying. In my experience, American governments and federal officials regularly lie to journalists about everything from why we're going to war to whether they're sneaking a look at our phone records or, nowadays, why they're putting us in jail. There was no way in hell that I, as a child of the '60s and a noncombatant member of the Vietnam generation and chief editor of the *Times,* was going to accept, as a matter of course, the assertions of government officials, who were always ready to say this or that *Times* reporter was wrong but I'm not going to tell you how. I addressed what I thought was my worst sin, what I called a "lapse of vigilance" on some of the myriad daily details of putting out the paper. If I had read the corrections column more closely, I'd have nailed Jayson without help from anyone. But that's a song for the Wudacudashuda. The plain fact is I chose to spend my time on the journalism. I never aspired to be executive copy editor of *The New York Times.* For one thing, the future of the *Times* depended on improving tomorrow's paper, not yesterday's.

I'm a political reporter. I can read an audience. The staff, at least the vocal part of it, wasn't buying. For example, I noticed a guy in the audience who applauded vigorously every time I was criticized. He was a beneficiary of one of my second chances as well. When I took over, I was told by editors who had interviewed him that he had been permanently written off as an applicant for employment because of admitting to a struggle with drugs earlier in his life. I hired him anyway because I liked his writing. Maybe I flew into a Bermuda Triangle of angry druggies, of which Jayson was only one corner. Later I found out that another reporter, the guy hammering me in *Newsweek,* had been treated for heroin addiction at the same rehab facility patronized by a college friend of mine. I had passed on a chance to hire this guy earlier in his career because I believed that he was easily spun by his sources. If I had known about the heroin, I might have hired him, too. Some people at the *Times* and commentators on Fox News said I should be fired because I was too easy on blacks. I think my soft spot for ex-junkies caused me a lot more trouble.

The most memorable point of the day for me was not the widely reported moment when Arthur pulled a stuffed moose from a bag and handed it to me as a symbol of our new era of kindness. Personally, I'll remember more fondly the last thing that Krystyna said to me as we left our window table at Charlotte. She took my hand tenderly, fixed me with her blue-eyed gaze and said, "Remember, your job for the next two hours is to resist every impulse to tell them to go fuck themselves." I'm not, as I have admitted, a detail man or notably patient or obedient, but those instructions I followed to a T.

III. THE STARBUCKS REVELATION

The next morning I stopped in the Starbucks at Eighth Avenue and Forty-third Street, where the service is inefficient but surly. I waited patiently for my venti iced decaf nonfat latte. The moment I stepped back on the sidewalk, the guy who had ripped me for not taking the word of U.S. attorneys was advancing toward me, a big smile on his face, his hand extended.

I looked at the hand as it came nearer. I held on to my latte. I knew this guy well. He was a talented editor. He had a good heart. I had recently offered him a big promotion, which he turned down because he was a single parent with custody of his kids. When my parents died, he sent me, by way of consolation, a book of poetry by Seamus Heaney. He had an idiosyncrasy that I tolerated because of his talent and because I had always thought there was too little freedom of speech inside the *Times*. He liked to offer impudent, even insulting insinuations about me in staff meetings, then follow up privately with fawning e-mails about what a fine guy I was. I considered not taking his hand. Then I realized that to him it represented today's private e-mail. I shook it.

We walked east on Forty-third toward the flags that flap over the doorway of the Times building. He talked in a rush of words about how he hoped I hadn't misunderstood the motivation of his remarks in the meeting. I pondered a question, and it was not either of the questions attributed to Lee in the mountains. Was I betrayed? Did I betray?

As we drew near the revolving doors at the entrance to the *Times,* I asked myself this: What is it about this place that has given this good man the soul of a bushwhacker? It took me some while to figure out why I remembered the encounter with such clarity. Upon the stroke of the moment that question popped into my head, I fell out of love with *The New York Times*. I don't mean I quit caring for it in terms of devotion to its values or dedication to its future success or being proud of the work we did there or being willing to soldier on in its behalf. I mean I fell out of love with the *Times* in the way people fall out of love, the mysterious, alchemical way described by a woman in James Salter's austere short story "Last Night": "Whatever holds people together was gone. She told him she could not help it. That was just the way it was." When hope dies, duty remains. When love dies, duty loses its savor.

IV. WHAT KIND OF MONEY
ARE WE TALKING ABOUT?

It was one of those late May evenings when New York seems to both hug you and summon you on toward some reward to be found in that city and nowhere else. Work that day had followed the usual Yeatsian paradigm of the post-Blair era, the worst lot howling, their betters silent. I was not offended by the silence of friends. They were simply doing what I had done in my years of climbing through the ranks, what I would have done in their place if I was in mid-career with a family to support and this kind of hailstorm was raging. They were waiting to see if the storm blew itself out. They were waiting to see who survived.

I was looking forward to martinis with Krystyna—Grey Goose for me, Belvedere for her—in the garden of our house in the West Village. Such was its encirclement by other buildings that it had the feel of a walled garden. We had planted it in the flora of a New Orleans garden, and in their protected mini-climate heated by air-conditioner vents and exhaust fans, the plants had thrived extravagantly, wantonly. It was a green outdoor living room, ferns towering and wisteria draping around a slate floor and a round table and folding chairs of the Parisian style.

I had amused myself on my way home by recalling Ben's question about Jayson. It reminded me of my fascination with the falling cats of New York. I had since learned that, in the warm months, three to five cats a week fall from the city's high-rises, some plunging more than thirty stories. But only a few die, and so far they have claimed no human victims. That is because cats fall at only sixty miles per hour, half the speed of humans. A pet-loving pedestrian or a strolling vet might survive a glancing blow from a falling cat, since a cat tends to glide a bit by extending its legs and tail. My career had been hit by a plummeting dwarf, falling straight and fast, and nothing is likely to survive that. Falling bodies are a grim subject in our neighborhood, but there is no double standard in X-rays, metaphors of departure or journalists caught in media hurricanes. If you're hit you're hit.

I had some news to serve with the martinis in the garden. Upon inquiring discreetly into the pension rules at the *Times,* I had learned that in this hurly-burly spring I had passed two milestones while my attention was focused on our wedding and subsequent honeymoon disruptions. By turning sixty on February 5, I had reached the minimal age for retirement under *Times* rules. On March 13, by reaching my twenty-fifth anniversary on the paper, I had passed the mark at which one qualifies for receiving 100 percent of the monthly pension benefit one has coming. Suddenly it did not matter that my dreams of a dot-com-financed early retirement had been dashed. I could still walk away if things went badly at the *Times,* and things were definitely going badly. In addition, our Greenwich Village house was gaining value. Savings and a modest inheritance from my parents had delivered the Pennsylvania house to us mortgage free. Then there was the monthly check we could have any time, not a staggering amount in post-Reagan America, but enough money for our needs. Workers of the world, you know exactly what kind of money we're talking about, and we had the Great Blalock's advice from beyond the grave about how to use it.

CHAPTER 41

A Year Later:
Salmon Fishing in the Ruins
of Empire

I have a photograph of my favorite moment in all the fishing I've
ever witnessed, and I'm not holding the rod in that picture. I'm
not even in it. More than anything that third day on the Kola
River, I wanted Krystyna to catch her first Atlantic salmon.
When we entered the expansive junction pool where the Kitsa
River tumbles into the main Kola, I told Krystyna's guide, Misha,
that I wanted her to take the first crack at the long, deep tongue
of slick water at the far end of the pool. That spot, sheltered by
boulders on one side, the steep shoreline on the other and by a lip
of submerged rock on its downstream end, was a natural bathtub
sitting atop a mile-long staircase of rapids. It was the first place a
salmon could rest, its muscles spent from a steep ascent against
masses of tumbling white water.

I had taken a fish there on our first day. When we drew the
same beat again in midweek, my mind immediately reserved that
place for Krystyna. She had fished herself to exhaustion for
three days, making lovely overhead and roll casts with her Spey
rod. Since that day four years earlier on the Penobscot and in the
two years since we'd moved in together, Krystyna had caught the
big sea-run browns in Patagonia with her fourteen-foot Sage and
taken sipping trout in Pennsylvania on a bamboo rod that weighs
less than a box of toothpicks. Offshore from Key Largo, she

caught sailfish. On the flats, she took the first bonefish she ever saw with her first cast. Along the way, I learned not to be jealous of smitten guides on three continents, and I also learned that when it came to fishing, there was no quit in my wife.

She demonstrated that one howling day in Argentina when the dashing Spaniard Diego Motter operated on the big fly that the wind slapped into her chin. It looked nasty, even surgically formidable, the thick hook having passed through and through tender flesh, rendering useless my previous hook-extraction experience. Standing knee deep in the Río Grande, I held her rod and steadied her while Diego pushed the barb clear and mashed it down with his pliers and then backed the hook out, leaving two tiny drops of blood to mark the entry and exit holes. I dabbed them away with Kleenex and looked closely at her fine-grained skin.

"No scars," I said.

We both congratulated Diego on his skill. Krystyna grabbed her rod and made ready to cast. She looked pale to me and, to an ever so slight degree, wobbly. I informed her that people had been known to faint and topple over after hook extractions. We agreed to take a break.

"You're very good at that, Diego," she said as the three of us found a lee spot in the sun. "Do you have to remove a lot of hooks from your clients?"

"Not until today," he said. "That's my first one."

"If I had known that," she said, "we'd be on our way to the airport to catch the plane to Buenos Aires."

I pointed out that B.A. is supposed to have the best plastic surgeons in the world, but none could have left a more flawless chin than Diego. B.A. also has a higher percentage of psychotherapists, per capita, than New York. I haven't sorted out why. Maybe it has to do with the tango or the secret police. In any event, Krystyna marched back to the river, casting into the fierce wind, this time with her chin zippered into the high neck of her wading jacket.

In Russia, the fact that Krystyna spoke the language only deepened the adulation of Misha and his partner, Alexei, who had drawn the short straw and had to row my raft. Alexei and I worked the deep runs in the T-intersection of the two streams. Several hundred yards across the river, Misha watched as Krystyna methodically worked her way through the magic pool. She was certain to be the first to fish it that day, or as certain as anything gets on the Kola, where poachers prowl up and down the Murmansk–St. Petersburg train track that parallels the river. I had told my guide that the moment Krystyna hooked a fish, I wanted to row over and take photographs. Anyone's first salmon is a big event, in part because it is possible to cast hundreds of times and never get a take.

Which was what happened to Krystyna throughout the afternoon. There was no point leaving, since this was the best pool on our beat and also our take-out point. After a couple of hours, we paddled over to join them. The guides conferred. We learned that she had moved a fish several times at the prime holding spot in the pool, a patch of slick water marking the tublike hydraulic eddy above the rapids. What was required was careful casting so you could get a clean swing of the fly across the three or four feet of good water before the fly got sucked into the rapids.

"We should rest the pool a little more, then you try this fish," Misha told me. "It is probably still there."

"I know," I said. That salmon was not likely to leave its sweet little aqueous pillow until nightfall. I looked at the sun. It was about to slide behind the ridge above the railroad track. For the moment, its light was hitting the holding spot at a harsh, glaring angle.

"That's a taking fish if you've moved it that much," I said. "Let's let the sun get off the water, and then I want Krystyna to try it again."

When the time came, I asked her to let me climb up to the railroad track before she began. The camera would have a perfect bird's-eye shot from thirty feet above the water. Misha and Alexei did all that any salmon guide can do in such a situation. They made a guess as to the best fly pattern, tied it on, sat on a log and smoked.

Krystyna began casting, first to the water well above the spot where the fish had last shown itself. You do this in case the salmon has moved up current, as fish in a comfortable holding area will do at times. Then the cast is lengthened incrementally, to cover every inch of the area in a systematic way. When it came time to put the fly in the prime position, only a roll cast would do, since the trees to Krystyna's back would snag her back cast if she went overhand. Some people who've fished a long time can't make a decent roll cast. Krystyna is not one of those people.

When it came time for her to cast sixty feet to the very heart of the heart of the good place, to cast at the optimum angle with precisely the right amount of line on the water, her cast was, in a word, ideal. The fly landed on the black water. The arc of its transit across the holy water would be as smooth as that of the brass ball at the end of a clock pendulum. As the fly moved with the current, I spoke quietly to myself, with a certainty inappropriate to fishing. "That's the perfect cast for this fish," I said, speaking of a fish we could not see, in a spot that might have been vacated. Yet I knew it was there, knew with a conviction stirred from the *anima mundi* by the archetypal perfection of the cast by this well-loved person that this fish was going to take the fly. For once, I was ready with the camera.

And just at that instant, Krystyna's fly was taken. The water boiled. Her rod arched over. The shutter clicked, and that, dear friends, is how I got a picture of my favorite moment in a lifetime of fishing, my splendid wife and the planet's handsomest fish dancing at opposite ends of a straight, yellow string.

As the salmon sat on the lip of the rapids, its four human admirers stood on the lip of a suspenseful adventure. The camera clicked time after time. Krystyna did what you are supposed to do with a fresh salmon that is doggedly holding bottom, which is to keep a tight line and not rush the beast. The guides expressed the hope that the fish, pressured by the tight line, would swim upstream, and it did for a bit. I had scrambled down from the railroad track when the salmon did what you never want them to do. It swung its head with the current, got the force of the river behind it and swam downstream.

"We'll have to follow it unless it stops," said Misha. Of the two, he spoke better English.

But Alexei's vocabulary was adequate for the occasion. "This fish not stopping," he said.

Following a fish down the steep, slick-bouldered shore of a raging cataract is never easy and often unwise. Even if you're in a boat and the rapids are navigable, you may have no time to react before the fleeing fish, speeded by the tripling force of its weight, its power and the current, breaks off. If you're on the shore and the descent is perilous and you are familiar with the salmon rivers of the world, you may quite honorably break the fish off on purpose, thus avoiding loss of all your line and the possibility of fractured rods or ankles, drenching or, in extreme but documented cases, drowning. As it happened, two Americans had died a couple of weeks earlier when their guide's anchor rope parted and their raft had been swept into just such a patch of water as this.

So, away we went. Misha and Alexei hopscotched down the shore, one finding a place for Krystyna and reaching back a hand for her while the other scrambled ahead to find the next spot. I came along behind, holding Krystyna's wading belt to keep her from falling as she hopped from rock to rock.

At this point, I thought of Edwin Valentine, and I thought well of him, indeed. Edwin was a New York street kid who fell in love with fishing at the Coney Island pier and had worked himself up to chief tackle rigger at the Urban Angler, the fly shop on lower Fifth Avenue. A few days before we left for Russia, he put four hundred yards of new, ultrafine Micron backing on my Tibor Gulfstream fly reel. This replaced two hundred yards of the large-diameter Dacron backing. I told the guides there was no point in giving up on this salmon when it got a big lead on us. We had plenty of backing. Edwin had readied us for just such a situation.

The four of us had progressed in the described fashion for a couple of hundred yards. Everything was going fine, until everything started going badly. The line had caught on a driftwood snag far out in the rapids. The fish was still taking line. We would not be able to continue our pursuit of it unless the line pulled free. It didn't.

Then Misha did something foolish, athletic and amazing. He began hopping from boulder to boulder, making his way across a river that clearly was not intended for foot traffic. He was probably young and strong enough to survive bouncing a mile or so downstream if he missed a rock, but it was still a damn sight more radical than anything I would have done for someone else's fish, even Krystyna's. He freed the line.

Krystyna wound frantically, coming tight on the fish again. The journey back to us was equally perilous for Misha, but he made it. The four of us continued our scrambling pursuit down the shoreline, coming in a minute or so to a place where the river's angle of descent was a little less steep. We were over a quarter mile from where we started. Misha spotted a patch of deeper, slower water hard against the bank where he thought he could net the fish. Alexei and I kept coming along with Krystyna. The labor of regaining all that line must have felt endless. But at last she brought the fish in close and led it into Misha's net. It was a male fish that did not need lies to lift it to twelve pounds. It was silver and shiny-fresh from the White Sea. Misha revived the fish by holding it steady in the current, using his boot top like a cradle under the fish's belly. We set it free to beat its way back up to its taking place.

We were all winded, but as soon as the fish was released, Alexei began running up the railroad tracks. It turned out he was worried that poachers would steal the rods and tackle we had left behind. Fishing in Russia can be like that. Unlike some of Russia's more remote and better managed salmon rivers, the Kola runs right through Murmansk, where 500,000 Russians are marooned in a dying economy. You can be in a beautiful, sylvan pool like the one where Krystyna got two twenty-pounders in a row from a sandy beach and then around the next bend see a decaying pumping station or an abandoned Red Army barracks. I don't want to make too much of this. I've had industrial-strength fishing in the United States, for smallmouth bass within sight of the cooling towers at Three Mile Island, for stripers under the thundering Williamsburg Bridge in Manhattan, for redfish among abandoned oil rigs in the Louisiana marshes. I'd be hard-pressed to say that the wreckage of the Soviet Union is uglier than those places. There is certainly no new construction on the Kola that is more deadly to sea life or more dangerous as terrorist targets than the liquefied natural gas terminals that Exxon, George W. Bush and Dick Cheney want to build in the major ports, bays and estuaries of America. So if it's chauvinistic to feel superior to the New Russia, it's nonetheless appropriate to be sad about what has happened along the namesake river of the Kola Peninsula. The camp owners are greedy, the wardens are winking and the poachers are working. The Kola is so loaded with nuclear waste, PCBs, dioxin and God knows what else that its poachers are probably poisoning themselves and their customers. Maybe things are better on the remote streams, but it's been a rough season on the Kola in the decade since Nat and I heard Mariusz Wróblewski's hopeful prediction that the New Russia would help protect "the unique places in the world."

In such a world as we have, one must find peace where one can, and in the right circumstances peace can come dropping slow in weary old Russia as well as at Innisfree. All along the Kola, the hillocks are covered with spongy green moss, thick and soft as a mattress. Every day, Misha and Alexei served a shore lunch of vegetable soup and hot tea, heated over a small gas stove. If you looked, you could always find a mossy mound for a pillow in perfect proximity to a cushioned dip of earth for easing your back.

I quickly became a connoisseur of these tundra hammocks and a devotee of falling asleep in them. The one I found at lunchtime on the day Krystyna chased the salmon down the river was the best of all. I mentioned waiting for the sun to drop that afternoon. The sky had cleared late in the day. Throughout the morning, a slow rain, hardly heavier than fog, fell on us as we fished and when we stopped for lunch. After lunch I lay on my back in a perfect undulation of moss. It supported my head, back and feet with equanimity. Clad in my waders and hooded Gore-Tex jacket and fleece gloves and with a slouch hat over my eyes, I was waterproof in a darkened tent that was, in effect, about an inch bigger than my body in all directions. I listened to the soft talk of the river passing and the guides down along its edge chatting in Russian. I heard the tiny drops of rain splatting on my jacket and going bump, bump, ta-bump against the dome of my hat. Krystyna lay curled beside me, dry inside her own gear, her head on my shoulder. I don't know if she slept, but I did, a sleep so relaxed, so pure, so subtle that I suspect only a baby or a cat could equal it.

I awakened to the same wet feathers of sound that had put me to sleep. I realized that I did not have a care in the world, and the thought did not startle me. Having these moments of feeling absolutely carefree and content within a world of wife, words and rivers had become customary without my realizing it. My newspaper days seemed long ago, far, far away, and—I struggled for an inner summation of a feeling so elusive yet now firmly stationary in my life—those days felt treasured but unmourned.

CHAPTER 42

The Last Editorial:
On Bear

Paul W. Bryant was not a man to sing the Song of the Wudacu-dashuda after a bitter defeat. Other Southern coaches made excuses—the wind in the fourth quarter, the mud in the middle of the field, the cowbells in the student section, the Yankee refer-ees. Coach Bryant would say "We had our chances to win the game" and move on. By chances, he did not mean unearned gifts. He meant opportunities to be seized; the rest was up to you. He understood that a game was not a continuous flow but a col-lection of decisive moments that had to be recognized and dominated. It's the same with covering a breaking news story. If you don't anticipate those moments in a developing news story and get your people moving to respond to them, your competi-tors will beat you like a drum, and they won't stop until you make them. The *Times*'s habit of cruising through critical inter-sections on automatic pilot was alarming to me as of March 13, 1978, the first full day I spent in the newsroom on Forty-third Street. A flat-lining newspaper is a vulnerable newspaper. It can also be a place of frustration for its most talented people. When I got fired, the strongest emotion I felt was anger at myself. I had lost a game I should have won against opponents I could have outsmarted. You can see how that kind of thinking could easily turn into a river. Heraclitus said you cannot step into the same river twice. This river you don't want to step into the first time. Better to paraphrase what the Bear always said after watching a nasty replay. I had my chances to win. That game is over.

After June 3, 2003, there was no rush in my new life as a civilian to name or blame that neutral force we call luck. I instantly realized that of all the things I had to lose—mate, family, health, friends, passions, zeal, contrariness, fly rods, my books, the words in my head to make another—I had lost the most expendable, a job at a newspaper. I immediately got kind notes from Fred Hiatt at *The Washington Post* and John Carroll at the *Los Angeles Times* inviting me to discuss writing columns for their respective newspapers. I was tempted. There was a presidential campaign coming. I had always loved the life of the campaign trail. What fun to go back out there and kick ass. For a few days, the blood of my Celtic ancestors roared in my veins. I might just paint half my body blue and take the field.

There was another temptation, which was to spend my life debating what had happened and who was to blame for this or that lapse. Since accountability, to which I had full title, trumps responsibility, there was no argument to be pursued there unless I wanted to waste days that could be devoted to pursuits other than masochism. As for the endless variables of blame, I understood the sociology of the situation as it applied to me. The *Times* is a tribal community with some aspects of the genuine cult. Those who wanted me out had no choice but to demonize me. It was a necessary recovery ritual for the newsroom and probably for any large organization when its members may be stunned or even a little ashamed about what they have witnessed. "If you think you're going to be remembered as a hard-charging guy with a heart of gold, you're living in a dreamworld," Bill Safire told me. I would have to settle for hard-charging, and even that would be disputed in an endless conversation in which whittling down my professional reputation was an institutional necessity.

"There are still advocates of Howellism in the paper, but they have to keep a very low profile," he said. "Whenever anyone talks about the paper's metabolism, everyone knows what it means. That's your word." The de-escalation of adjectives would only intensify after I published an article in *The Atlantic Monthly* warning that the *Times* could be in financial trouble if it did not make the changes Arthur and I had discussed. As a man who had launched a hundred thousand adjectives in my time, I had no karmic right of appeal or any claim on clemency, especially in our nation's capital. Among politicians of both parties who had been the recipients of said adjectives, one commentator said at the news of my dismissal, "You couldn't cut the Schadenfreude with a chain saw." Upon mature reflection, there were obvious reasons for dropping out of the conversation about events at the newspaper. It was interminable. It was irresolvable. It mattered only to a few hundred people in and around the *Times* newsroom. Even they were already losing interest in it, and the world beyond had never given a damn. Everybody in the great world was thinking about the same thing I was thinking about: What do I do next? What's going to happen to me next? And out of all the billions around the world asking that question, I had been drawn by the indifferent gravity of luck into the orbit of the very, very small number of people who could answer it this way: Something different. I chose to find a whole new life—a new, whole life—instead of the twilight life of columns, journalism seminars, talk shows, op-ed pieces, the occasional book if I had time to write. This was my real chance to ride the main current, to become untethered from "occasional," from that world in which desire must always yield to conditionality.

And what about that other passenger of gravity with whom I had intersected as a fish intersects with a fly? Little Jayson Blair had taken only one thing from me. It was not my job, nor the space occupied by my loved ones or true friends. What I lost was a benign circuitry of connection with people at the *Times,* dating back over a quarter of a century in some of our lives, and it was not without value. There was a group of people with whom I had worked in close and sometimes glorious harmony. We were proud of the papers we made together. We knew one another's lovers, spouses, children, parents. In various overlapping combinations, we went to one another's weddings, birthdays, graduations, bar and bat mitzvahs, christenings. Our sociability would have lasted until the end for all of us. Now, in all probability, I will not be at their funerals nor they at mine. These things happen in our land. People live longer nowadays and work and reside in many different places. They do not stay home the way my grandfather did. In this going and coming, you may be required to run through several sets of colleagues in your time.

Jayson had only done what the owners of truncated personalities must sometimes do. He had entered our lives without invitation and destroyed the bonds of collegiality that might have held for years. That is where the sin, more aptly the sickness, of the incomplete man or woman resides, in the ability to inject a pathology into the lives of others, without guilt. In this case, the worst had not happened to me or anyone I knew. The uninvited intruder had not taken our friends or interrupted our loves. That can happen when you are visited by someone within whom the incomplete places have filled with malice.

Blessed are we, my friends and colleagues alike, whose lives have not been touched by what can happen when the nurse who differs from other nurses in only one way slips into the hospital room of the unattended patient or the child-snatcher stops randomly at the 7-Eleven or the pilots who wish to land in the garden of the seventy-two virgins get hold of airplanes. Blessed are those among us who have lost neither the love nor the lives of our precious ones in insane circumstances, nor been otherwise cheated of the ability to fish fleeting moments of imperial joy from the three rivers that beckon us. We have yet a chance to play on Coach Bryant's terms, which is to say with passion and purpose, and thereby finish our lives at a place by the riverside where we can, at long last, put a name to the luck that has found us.

CHAPTER 43

Two Years Later:
Feeling the Grab of the Rainbow

As the lives of fishermen go, Chris Branham has had an atypical one: born in the Kenyan Aberdares, educated in England, adopted in his late teens by the owners of an Alaskan lodge. There are no Pinkerton moments when Chris takes us by Helio Courier floatplane to the Alagnak River, which at certain times of the year, indeed, at this particular time on June 23, 2005, offers the best rainbow trout fishing on the Katmai Peninsula. These planes can stay in the air at forty miles per hour and land as confidently as a mallard. Krystyna and I wait while Chris anchors the plane and transfers our gear to another of those jet-powered johnboats made in the great state that produced both Bill Clinton and the largest brown trout ever caught in the continental United States.

The Alagnak twists through the tundra, its water as clear yet greenly viscous as that of any mangrove creek in the Bahamas. With the same Spey rods we used in Patagonia and Russia, Krystyna and I are swinging flies across the current. We are using Articulated Leeches, strips of rabbit fur with a single stinger hook concealed in the tail of each fly. Later in the year, we would be using the Egg-sucking Purple Leech, a.k.a. the Lawyer. The fish are biting so fast that you would want to lie down in the boat to change flies.

But they are not biting hard. Sometimes a fish will track the fly in its arcing swing, nipping it repeatedly. As with salmon, you must wait until you feel the weight of the fish. After three nips and a little heaviness at the end of the line, I strike and miss. The fly continues to swing. More nips, and finally, at the very end of the swing, the fish loads up the line. I hand-set so as not to pull it away. A large rainbow comes out of the water several times.

"Good job. Good fish," Chris says. Then it throws the hook.

"That's all right," he said. "You made him grab. That's what it's all about in fishing, the grab."

Attend once again, taxpaying owners of the last American wilderness, to the power of consummating moments. I think I've been addicted to them since the day I hit the baseball at Avondale Park and, at about the same time in my life, picked up fly casting. The thunk of the bat, the feeling in your forearm when the rod bends to the weight of the line extending behind you and then ejaculates it into a plein-air world. You want it to last, and because it can't, you know you're going to have to repeat it, over and over. You will need skill. You will need practice. You will need chances. You cannot prolong the grab, the take, the hit or even the extenuated moment when the rod you hold is a living thing in a living world. You can only be in those moments while they last, and each one could be the final one of your life.

That's why if, gun to my head, I had to choose between writing and fishing, I would choose writing. The instruments for replicating the feeling you get from writing—the flow—are all within your head. On a good run, you can make it last an hour, two hours, even four. Then it will be gone. The flow stops. But the next morning you can summon it again. The flow, the zone, the roll—the point is to get in there and ride, ride, ride, time suspended, the words coming in a rush. Every time it happens, your state of mind should be sacramental. If there's one thing we learn from the American trinity—Faulkner, Hemingway, Fitzgerald—it is that the gift can be lost through carelessness, drink or the unavoidable ravages of age. Their gifts were huge. By comparison, your gift and mine will be small. Even so, we must not abuse this gift. We must not deny it. We must serve it.

A Fine Madness by Elliott Baker is a novel about a poet, Samson Shillitoe, who thinks he has lost the flow. He scrambles for money, fornicates, drinks when he should be writing. He winds up in a mental institution, where he is lobotomized. Upon his release, he has a financial windfall that means there'd be "no more time wasted on meaningless labor."

> For the first time in his life he'd be completely independent with poetry his only care. Then he remembered what was wrong, the one undetermined factor. Was he still a poet? Or had they sliced out the tissue on which all his plans depended?

The thought terrifies him. He is on an airplane on his way to the newly prosperous life in Montana when it strikes. His adoring mistress, Rhoda, is telling him she is pregnant with their child. But he cannot comprehend the news because he has been paralyzed by uncertainty. Before the lobotomy, he had finished three parts of what he envisioned as an epic poem.

> A tug, a whisper, of uneasiness. Something was screwed up. But the plane was steady. He tracked the blinking danger light and came to Rhoda's glow. Her mouth was still flapping, but she was drowned out by the turmoil inside him—swelling, buffeting him, stretching his skin until it screeched. Then the fourth part of the poem broke free, its wild wind carrying him higher and higher. And the words, like hard-brined fists of fire, beat back at the sun.

Now, that's what I call a happy ending.

And we may be sure that Elliott Baker knew whereof he spoke. Note that no mention is made of publishing the poem. The urge to publish, to address the world, burns in the young. Later, the poem gets written, the book finished, the score completed because the maker wants to be assured that he or she can still hear the music in the head, and not just hear it but summon it. The words on this page would have been written whether or not anyone was ever going to read them. I needed to feel them coming out. That is why, as the Great Blalock told me long ago, fly fishing is not about catching fish. We'd still make the cast if the last fish had fled to the deepest, most unreachable waters of the earth.

CHAPTER 44

We Shall Be Released

Since lies have played such a prominent role in my life, there's no way around telling about the argument between Tennant and me over how we hooked the marlin at Christmas Island. A year or so after we got back from that South Pacific Paradise of Fish and Birds, Tennant and I were fly fishing for striped bass under the lighthouse at Montauk Point. The trip entered our conversation when Tennant caught a false albacore, a hard-running fish that can wear you out on a fly rod.

"I don't see how you did that for seven and a half hours," he said, flopping the wrist of his rod hand. "By the way," he said, "you're wrong about how you hooked the marlin." Tennant had been reading my first-draft account of that entire day. I wanted him to check the accuracy of my memory as to what happened when, who said what and so on.

"I remember we were doing some trolling, then Tuna said, 'Pick up the lines, we're moving.' The object was to resume trolling in another place," Tennant said. "As we were moving, suddenly these fish surfaced, and before we could get set up with the trolling rods, you reached down and got your fly rod and made a cast, and with the first or second cast, you hooked that fish. We may just have different memories, but I think you cast that fly."

Clearly one of us had soaked his head in the river of forgetfulness. I may joke about the Holy Rules of Fly Fishing, but it gives me no pleasure to break any of them. In fact, it afflicts me with guilt and the need to confess, which is why I admitted trolling with my fly rod off Christmas Island. It's not a felony to troll with a fly rod, but you damn sure can't count such a fish as a fly-rod fish. As I mentioned, the International Game Fish Association requires that the boat engine be in neutral before a cast is made and that the fly be moved through the water by hand-stripping the line, not by the motion of the boat. Tennant referred mildly to our disagreement in the margin notes to that first draft: "We may just have divergent memories."

Then he started sending additional annotations. Within a few months, he hardened his stance in a most uncharacteristic way. Tennant is one of the most open-minded people I know, which is fortunate because in my view he doesn't have the world's greatest memory. He would tell you, of course, that it is I who have the porous memory and am obstinate about admitting it. In the follow-up annotations on later drafts, he retracted his "divergent memories" observation.

This is what he wrote in the margin in a tiny, meticulous hand that reminded me of his father's comments in the margins of exam papers: "I said this, but now I regret it–[mentioning] the possibility of being wrong. I know I am right. I am right. You are wrong. My memory on this is so clear."

Once he got warmed up, Tennant, who has the historian's penchant for expanding the documentary record, pressed his campaign to discredit my claim to piscatorial sinning. I was no longer just "wrong." In a follow-up letter, I became "dead wrong about your recollection versus my recollection on the Christmas Island fish. Tuna had cut the motor and we were just preparing to troll when the fish surfaced. Instantly, you picked up a fly rod, made one false cast, and then placed the fly squarely in the area of fish activity, strikes, etc. It was not a long cast. After that, you are right. Once the fish was on, Tuna said 'Bonito,' etc."

I began to identify with those habitual confessors who try to talk their way into jail. Once it became a mnemonic mano a mano between me and Tennant, it didn't seem to matter that I was trying to confess. Why would I tell on myself if I hadn't really been trolling my fly in a way I knew to be outside the rule book? In subsequent communications, Tennant developed a theory. I was suffering from fatigue-induced delusions.

During Christmas Island fight, you were so focused and intense it's *no wonder* that your memory on how it all started is *slightly flawed* [my italics throughout]. To wit, you also have *inaccurate recollections* on food/water: you had three sips of water during the entire fight; I remember this because I know you were in a situation that would encourage cramping, and I worried that you would get dehydrated (for lack of water), thus increasing your chances of cramping. Also, you had either two or three bites from a p.b.j. sandwich—not ham. We had eaten the ham during earlier trolling, even though it was early to be eating. I was holding the water bottle to your mouth and holding sandwiches to your mouth so that you could keep both hands on the rod.

What was I to make of this? What are *you,* diligent readers, to make of it? Given his reverence for facts, there's not a chance that Tennant thought he was lying. Moreover, his statements did not have the clumsy feel of spontaneous confabulation, as defined in the earlier-referenced *Lies! Lies!! Lies!!!* by Dr. Charles V. Ford. As a practitioner and beneficiary of spontaneous confabulation, I recognized that Tennant's detailed memories were masterpieces of verisimilitude, superior in every way to the confabulation to which I had resorted in wooing Krystyna, the one about my burning interest in Polish fly fishing. What could be clumsier than that statement or, come to think of it, more effective? Still, the best that could be said of it, in terms of quality, was that it had the spontaneous energy born of desperation. Who has found a great love who would not lie to keep it? Given all that proceeded from the day we met at that sometime citadel of truth, *The New York Times,* I'd do the same again.

But in all other areas of my life—even fishing—I have labored to be an honest man, not only honest but exacting in that honesty, even to the point of resisting any flattering alteration of how my fly got into that fish's mouth. I assure you my account is correct, but I do not impugn the integrity of my friend. He, too, is a man with a satisfied mind. Tennant's version has the feel of factual reality—or finely wrought fiction. In regard to these qualities, I hope, it is no different than my own. By way of resolving this final paradox of my unlikely tale, I point you once again toward Dr. Ford's book and his valuable chapter "False Memories, False Accusations and False Confessions." He observes, "Although most of the general public and even many psychologists view memory as something that is fixed in the brain (like a computer file), research has shown that memory is continuously being reconstructed. Old memories are updated with new perceptions, and prior memory traces are replaced. This process occurs outside of conscious awareness, and the individual does not perceive the new memory as new. This finding has enormous importance for the courtroom and the psychotherapist's office."

He might have added, given the mutability of memory and therefore of "facts" as we generally conceive of them, the implications for journalism and fish stories are not small. I had plunged once again into Dr. Ford's book, seeking some sort of breakthrough in the forensics of mendacity. I felt a twinge of despair as the good doctor came to his "bottom line" on page 195. There would never be any way to tell which of us was correct since "one person's self-deception or overt lies can become another person's firmly held memories and 'truth.'" And if Alabama's foremost authority on the subject, studying the citizens of that paradise of fibs, falsehoods, fabrications, tall tales, hogwash, moonshine, baloney, taradiddles, concoctions, stretchers and whoppers, cannot tell us how to choose among truth, lies, stretchers and the sincerely misremembered, who among us can?

Let's not make too much of it. What Dr. Ford is trying to tell us is that there are many channels in the river of forgetfulness, some braiding, some diverging. And anyway, the marlin that leaps yet in my memory, three times from the top of a wave, was just another fish that got away, except for one thing. It released me.

Henryville, Pennsylvania
August 17, 2005

Index

ABOUT THE AUTHOR

Howell Raines is a Pulitzer Prize winner who was a journalist for almost forty years. His career culminated at *The New York Times,* where he worked as the editorial page editor before taking over as executive editor. He is the author of three previous books, including *Fly Fishing Through the Midlife Crisis,* which was a *New York Times* bestseller. He and his wife live in the Pocono Mountains.